New Yiddish Library

The New Yiddish Library is a joint project of the Fund for the Translation of Jewish Literature and the National Yiddish Book Center.

Additional support comes from The Kaplen Foundation and the Felix Posen Fund for the Translation of Modern Yiddish Literature.

SERIES EDITOR: DAVID G. ROSKIES

The Cross
and Other
Jewish
Stories

LAMED SHAPIRO

EDITED AND WITH AN

INTRODUCTION BY

LEAH GARRETT

YALE UNIVERSITY PRESS

NEW HAVEN AND LONDON

Set in Scala type by The Composing Room of Michigan, Inc. Printed in
the United States of America.

Library of Congress Cataloging-in-Publication Data
Shapiro, Lamed, 1878–1948.
The cross and other Jewish stories / Lamed Shapiro ; edited and with an
Introduction by Leah Garrett ; with translations by Heather Valencia,
Jeremy Dauber, David G. Roskies, Joseph Sherman, Lawrence Rosen-
wald, Reuben Bercovitch, Irving Howe and Eliezer Greenberg, Bernard
Guilbert Guerney, and Norbert Guterman.
p.   cm.—(New Yiddish library)
Includes bibliographical references.
ISBN-13: 978-0-300-11069-2 (hardcover : alk. paper)
1. Shapiro, Lamed, 1878–1948—Translations into English.   I. Title.
PJ5129.S43C76   2006
839'.133—dc22
                                                        2006018701

Credits: "White Chalah," by Lamed Shapiro, translated by Norbert Guterman, "Smoke," by Lamed Shapiro, translated by Irving Howe and Eliezer Greenberg, copyright 1953, 1954, 1989 by Viking Penguin, renewed
© 1981, 1982 by Irving Howe and Eva Greenberg; "The Rebbe and the
Rebbetsin," by Lamed Shapiro, translated by Irving Howe and Eliezer
Greenberg, copyright 1953, 1954, 1989 by Viking Penguin, renewed
© 1981, 1982 by Irving Howe and Eva Greenberg; "Eating Days," by
Lamed Shapiro, translated by Bernard Guilbert Guerney, copyright
1953, 1954, 1989 by Viking Penguin, renewed © 1981, 1982 by Irving
Howe and Eva Greenberg, from A TREASURY OF YIDDISH STORIES, by
Irving Howe and Eliezer Greenberg, editors, copyright 1953, 1954,
1989 by Viking Penguin, renewed © 1981, 1982 by Irving Howe and
Eva Greenberg. Used by permission of Viking Penguin, a division of
Penguin Group (USA) Inc.; "The Chair," by Lamed Shapiro, translated
by Reuben Bercovitch, copyright 2004 by Reuben Bercovitch.

A catalogue record for this book is available from the British Library.

The paper in this book meets the guidelines for permanence and dura-
bility of the Committee on Production Guidelines for Book Longevity of
the Council on Library Resources.

10 9 8 7 6 5 4 3 2 1

◆◆◆ Contents

♦ ♦ ♦ *Acknowledgments*

First and foremost I wish to thank my remarkable translators: Heather Valencia, Joseph Sherman, Lawrence Rosenwald, Reuben Bercovitch, Jeremy Dauber, and David G. Roskies. Through their diligent and creative work, they remind us that the translator, too, is an artist and master of the word. Lawrence Rosenwald wishes to acknowledge as well the assistance of Harry Bochner with the story "New Yorkish." In some cases, the annotations have been generously provided by the translators themselves.

I am grateful to the following people for helping me to fill in the many gaps in Shapiro's biography: Esther Frank; Brad Hill and the librarians at YIVO; Itzik Gottesman; Ruth R. Wisse; the librarians at the University of Denver; and the Medem Library in Paris.

My thanks to friends and colleagues who read parts of the manuscript or who served as sounding boards as I grappled with Shapiro's life and works: Carol Helstotsky, Eric Gould, David Shneer, Gloria Farler, Mikhail Krutikov, and Jeremy Dauber. Thanks as well to the English and Judaic Studies faculty at the University of Denver for their support.

At the Center for Judaic Studies at the University of Denver, Patricia Larsen was of great help in administrative matters, and Thyria Wilson worked hard and carefully on the glossary of terms. The staff of the

National Yiddish Book Center were of aid to me at every stage. Particular thanks go to Aaron Lansky, Nancy Sherman, and Catherine Madsen.

I am profoundly indebted to David G. Roskies, the editor of the New Yiddish Library, for reading and rereading the manuscript, for his insights and advice, and for the many long hours he devoted to getting this volume up to speed.

My husband and daughters were a constant source of support, patience, and good humor. This book is dedicated to my mother, Susan Vladeck, and to the memory of my beloved grandmother Irene Klein and my grandfather Abraham Klein. Together they awoke in me a love for Yiddish and Jewish culture.

◆ ◆ ◆ *Introduction*

LEAH GARRETT

A Jewish immigrant stands on the deck of a ship bound for the United States. Behind him lies a home visited by violence and destruction; ahead of him, a new world beckoning with the promise of limitless reinvention. Searching for a means to express the push-and-pull of past and future, he finds a reflection of his inner turmoil in the ocean below:

> Restlessly, the thick-dark waves capped with gray heads of foam hurl themselves one upon another. Harsh is the gloom of the mournful sea, and great its vexation.
>
> Little man, where are you crawling to? Little man, what are you striving to reach? You've set off over the mighty waters in the shell of a nut. O you pitiful wretch!

Wherever they find themselves, whether in a seedy yeshiva or a noisy cafeteria, and whoever they are—bespectacled students or bearded sages, muscular butchers or disgruntled union men—the characters who people the fiction of Lamed Shapiro have set out over mighty, mournful waters in the shell of a nut. Shapiro's writings graphically render the struggle of the modern Jew thrust into a desperate search for meaning at the very moment when the traditional community is decaying from within and threatened by destruction from without.

Like the young man fleeing his ravaged home, Lamed Shapiro was a Romantic manqué. How much happier he would have been as a Wordsworth, who found serenity in nature. As a Jew in the modern world, what he found instead was radical instability. For Shapiro, this conflict was inescapable, whether in the violence of pogroms or in the chaotic fate awaiting immigrants in the new world. Shapiro's own life—marked by radical dislocations, always in danger of spiraling out of control—is one of the most disturbing in the annals of modern Jewish writing.

Throughout his seventy turbulent years, Lamed Shapiro suffered from bouts of depression, some so severe that they led him to attempt suicide. When depressed, he would reject offers of help, isolate himself, and stop writing. Then, instead of returning to his desk, he would set himself obsessively on such seemingly impossible tasks as the reinvention of color photography. Friends would find him skinny and agitated from lack of sleep; in later life, his periods of morbid gloom were marked by bouts of heavy drinking. Small wonder that, when compared with most other Yiddish writers, his literary output was rather slim.

Nonetheless, the critics were nearly universal in their praise. They admired Shapiro's stories for their content and, above all, for their form and the "silence," "discipline," "stillness," and "control" of their unique style.[1] Here lay Shapiro's primary contribution to Yiddish literature: a new way of showing the discord of Jewish life in the modern world through a controlled (or, as the poet Jacob Glatstein termed it, "claustrophobic") poetic voice. A. Tabachnik articulated the critical consensus when he wrote: "There is no Yiddish writer, not even David Bergelson, who stands out with the degree of self-conscious mastery, of stylistic precision, of artistic control and discipline, as does Lamed Shapiro."[2]

Levi Joshua Shapiro was born to Orthodox parents on March 10, 1878, in the Ukrainian shtetl of Rzhishchev, sixty-two kilometers southeast of Kiev.[3] The 1939 census counted a Jewish population of 1,608 out of a general population of over 20,000 in Rzhishchev. The shtetl, surrounded by forests, adjoined the mighty Dneiper, a river that would later play a prominent role in Shapiro's stories.

Khaya Bluma, Levi's mother, was the second wife of his father, Aryeh Leyb, who had two sons by a previous marriage. She regarded Levi as her favorite son, and the boy reciprocated her devotion. Their relationship remained intense and intimate as long as she lived—and also tempestuous, an Oedipal struggle that found powerful expression in his writings, where Jewish mothers are often depicted as sadistic hags who torment their children to distraction.

The life of a Jewish male from a good home ought to have been devoted to the study of the Talmud, followed by an arranged marriage and a career in the family business. But from the age of eight, Shapiro was irresistibly drawn to literature. Like other young rebels of his generation, he was caught up in reading and then in composing heretical works, first in Hebrew, then in Russian, and finally in Yiddish.

As an adolescent, Levi fell under the spell of the Russian nihilist writer Dmitrii Pisarev (1840–1868). Pisarev had issued a clarion call for realistic renderings of life based on honest self-analysis. His heroes were young men and women at war with the established order. It was Pisarev, paradoxically, who showed the young hopeful from the shtetl the literary potential of his own mother tongue. As Shapiro would recall, Pisarev "turned my glance away from the morning star that sings its chorus—to the poor world, the world of my true surroundings." Indeed, if the purpose of literature was the honest rendering of real human experience, then there was no better tool than Yiddish.

In 1896, at the age of eighteen, Levi Shapiro realized his "path lay with Yiddish literature"[4] and made the young Jewish writer's archetypal move to the bustling metropolis of Warsaw, a provincial capital of the Russian Empire and the center of a burgeoning Jewish culture in several languages. No less archetypally, he promptly undertook a pilgrimage to the great Yiddish writer I. L. Peretz (1852–1915). Intent upon appearing the urbanite, the small town yokel got all dressed up,

> wearing an outfit that was a cross between a long jacket and a dress coat, and a hat with a shiny beak, like a real Russian student. In this get-up, I rang the doorbell of Number One, next to a plaque that read: "I. L. Peretz receives visitors at four in the afternoon." The door opened to Peretz himself. Peretz's large eyes became even bigger when he saw my get-up. Why

that look of astonishment? I asked myself. I realized that in my attire I looked like Genghis Khan.[5]

They spent the afternoon discussing the bright potential of Yiddish letters.

Two years of hunger and chronic unemployment followed, after which Shapiro quit the metropolis and returned home to Rzhishchev. The next period in his life is poorly documented. A failed love relationship resulted in his first attempted suicide—by drinking iodine, the method then favored by young Russians of both sexes. While at home, he managed to avoid the draft and to publish his first piece: an entry in Russian for a joke contest. The one-ruble honorarium staved off his hunger for a few days. He had intended his stay to last only a few months. Instead, he remained at home for five long years.

Finally, in 1903, at the age of twenty-five, Shapiro returned to Warsaw, there to publish his first Yiddish stories, "Wings" (1903) and "Itsikl Mamzer" and "Tiger" (1904), in journals edited by Avrom Reisen and Peretz. In Warsaw, Shapiro lived with the Yiddish-Hebrew writer Hirsh Dovid Nomberg (1876–1927), who tried to convince him to change his name. "What kind of name is Shapiro for a writer?" Nomberg protested. "A writer needs to have a name that will make on impression on the reader's mind. Not Shapiro. There are hundreds of Shapiros."

"It will be one or the other," the dime-a-dozen Shapiro replied, "either L. Shapiro will become a name to the reader, or it will be nothing to him."[6] While "Shapiro" may not have captured the imagination of the Jewish public, the sole initial "Lamed" (the letter "L" in the Jewish alphabet) became something of a modernist affect, akin to that adopted by the American poet e. e. cummings.

Shapiro's second sojourn in Warsaw ended abruptly, in the epoch-making year of 1905. It was a time of revolutionary upheaval in Russia as the granting of civil liberties was followed by the shock of pogrom violence against Jews, more widespread and brutal than anything before. Late that year, Shapiro joined a wave of young emigrants fleeing Mother Russia to start a new life in America. Shapiro's leave-taking was different from most in two crucial respects. While many could boast a revolutionary past, Shapiro fled for reasons of economic failure. Moreover, he did not undertake the trip alone but with his mother in tow, though it is not clear whether this was out of a sense of duty or because he feared venturing into the great world without Khaya Bluma at his side. Khaya Bluma was to live with her son for the next two decades until her death in 1925, when Shapiro was forty-seven.

En route to America, Shapiro spent four months in London, a brief but extremely productive sojourn. There he befriended the Hebrew-Yiddish writer and revolutionary Yosef Hayyim Brenner (1881–1921), one of the founders of modern Hebrew prose and an uncompromising critic of Jewish life. Brenner's fiction, like that of Berdyczewski, Gnessin, Schneour, Berkovitsh, and Nomberg, was peopled by variations on the type of the *talush*, the "dangling," alienated young man adrift within Jewish and modern life. In London, Brenner and Shapiro debated the relative merits of Yiddish and Hebrew literature. By now, Shapiro was firmly convinced that Yiddish, as a supple, literary language, was the obvious choice for a writer committed to the representation of contemporary Jewish life.[7]

In London, Shapiro enjoyed total freedom of expression for the first time, and it was there that he began to make his mark as a new voice in Yiddish literature. While working for the anarchist journal *Di fraye arbeter velt* (The Free Workers' World), edited by Brenner, he published "Self-Defense," a poem inspired by the 1905 pogrom in Zhitomir in which twenty-nine Jews had been killed and numerous Jewish women raped and tortured. The pogrom theme was hardly new to Jewish literature; in 1903, the great Hebrew-Yiddish poet Hayyim Nahman Bialik (1873–1934) had published a ferocious response to the Kishinev pogrom, "In the City of Slaughter." Like Bialik, Shapiro raised earthly violence to a metaphysical plane, implicating God in the horrific fate visited upon the Jews. But while, in Bialik, the poet's anger is directed at Jewish passivity, in "Self Defense" the speaker implores God to give Jews the strength to fight and kill their oppressors.

Shapiro himself was never to witness anti-Jewish violence, never to take up arms against pogromists, never to raise anything but his pen in protest. And yet, already in this early, declarative poem, he depicts violence as a primitive, intoxicating fury that Jews must confront and internalize for the sake of their own liberation. Detached from direct experience, Shapiro was to spend the next decade trying to fathom the seductive force of this dark menace.

In New York, accompanied by his mother, Shapiro soon found his niche among a group of Yiddish-speaking poets, prose writers, critics, and artists, the so-called *Yunge*, or Young Ones, who together would launch an aesthetic revolution in Jewish life.[8] Entering what was for him an unusually productive period, Shapiro published four pogrom stories: "The Kiss" (1907), "Pour Out Thy Wrath" (1908), "The Cross" (1909), and "In the Dead Town" (1910). For a brief time he was employed at the *Forverts*, the largest Yiddish daily, but he had a falling-out with Abraham Cahan, the paper's domineering editor. His later New York stories would consistently challenge and lampoon the central role of the newspaper in Yiddish life.

During this time Shapiro met and fell in love with Freydl, who abandoned a husband and two children in order to link her fate to his.[9] Together they began looking for work, moving to Chicago in 1909, where they ran a restaurant. There, in the course of three feverish days, Shapiro wrote his most celebrated pogrom story, "The Cross," which established him as a major Yiddish writer in the same league as Sholem Asch (1880–1957). "The Cross" tells the story of a Jew who witnesses his mother being raped and killed during a pogrom, and then the attackers carve a cross into his forehead. In response to these traumatizing events, he rapes and kills the girl he is in love with.

Chaim Zhitlovsky (1865–1943), the editor of the New York–based *Dos naye lebn* (The New Life) and a leading intellectual, published "The Cross" as a companion piece to Asch's sentimental-heroic "In a Carnival Night." This editorial juxtaposition sparked a spirited debate on the "crucifix question": was the Christian cross to be located, as with Shapiro, at the nexus of modern violence, or did it, as in Asch, hold out the promise for a historic reconciliation?[10] Shapiro's name was forever after associated with the view of the crucifix as a malevolent symbol.

When the Chicago restaurant closed in 1909, he and Freydl returned—not to New York, but all the way to Warsaw. (Happily for the couple, Khaya Bluma did not accompany them.) At first Warsaw fulfilled its promise. Shapiro became co-editor of the important Yiddish paper *Der fraynd* (The Friend), published his semiautobiographical "At Sea," about the passage to America of a sensitive young artist, printed a number of his pogrom stories in chapbook form, and collected these and other early works in *Noveln*.[11] He also began producing accomplished translations into Yiddish of world literature: Walter Scott's *Ivanhoe*, published in 1911 in Warsaw, and Rudyard Kipling's *The Jungle Book*, published the same year in Vilna. But the trip to Warsaw ended in economic failure. Hoping to settle permanently in Switzerland, he and Freydl opened a restaurant in Zurich in 1910. By 1911 they were back in New York.

This time the couple opened a coffeehouse in lower Manhattan called The Center, which was frequented by the poets, prose writers, and critics of *Di yunge*. The reviews were mixed. "The food was not tasty, the cleanliness left something to be desired," recalled S. Miller, "but [we ate there] for the sake of a colleague . . . who needed a handout."[12] Zishe Weinper remembered things differently: "L. Shapiro slowly created a natural zone where both sides could meet—the members of The Young group, as well as the elders. The Shapiro family had transformed the place into a corner for writers. After one a.m., only writers remained. Then L. Shapiro would turn to us and say: 'And now I'm no restauranteur,' meaning that those who were still left after the clock struck one could drink their tea or coffee without paying."[13]

It was a fine way to link the generations but a bad way to run a business. Over and over again, Shapiro tried (and failed) to make a living by serving food. His urge to run a restaurant may have reflected a desire to establish a mini–salon culture where he could interact with the public on his own terms, mixing physical and spiritual sustenance.[14]

In 1912 the couple and Khaya Bluma headed west. In Los Angeles, the small local group of Yiddish writers tried unsuccessfully to find him a job. When that failed they held a fund-raiser, but Shapiro, eccentric as always, did not show up for the banquet. He and Freydl returned that year to New York. The years of poverty and failure were taking their toll. A bitter, angry man, Shapiro turned next to selling used books.

The singular achievement of this period was a collection of stories, *The Jewish Regime and Other Items* (1919), which included the contents of his earlier collection plus three masterpieces, "Smoke," "White

Challah," and the title story. Shapiro proclaimed the latter two his final pogrom tales—and they were.

In 1921, Freydl, the now forty-three-year-old Lamed, and his mother again moved to Los Angeles. Unlike in New York, where well-known Yiddish writers were a dime a dozen, Shapiro was now a "big fish in a small pond." Yet rather than devoting his energies to his writing, he threw himself into the effort to invent a new way to develop color film (a process which already existed, having been invented in Germany). The idea of getting rich quick by finding a means of faithful reproduction may have held special appeal for a writer who was himself seeking to be as realistic a writer as possible.

Friends who saw him during this time reported a thin, disheveled, chain-smoking Shapiro obsessively working on his invention while the earthy Freydl took care of daily life and made their home a haven for visitors.

The year 1925 saw the death of Shapiro's mother. In the same year, the writer Leyvik Chanukov (1892–1958) paid him a visit at the behest of Zalmen Reyzen, who needed more information on Shapiro for his biographical dictionary of modern Yiddish writers. Shapiro told Chanukov that he had stopped writing altogether because he had been "burned" by the pressure to write always another pogrom tale, a genre that had been for him merely youthful indulgence. The only thing that mattered to him was fidelity to real life: "If I were to write now, my path would be 100-percent realism. I would erase all external influences. Realism—this must be the essence of our prose."[15]

Shapiro referred to his wife as "holy Freydl." Theirs was both a great and tragic love story, and her death from diabetes in 1927 nearly destroyed him. Without her, he became confused and alienated from the loyal friends who sought to save him from himself. Freydl had been not only Lamed's best friend, the woman who had abandoned a husband and two children for his sake, but a surrogate mother, a warm, funny, joyous presence. Her death left him both profoundly lonely and guilty for his part in the breakup of her family.

"What did your wife die of?" his longtime friend Rashel Hirshkan-Miller asked Shapiro at a seder held soon after Freydl's death. Shapiro had been filling his wine glass much more frequently than required by the seder ritual, and had eaten much less than the other assembled guests. "From what, you ask?" his eyes filled with tears and he yelled out, "She died of poverty, of squalor, from need, and from more—from compassion for me. Like my mother, so too my Freydl." Years after Freydl died, Shapiro published privately an exquisite collection of penitential poems in her memory, *From the Women's Prayer Book* (1941).[16]

Following Freydl's death Shapiro returned to New York where, for a time, Communism filled the vacuum in his life. In 1920 he had served as the literary editor of the Communist journal *Funken* (Sparks), writing under the pseudonym Y. Zolot (Russian for "gold"). Then came the anti-Jewish Arab riots of 1929, which marked a turning point in the Yiddish love affair with the Communist Party. On Moscow's orders, the Communist paper *Freiheit* (Freedom) redefined the murder of Jewish civilians and scores of yeshiva students in Palestine as the start of an "Arab Revolution" and castigated the "Jewish Fascists" who had supposedly provoked the bloodshed. Yet when a group of Yiddish writers broke with the *Freiheit* in response to these statements, they did so by "accus[ing] the paper of shifting its policy against the wishes of the Communist regime." What they could not do was to bring themselves to "question their faith in the Communist ideal." Shapiro was among them.[17]

In 1931, at the age of fifty-three, Shapiro published a third story collection, *New Yorkish,* which contains some of his most ruminative and mature pieces: "Eating Days," about a decaying yeshiva in Eastern Europe and the young men who long to escape from it; and two narratives about Jewish life in New York City, the title story, and "Doc." The latter is a series of parodic vignettes about Benny Milgroym—Benny "Pomegranate"—a cigar-maker-turned-demi-doctor who serves as Shapiro's vehicle to lampoon American-style romance, bourgeois aspirations, and, most emphatically, the literary aspirations of Yiddish-speaking immigrants.

"Doc" was Shapiro's requiem to the hopes of a secular Yiddish culture in America. There remained but one road out of the morass of vulgarity, bourgeois accommodation, and false hopes: the Soviet Union. What most attracted him to the great experiment in the U.S.S.R. was its much-publicized support for creative artists. He declared his intention of relocating to this land where serious writers could earn a living from their writing. And whenever, in conversation, anyone raised the subject of Birobodzhan—the so-called Jewish Autonomous Region just north of Manchuria that was Stalin's version of a Soviet Zion—Shapiro's face would light up. "Even his voice would sound stronger, more assertive," reported one of his loyal friends. "The ironic, bitter smile would disappear. . . . He believed in the place—and what a healthy man he would then appear![18]

Eventually, Shapiro came to lament the Communist Party's recourse to censorship as practiced by the *Freiheit,* and he objected to the Communist blind spot for the experiences of the individual. "I would wish that our Proletariat poets," he proclaimed, "would seek and find the path to the two billion individuals who comprise the humans of this world."[19] "Let me write my work!" he exclaimed in private conversation to the critic B. Rivkin in 1936. "Politicos, who turn to the masses, should do their job, obeying the commands of the masses. But we are artists, and the job of the artist is to find in regular life the irregular, to reveal the deep sense and truth of life."[20]

In 1933, after raising funds from his friends and admirers, Shapiro brought out *Studio,* a journal, he claimed, that would be unlike any other. This editorial project rejuvenated him. *Studio* contained stories, poems, and discussions on literary affairs, with Shapiro himself writing stunningly incisive essays under the pseudonyms Lamed Shin, Yud Zayn, and Yud Zolot. Here he also published the long tales "The Chair" and "The American Devil," the latter from his unfinished novel of the same name. The first two issues featured some of the most prominent names in American Yiddish letters: Moshe-Leyb Halpern, Jacob Glatstein, Eliezer Greenberg, B. Rivkin, and Shmuel Niger. But Shapiro's combative style and often catty discussions of the literary scene began to take their toll, making others reluctant to share their material with him. By the third and final issue, the predominant voice was that of Shapiro himself, and another of his creative projects had ended in failure.

Studio charts the shifting and conflicted relationship of Shapiro to the Communist Party. It was a utopian, typically "Shapiro-ish" venture.

Downplaying the role of ideology, Shapiro believed he could champion the freedom of the individual, including the individual artist. Indeed, while staking out various pro-Soviet positions—love of the "common man," faith in the Birobidzhan project—the journal was able to attract a readership drawn from all parties: the leftists, the rightists, a few Zionists, a handful of traditional Jews.[21] Shapiro believed that his literary journal—like literature in general—could break down the barriers between men.[22] But this balancing act between Stalinism and the transcendent value of the individual was one that would become increasingly precarious in the 1930s, and in this Shapiro, like other left-wing Yiddishists, was hardly alone.

For the next few years, he lived primarily off the handouts of friends who saw him as the "great writer." The great writer was, however, falling apart physically; he drank and smoked heavily, and, after being hit by a car, relied on a cane.[23] With the friends he had not yet alienated he spoke of writing *the* great American novel. Many were beginning to see him as a tragic figure.

In 1937, Shapiro was invited to work for the Federal Writers' Project, a program of the Works Progress Administration (WPA), which employed artists and writers during the Depression. The Yiddish Writers' Group, to which Shapiro belonged, was given the task of creating a survey and analysis of Jewish fraternal organizations; the result was published in 1938 as *The Jewish Landsmanschaften of New York*.[24] In 1939, the group brought out a second book, *Jewish Families and Family Circles of New York*.[25]

Shapiro's essays for the Landsmanschaft project are written simply but in an improvisational style very much at odds with the scholarly tone of the rest of the volume, which makes "substantial contributions to American social history."[26] In "Immigration and the Landsmanschaft," for example, Shapiro pithily contrasts Jewish with non-Jewish immigrants to America: "Others came with the pickaxe, the Jew came with the needle." He also offers a survey of Yiddish literature and the Jewish family in America. While his writings for the WPA present an idealized, folksy portrait of American Jewish life, here and there he manages to sneak in barbs at the United States, the home of the Ku

Klux Klan and a place where anti-Semitism can rear its ugly head.[27] In the meantime, he called in sick on numerous occasions because of heavy drinking, and was continually pleading with the WPA to extend his contract.[28] Friends in the Writers' Project sought to protect him from dismissal for alcoholism.

In the late 1930s Shapiro outlined his still-unfinished American novel, *The American Devil*. The main character, the "thread" holding it all together, was his American *baal-guf*, or physically imposing type, Jake Bereza. Originally titled "Suzie from the Bronx," the novel was to be encyclopedic in range, representing the differential response of working-class and wealthy New York Jews to the economic and cultural crises in America and to the survival of the Jewish settlement in Palestine. Shapiro characterized Suzie, Jake's love interest, as the "Yiddish Madame Bovary."[29] The master of the small, controlled gesture, Shapiro was here trying to reinvent himself as an American naturalist, with a panoramic vision of class disparity. Small wonder that the novel remained unfinished.

During these years, Shapiro's rent at the Broadway Central Hotel in lower Manhattan was paid by Noah and Sonya Nakhbush. Noah, a veteran Yiddish actor from the famed Vilna Troupe, had immigrated to America in 1923 and performed solo recitals of Yiddish literature (he even landed a part in a Yiddish film).[30] When Shapiro returned to Los Angeles, the Nakhbushes accompanied him and took him in as a permanent boarder. With his mother and Freydl gone, Shapiro now found in Sonya a woman willing to devote her life to taking care of a brilliant but temperamental child.

Shapiro's life of wandering had by now taken him from the Ukrainian hinterland to Warsaw, back to the Ukraine, back to Warsaw, to London, to New York, to Chicago, to Warsaw, to Zurich, to New York, to Los Angeles, to New York, and finally back to Los Angeles. The man whose American writings were devoted to unmasking the shallowness of the American dream would end his life in the land of eternal sunshine.

Once resettled in Los Angeles at the age of sixty-eight, Shapiro managed to produce one last, highly suggestive volume of literary essays, *The Writer Goes to School* (1945), largely reworked from the pages of *Studio*. Although the collection does not deliver on its promise to trace the education of a writer from start to finish, the title essay explicates Shapiro's poetics of prose in a remarkably analytic and urbane style.

The forties were a period of disillusionment with the radical Left, and a period of sober realignment with the fate of his fellow Jews. "Certainly I'm a Communist," Shapiro readily acknowledged, "but the problem is that the Bolsheviks aren't the Communists that the [first-century] Essenes were. I have seen how Communism, like all our idealistic dreams, is transformed once it gets pulled from the heavens down to earth."[31]

But the fate of a Yiddish writer, even and especially an aging Yiddish writer in Los Angeles, could not be severed from the fate of European Jewry. In the face of their destruction, how could one still portray the Jews as implicated in the violence perpetrated against them? In the face of their utter helplessness, how could one still believe in the liberation of the Jews by and through brute violence? In poems left unpublished, Shapiro evoked an ever-growing abyss between Gentiles and Jews and a cycle of anti-Jewish violence that continued unabated from the mythic times of Haman, to the murderous cossacks Chmielnitsky and Gonta of the seventeenth and eighteenth centuries, all the way to Hitler. Verse had always served Shapiro as his most direct vehicle for addressing the deity, and he now projected his sense of Jewish powerlessness onto the Jewish God. In a poem from 1942, Shapiro composed a personal "Prayer" to the now-impotent God of Israel, asking Him at least to preserve the suppleness, the interiority, the emotional directness of the poet's Yiddish "word."[32]

For all that, Shapiro remained brutally honest until the very end. "I am among you—" he wrote,

And hundreds of miles apart.
I see you through morning and early evening fog,
For otherwise I could not possibly tolerate your presence.
I am among you,
And see you through the fumes of alcohol and nicotine.[33]

In 1946, after losing sensation in his legs and spending days hallucinating in a hospital, Shapiro moved into a converted garage at his friend V. Kessner's house, where he lived until his death. A year later, driven once again by depression, he attempted suicide with sleeping pills. Much to his and his doctor's surprise, he survived and, at least temporarily, found a new lease on life.

On August 24, 1948, however, he lay dying in his garage home in the Los Angeles foothills, surrounded by the clutter of his many failed attempts to create a new process for color photography. "I will not die," he insisted over and over again. The next morning, he succumbed to the prolonged effects of years of alcoholism. His last wish was to lie by Freydl's grave. Thus he was buried in an old cemetery next to a park.[34]

In Los Angeles, Shapiro's literary concerns had been carefully watched over by his most ardent supporter and greatest friend, the writer S. Miller. After his death, it was Miller who oversaw the publication of his posthumous works, *Ksovim,* and wrote the first biography.

II

When the idea for a story took hold of him, Lamed Shapiro reached for any surface he could lay his hands on: the margins of newspapers, the back of a menu, hotel stationery. He often wrote on scraps of paper that he then taped together into one extremely long document, somewhat resembling a primitive quilt. Yet much of his prose fiction came out in nearly finished form. The final, published version of "At Sea," for example, displays hardly any changes when compared with the first draft. (His essays, by contrast, were heavily edited.) Like his life, Shapiro's writing was marked by frenzied activity, the multiple scraps of paper bearing witness to a man possessed by an idea and unable to stop until he expressed it. More often than not, such bursts of activity were followed by dry periods of artistic silence.

Shapiro was a prolific reader of Jewish and world literature. Peretz, the architect and personal embodiment of a modern Yiddish aesthetic, was his decisive influence.[35] Inspired by the older writer's example, Shapiro saw the short story as the ideal vehicle for rendering the Jewish experience in a changing world; he would use a spare, urbane, and extremely polished style to convey the "truth" of a world running headlong toward modernity—and madness.

Peretz was the last of a generation of Jewish writers who could be all things to all people. The next generation went down two separate paths: the lyrical-impressionists in one direction, the naturalists in another. The latter—Schneour, Opatoshu, Weissenberg, Warshawski—sought their subjects on the margins of Jewish society, among horse thieves, peddlers, Jews who were all brawn and no brains, and portrayed a gallery of unsavory characters governed by their passions and victims of their environment. Shapiro the impressionist went them two better, by describing the transformation of a sensitive intellectual into a man of iron and by exposing the brutalized inner landscape of an illiterate, speechless Ukrainian peasant.

Literary impressionism was inspired by French art, notably the works of Monet. Yiddish and Hebrew authors learned the literary version of this technique from turn-of-the-century Russian and Scandinavian writers. The typical hero was a passive, highly sensitive young man or woman who viewed the world through a window, a fog, a passing train. Such sensory impressions were the locus of reality. In these slow-moving stories the most active force was the narrator, usually a highly literate, urbane consciousness who exerted absolute control over the speech, actions, perceptions, and moods of the characters, even while endowing inanimate objects with independent existence. Together with his compatriot and contemporary David Bergelson (1886–1952), Shapiro pioneered and perfected the art of literary impressionism in modern Yiddish fiction.[36]

Shapiro's theme of sexual violence may owe something to still another literary trend popular in the years when he was coming of age: Russian Boulevard writing, an offshoot of the Decadent School, which focused on street life. Following the failed revolution of 1905 and the loosening of official censorship, Russian society became obsessed with questions of sexuality in all its permutations. Literature was rife with hitherto taboo subjects like homosexuality and infidelity. Boulevard writing was marked by tales of sexual violence, prostitution and rape, multiple partners, and sexually transmitted disease.[37]

Shapiro's stories are marked by the same mingling of sex and violence, high and low. But while Boulevard writing located the "animalistic" aspect of humans in their sexual behavior, Shapiro typically finds it in acts of violence. In such stories as "The Kiss," "Pour Out Thy

Wrath," "The Cross," and "White Challah," anti-Jewish violence is seductive and sexualized, and, in a further deviation from Shapiro's Russian models, directed not against women specifically but against Jews. Moreover, whereas in Boulevard writing the violence infects its victim by transforming her into a prostitute, in Shapiro's stories the attacked Jew becomes a perpetrator of violence.

Thematically, I have chosen to group Shapiro's short fiction under the following three headings: pogrom stories, the Old World, and the New World.[38]

Pogrom Stories

The critic Shmuel Niger once spoke of "the mystery of rage" in Shapiro's "The Cross": "the blind, crazy, force that makes a mockery of man and makes a mere game of his desires."[39] In Shapiro's imploding universe, no one is spared the corrosive effects of this violent rage: neither male nor female, young nor old, Gentile nor Jew. As Ruth Wisse has written, "The Cross" was Shapiro's attempt to confront the pogrom not as something utterly counter to Jewish experience "but as a form of energy that would have to be assimilated if Jews were ever to escape its fury."[40]

Thus, when the pogromist in "The Kiss" forces the Jew to kiss his feet, he is making a mockery of Christ's humility in washing the feet of John the Baptist.[41] The cross, the central icon of Christianity and the embodiment of brotherly love and self-transcendence, has become instead an emblem of anti-Jewish violence. But when the main narrator likens the cross to the tefillin, which contain the biblical credo "And thou shalt love the Lord thy God . . . ," we become painfully aware of the Jew's own "conflicted identity" in the presence of brutish reality, with its capacity to undo and invert every fixed value. "As the cross comprises both Jewish covenant (tefillin) and Christian redemption, so the narrator is both Jew and Gentile, victim and pogromist."[42] In "White Challah," the loaf of bread required for the Sabbath is transformed into the physical embodiment of pagan-Christian sacrifice. Part human sacrifice, part Eucharist, the most familiar of Jewish symbols becomes an emblem of cannibalistic violence. Christian violence against Jews

was not to be understood, according to Shapiro, as an outburst of dia-
bolical, ancient evil, but as "the manifestation of the eternal conflict between Christians and Jews, almost as the natural, intelligible conduct
given the present conditions."[43]

Violence in these stories is ubiquitous and crosses all boundaries. It
affects the tangible, external world of the body, producing an unwanted
child or a permanent scar on the forehead. It affects the landscape, dev-
astated as if by a whirlwind. It affects the realm of shared cultural symbols, changing forever the meaning of tefillin and cross, of the nature
of religion itself.

The Old World

Most of Shapiro's shtetls are not to be found on any map. Zagoria-
Vitrok is glossed as meaning "Beyond the Windmill Hills," but its Jewish incarnation, Zahoria, resonates with "Zohar," a mystical source of
light. Krivodov, left unexplained, means "Crooked Oak." Once, all geo-
graphic place names in Yiddish fiction were satiric: Foolstown, Beg-
garsburgh, Rougesville. In Shapiro's fiction, they become states of
mind and symbols of both renewal and loss. The same waterway that
can carry Jews away from the shtetl is a symbol of change that augurs
the town's breakdown.

In Shapiro's tales the shtetl is sick: it is at the beginning of its illness,
or it is dying, or it is dead. In none is it a vibrant place with a promise of
a bright future. In "Eating Days," violence occurs within the privacy of
home and school, and young people must leave in order to find a meaningful life. Even the "Rebbe and the Rebbetzin," with its loving portrait
of a traditional Jewish couple, suggests a future as barren as the rab-
binic couple itself. In a story that begins with the words of a fairy tale,
"Once upon a time," the shtetl is more mythical than real.

The New World

Shapiro's novella "At Sea," first published in Warsaw when he was
thirty-one, connects his Old World and American stories. "At Sea" is a
lyrical tale of immigrant passage. The unnamed narrator is situated
within three locales of self-examination: the old country, where a

pogrom has wreaked havoc on all the generations, and which now exists only in memory; the ocean, representing a present moment of romantic reverie; and the new world, the locus of both fear and longing. The ocean crossing is punctuated by suicide, dramatic encounters, the sighting of a glacier, and ruminations about the cosmos, moments reminiscent of the genre of the romantic quest. But the transitory nature of the voyage matches the immigrant's profound emotional and psychological disorientation.

Once in New York, the protagonist of "The Chair" and "New Yorkish" is still at sea, trying and failing to find his footing. The hustle and bustle of the city becomes for him an impressionist-sensory landscape bordering on chaos. To be sure, his life is no longer filled with the threat of physical violence, and that is no small blessing. "Pogroms, revolutions, wars, come and go," Shapiro argued toward the end of his life, continuing: "And they occupy a relatively short expanse of time. Life's longer path in the human world is sedate, leisurely, 'regular.' . . . Anyway, life, just as it is, is a daily tour from the kitchen to the bathroom and back again, with all the trimmings, with all the attendant nonsense. . . . Our desire to beautify life, to make it significant, is our subjective contribution to the objective world."[44] Thus, he maintained on a rare positive note, his job as a writer was to "collect the regular."[45]

Yet his work tells a different tale. Rather than respond to the stimuli of external reality by leading richly subjective and introspective lives, his New World characters pursue futile attempts to find meaning in the world. It is as if the bright lights of New York have stymied the ability of these young Jews to establish a deep and honest inner landscape. Inarticulate, they are unable to find consolation in Jewish texts, or even to take stock of their lives with a clear and critical eye. In Shapiro's earlier works, characters who were on the move were the best equipped to navigate their inner worlds. Stasis of the soul set in when the body was still. Not so in the tales of New York.

Overall, Shapiro's America is a fractured world where meaning slips away and where men like Manny, the protagonist of "New Yorkish," are caught up in the confusion of modern existence. Manny, the only New York Jew with the capacity for self-analysis, imbued with a rich inner life, is the most isolated from his surroundings. Although Manny readily avails himself of America's manifold pleasures—a vulgar vaudeville show, a one-night stand, *treyf* food—he is also a man of intellectual aspirations. His private world is replete with images from European high culture: "The Ninth Symphony," he says dismissively, "or *Tristan*, or whatever else there may be—without an ear of skin and meat they're nothing, and stuffed *kishkes* console the . . . soul." It is impossible to achieve a proper balance between the stuff of spiritual sustenance and good kosher cuisine, and in the end neither is attainable. For this alienated Jewish intellectual in America nothing can nourish the soul: not the world of American popular and consumer culture, or the world of European high art. Dolores has offered him a moment's respite, but he ultimately rejects her love. Our intellectual hero is left bewildered by his experience of sudden loss.

These American Jewish men have reached the end of the road. Refugees from the shtetl, they had every reason to hope that in America, the land of limitless reinvention, they would find fulfillment. Instead, they have been cast adrift among the corrosive freedoms of the city. American Judaism has become a rabbi in a wheelchair, making a cameo appearance in Jake's nightmare about Sacco and Vanzetti in "The Chair."

By joining the "modern world" they have lost the ability to understand both their internal and external realities. The tides of modern life, while exhilarating, ultimately drown them.

Aspiring to become a true "realist," Shapiro once imagined himself as "The Painter," an unnamed youthful protagonist who is tortured by the desire to realistically render the world, even as he yearns for romantic vistas. How to reconcile the animal-in-man, the human potential for violence, this story asks, with the search for beauty? There is no possible reconciliation. At story's end the painter discovers to his horror that the pristine majestic landscape is marked by a diffuse stain that threatens to blight the world and return it to primordial darkness.[46]

Penned in 1906, this darkly shifting landscape was a portent of the artistic struggle to come. As he matured and mastered the art of expressing the inexpressible, Shapiro achieved a unique blend of naturalism and impressionism. It was is if two other masters of the modernist short story, Isaac Babel and Delmore Schwartz, were fighting it out inside him; the Old World and the New; extremes of human behavior and the pursuit of evanescent beauty. The truth that Shapiro reveals in his best stories is that moments of self-transcendence are few and far between—Menashe enjoying his last smoke as if it were his first; the yeshiva student intoxicated by the sight of female flesh; Manny perceiving Dolores's unadulterated offer of love at the very instant of losing it; Sloveh hearing a familiar Jewish voice penetrate the chaos; a myrtle that blossoms anew against all odds—and that such moments are verifiable only within the sensory perception of the beholder or listener, as the dictates of literary impressionism required. Add to that Shapiro's own uncompromising goal to merge a series of vignettes into a seamless narrative. "The plan," as he described it, "is to give each section its own closure, each chapter being like a closed story, such that the end should circle back to the beginning, like an armband of rings."[47] The attentive reader of *The Cross and Other Jewish Stories* will discover how Shapiro utilized this extremely demanding form both in single-stranded narratives like "Smoke," and in deliciously complex ones like "Eating Days," "The Jewish Regime," "At Sea," and "The Chair." Within a world—and a personal life—marked by chaos and confusion, Lamed Shapiro was able to uncover an incorruptible human essence or a metaphysical symbol that would henceforth be recoverable, in living color, through the perfect medium of his art.

NOTES

1. See Jacob Glatstein's *In tokh genumen: eseyen 1945–1947* (New York: Farlag matones, 1947), p. 119; Eliezer Greenberg's "Bay undz un arum undz" *Getseltn* 3 (1945): 103—[106]; Shmuel Niger's "L. Shapiro," in *Vegn yidishe shrayber*, vol. 2 (Warsaw: Central, 1912), pp. 103–122; and Y. Rappaport, "L. Shapiros perzenlekhkeyt," *Di tsukunft* (October, 1962): p. 367.

2. Abraham Tabachnik, "Lamed Shapiro," in his *Dikhter un dikhtung* (New York, 1965), p. 421.

3. These are the major biographical sources on Lamed Shapiro. The most detailed is the "Biografishe notitsn," written by Sh. Miller, Shapiro's closest

friend. They are found in the posthumous collection of Shapiro's *Ksovim*, ed. Sh. Miller (Los Angeles: L. Shapiro Ksovim Komitet, 1949), pp. 7–18. Additional biographical information can be found in the following lexicons and encyclopedias: Zalmen Reyzen's *Leksikon fun der yidisher literatur, prese un filolgye*, vol. 4 (Vilna: Kletskin Farlag, 1929), pp. 465–69; *Leksikon fun der nayer yidisher literatur*, vol. 8 (New York: Alveltlekher yidisher kultur-kongres, 1981), pp. 533–36; *Encyclopaedia Judaica*, vol. 14 (Jerusalem: Keter, 1971), pp. 1304–05, and Jules Chametzky, John Felstiner, Hilene Flanzbaum, and Kathryn Hellerstein, eds. *Jewish American Literature: A Norton Anthology* (New York: Norton, 2001), p. 154–55; and Esther Frank's MA thesis, "An Analysis of Four Short Stories by Lamed Shapiro," Working Papers in Yiddish and East European Jewish Studies, number 28 (New York: Yivo, 1978).

4. Shapiro discusses his literary awakening in *Der shrayber geyt in kheyder* (Los Angeles: Farlag Aleyn, 1945), pp. 7–8.

5. Ibid, p. 8.

6. Quoted in Sh. Miller's "Biografishe notitsn," *Ksovim*, p. 9.

7. Ibid., 97–98.

8. For the most comprehensive examination of the life and work of *Di yunge*, see Ruth Wisse, *A Little Love in Big Manhattan* (Cambridge: Harvard University Press, 1988).

9. Unfortunately I was unable to discover Freydl's second name in any of the archives.

10. For the full discussion, see Chaim Zhitlovsky's "Kritik un bibliografye: Sholem Ashs 'In a karnaval nakht' un L. Shapiros 'Der tseylem,'" in *Dos naye lebn* (June 1909): pp. 37–46.

11. L. Shapiro, *Noveln* (1909).

12. Sh. Miller, "Biografishe notitsn," in *Ksovim*, p. 11.

13. Zishe Weinper, *Moyshe Leyb Halpern* (New York: Astoria Press, 1940), p. 92.

14. My graduate student Gloria Farler shared this insight with me.

15. Leyvik Chanukov, "Mayn ershte bagegenish mit Lamed Shapiro," in his *Literarishe eseyen* (New York: IKUF, 1960), p. 42.

16. L. Shapiro, *Fun korbn-minkhe* (New York: Farlag Aleyn, 1941).

17. Ruth R. Wisse, "Drowning in the Red Sea: The Lasting Legacy of Jewish Communism," unpublished manuscript.

18. Rashel Hirshkan-Miller, "Mayn bakantshaft mit L. Shapiro," *Zamlungen* 20 (1960): 72–73.

19. Lamed Shin, "Shraybtish," *Studio* 1.1 (1934): 114.

20. As quoted in Mina Bordo-Rivkin, ed., *B. Rivkin: Lebn un shafn* (Chicago: Farlag L. M. Shteyn, 1953), p. 124.

21. L. Shapiro, "Kriyes yam-suf," *Studio* 1.2 (1934): 118.

22. Ibid., p. 119.

23. Y. Bronshteyn, "L. Shapiro," in *Fun eygn hoyz: eseyen un mentshn vos ikh hob gekent* (Tel Aviv: Menorah, 1963), pp. 194–95.

24. *The Jewish Landsmanschaften of New York* (Di yidishe landsmanshaftn fun nyu york) (New York: I. L. Peretz Yiddish Writers' Union, 1938).

25. *Jewish Families and Family Circles of New York* (Yidishe familyes un familye krayzn fun nyu york) (New York: Yiddish Writers Union, 1939).

26. Ibid., p. 10.

27. Shapiro's work for the WPA can be found in the Lamed Shapiro archive at the Yivo Institute, Box 2, folders 36–37.

28. For these letters, see ibid., Box 2, folder 36.

29. See Tabachnik, "Lamed Shapiro," *Dikhter un dikhtung*, p. 422.

30. Noah Nakhbush's biography can be found in Zalmen Zylbercweig's *Leksikon fun yidishn teater*, vol. 2 (Warsaw: Farlag Elisheva, 1934), p. 1404.

31. L. Shapiro, "Mentsh—velt," *Ksovim*, p. 380–81.

32. See the poems "Shma koleynu," "Der mabl," and "A tfile" in *Ksovim*, pp. 56–59.

33. "Mayne fartogn," ibid., p. 61.

34. Bronshteyn, "L. Shapiro," in *Fun eygn hoyz*, p. 196.

35. See Ruth R. Wisse, *I. L. Peretz and the Making of Modern Jewish Culture* (Seattle: University of Washington Press, 1991).

36. For an analysis of the second-generation writers generally, and David Bergelson in particular, see Mikhail Krutikov's *Yiddish Fiction and the Crisis of Modernity, 1905–1914* (Stanford: Stanford University Press, 2001), pp. 38–49, 210–16.

37. For a discussion of boulevard writing, see Laura Engelstein, *The Keys to Happiness: Sex and the Search for Modernity in Fin-de-Siècle Russia* (Ithaca: Cornell University Press, 1992), pp. 359–420.

38. The Yiddish versions of the stories translated in *The Cross and Other Jewish Stories* are located in Lamed Shapiro's story collections: In *Noveln*

(which is dated 1909 but which came out in 1910) are found "The Cross," "Pour Out Thy Wrath," "In the Dead Town," "The Kiss," "The Rebbe and the Rebbetsin," "The Man and His Servant," "Between Fields," and "At Sea." *Di yidishe melukhe un andere zakhn* (The Jewish Regime and Other Stories) (New York: Farlag "Nay-tsayt," 1919) contains all the same stories as found in *Noveln* plus "White Challah," "The Jewish Regime," "Smoke," and "Myrtle." In *New Yorkish* (New York: Astoria Press, 1931) are found "Eating Days" and "New Yorkish." The story "The Chair" can be found in the journal that Shapiro edited (*Studio* 1.1 [1934]: 1–23). The story "Tiger" can be found in the posthumous collection *Ksovim* (Writings), edited by Sh. Miller (Los Angeles: L. Shapiro Ksovim Komitet, 1949).

39. Shmuel Niger, "L. Shapiro," in *Vegn yidishe shrayber,* vol. 2, p. 114.

40. Ruth R. Wisse, "Speaking of the Devil in Yiddish Literature," in *Studies in Contemporary Jewry,* vol. 18, *Jews and Violence: Images, Ideologies, Realities,* ed. Peter Y. Medding (New York: Oxford University Press, 2002), 65.

41. See Robert Wolf, "A Yiddish Manichaean: The Dualistic Fiction of Lamed Shapiro," Ph.D. diss., Columbia University, 1994, p. 100.

42. Ibid., p. 161.

43. Avrom Novershtern, "Di pogrom-tematik in di verk fun Lamed Shapiro," *Di goldene keyt* 106 (1981): 135.

44. L. Shapiro, *Der shrayber geyt in kheyder,* p. 32.

45. Ibid., p. 35.

46. See "Der moler," *Ksovim,* pp. 120–25.

47. L. Shapiro, *Der shrayber geyt in kheyder,* p. 30.

Pogrom Tales

1

His appearance:

A gigantic figure, big-boned but not fat, thin really. Sunburned, with sharp cheekbones and dark eyes. The hair on his head was almost entirely gray, but oddly young, thick, lushly grown, and slightly curly. A child's smile on his lips and an old man's tiny wrinkles around the eyes.

And then: on his wide forehead a sharply etched brown cross. It was a badly healed wound—two slashes of a knife, one across the other.

We met on the roof of a train car which was crossing through one of America's eastern states. And as we were both "tramping" cross-country, we agreed to do it together until we got tired of each other. I knew he was a Russian Jew just like me, and I didn't ask anything else. People like us live the kind of life where you don't need passports.

That summer we saw practically the entire United States. By day we used to travel on foot, cutting through woods, and bathing in the rivers we found along the way. The farmers provided food. That is, some of them gave, and we stole from the rest—chickens, geese, ducks. Afterwards we'd roast them over a fire somewhere in the woods or on the "prairie." And there were also days when, with no other choice, we made do with forest berries.

Sleep came whenever night fell: in the open fields or under a tree somewhere in the woods. Sometimes on dark nights we "hopped a train." That is, we went onto the roof of a car and hitched a little ride. The train flew like an arrow. A sharp wind hit us in the face, carrying the smoke of the locomotive in bits of cloud, dotted with many sparks. The prairie ran and circled around us, and breathed deep, and spoke quickly and quietly, with a multitude of sounds in a multitude of tongues. Distant planets sparkled over us and thoughts entered and swum about our heads, such strange thoughts, wild and open as the voices of the prairie: they seemed each unconnected to the next, they seemed knotted and linked and ringed together. And at the same time, beneath us, in the cars, people sat and reclined, many people, whose path was set and whose thoughts were confined; they knew from whence they came and whither they went, and they told of it to each other and yawned while they would do it, and they would slumber, not knowing that above, atop their heads, there were two free birds resting a while on their way. From where? Whither? At dawn we would jump down onto the ground and go to snatch a chicken or catch fish with makeshift poles.

On one of the last days in August I was lying naked on the sand on the bank of a deep and narrow river and was drying myself in the sun. My friend was still in the river and was making such a ruckus that it seemed like a whole gang of kids were bathing there. Afterwards he got out onto the bank, fresh and gleaming from head to toe. The brown cross on his forehead stood out particularly distinctly. We lay on the sand next to one another for a little while, lay there and kept quiet. I wanted and didn't want to ask him what sort of mark that was on his forehead. Finally, I posed my question.

He raised his head from the sand and gave me a curious look with a hint of mockery.

—You won't get scared?

I hadn't been shocked by anything for years.

—Tell me, I said.

2

My father died when I was a couple of months old. From what I heard about him, I understand that he was a "*somebody.*" A man from another world. I carry around his picture—one entirely made up by yours truly—in my imagination, because, like I said, he was a somebody. Anyway, the story I'm going to tell isn't about him.

My mother was a thin Jewish woman, tall, big-boned, dry and gloomy. She had a little store. She fed me, paid my tuition, and hit me plenty, because I didn't grow up the way she wanted.

What was it she wanted? I'm not completely clear on that. I think she probably wasn't clear herself. She always used to fight with my father, but when he died, she, a thirty-two-year-old woman, used to shake her head at any suggested matches:

—No, after *him* it's not right, I don't need anybody, and how can I take a stepfather for my child?

She never remarried. So I, naturally, had to be like my father, only without his faults. He never really belonged in this world of ours, he was, she used to say, "too passionate." And so the story went. She used to beat me brutally, without mercy. Once—I was about twelve then—she started to beat me with an iron pole that she used to close the shutters of her shop from the inside. I got furious and hit her back. She stood there pale, with big eyes, looking at me. From then on she didn't hit me any more.

The atmosphere between us in the house got even colder and tenser than before. About half a year later I went out "into the world."

Describing everything would take too long and it wouldn't be interesting either. Let me get to the main point. Fifteen years later, I was living in a big city in the south of Russia. I was a medical student and lived off tutoring. I took my mother in, but she was only living with me, she was taking care of herself: she bought and sold used clothing at the market. She didn't have anything to be ashamed of about the living she made, but she looked down on all the other old clothes dealers: who is *she?* Who are *they?*

She was as cold to me as before, at least on the outside, and I was just as cold to her. It even seemed to me that I hated her a little.

But if you went a bit deeper, she didn't bother me as much. I lived in an entirely different world.

3

It was a minor matter: we wanted to remake the world. First Russia, then the world. In the meantime we focused on Russia.

At that time the whole country was feverish with excitement. Larger and larger groups of people were being pulled into the stream, and above their heads exploded, more and more often, like a rocket, the hot, red, fire of individual heroic acts. Well-established heads, high and low, were falling one after another, and the old order was responding, and responding well, among other ways by pogroms against the Jews. The pogroms made no particular impression on me: we had a word for them then, "counter-revolution." It explained everything perfectly. Yes, I had never at the time actually lived through a pogrom: our city was still waiting for its turn.

I was a representative in the local committee of one of the parties. This wasn't enough for me. A thought, sharp as a knife, had slowly but surely cut its way into the depths of my brain. What was it? I wasn't clear exactly and in the meantime I didn't want to know. I just had the feeling that my muscles were becoming stiffer, tenser, and I once found that I absentmindedly had used my bare hands to shatter the back of a chair in one of the houses where I was giving lessons. I was left standing there completely confused. Another time my student asked me, wonderingly, "Who's Mina . . . ?"—and I understood that, lost in thought, I had said the name "Mina" out loud. And I also understood, that though my thoughts were about *one* thing and "Mina" was seemingly just a girl's name, that thought was always connected to Mina's picture, to the sounds that come together with the name "Mina." That particular feeling of significance and importance that was always in the air when Mina was present.

Besides me, the committee consisted of four men and one woman. I don't know what color eyes the men had, but Mina's were blue, bright blue, and at certain moments they grew dark, black and finally deep, pitch black, like a pit. Black hair, a regular, graceful figure, and some-thing slow and serious in her movements.

At our meetings she didn't argue much. She used to make a sugges-tion, or give her opinion about a situation in two or three pithy phrases, and then sit quiet and attentive with her shortsighted eyes squinting slightly. And very often it turned out that, after a long time, once we had heatedly debated and gone over the question and had cleared up all the misunderstandings, we, a little amazed, came to the same conclusion that had already been formulated in Mina's two or three pithy sentences.

She was a daughter of a senior Russian official. That was all we knew about her. At the door of our underground cell each of us would throw away our personal lives, like an overcoat in the foyer.

4

In our city the cloud of a pogrom was quickly approaching the Jews. Strange sounds swirled around the city, sharp and quiet sounds, like the hissing of a snake. People went around with their ears perked up, with quick, sideways looks, and gestured with their noses as if detect-ing a suspicious odor. But quietly and with cunning.

One hot afternoon we gathered together for an additional meeting at Mina's apartment, which also served as our underground cell's head-quarters. The meeting didn't last long: short deliberations, no debates, and a decision to organize in self-defense as quickly as possible. In the course of the meeting I noticed Mina glancing at me occasionally. When the members of the committee began to leave, she gave me a sign that I should stay behind.

I remained there with my hat on my head, leaning my back and both hands against the table, while Mina, with her head bent and her hair spreading over her breast, paced back and forth across the room. We were quiet. After a while, she raised her head, stopped, and looked straight at me. She was pale, very pale, and her eyes were dark and black, as only Mina's eyes could be.

I felt cold. In a flash, as if illuminated by a strong and sudden out-break of fire, my thoughts became clear to me: to become one of the "rockets" who light the way of the revolution, and who pay the price doing it.

And Mina was the first to understand! She saw it on my face, before it was even clear to me. Why . . . ?

—Have you decided? She asked after a while, with a voice half hushed.

—Decided. I answered slowly and firmly, feeling like the decision was being made that very second.

She looked at me for a while, and started pacing around the room again. After a few minutes she became as serious and still as always.

—Anyway, we'll still see one another, she said and gave me her hand.

Going home to mother, I felt that every bone in my body was singing. And I thought about the strange fate of a person, whose life's short path takes him between one woman he practically hates to another that he's beginning to love.

Before I opened the door of my apartment, I took a look at the city. The sun was just going down, and a light, delicate veil, spun of gold and happiness, lay in soft folds on the streets and the houses. Our city was a beautiful city.

5

We were too late. That very same night the pogrom broke out. Suddenly, like an explosion from a buried mine, and right in the area where I lived.

The first screams were mixed up with the haze of the dream I was having. Then I suddenly figured it out, got out of bed, lit a fire, and started quickly getting dressed. At that moment my mother sat up in bed and gave me a funny look.

I felt creepy. It was like she was looking at me coldly and ironically, as if the pogrom were aimed at me and not her. I stood there motionless for a minute, half-dressed. I looked at her, confused. And at that very moment the house trembled, as if it were in the arms of a storm.

The windows exploded with a crash, one door was smashed after another, and a gang of pogromists tore into us along with a foaming wave of broken screams and cries from the street.

I'm a strong man. But until that night I had never had to hit someone in anger. Until that night I didn't know the meaning of true rage which intoxicates, like powerful wine; of anger, that instantly boils your blood, that fires up your whole body, that hits you in the head and pervades all your thoughts. When the pogromists, a varied group, young, old, some with "homemade" weapons and some without weapons at all, attacked me, at first I coldly defended myself. But I was dazed at the same time, as if I didn't exactly understand what it was they wanted from me. Suddenly, after some little thing—I think that someone smashed my writing utensils on the ground—a white heat took control of my whole body, my head started to get dizzy and my hand raised up of its own accord. Across from me there was this short little goy, not very big at all, with a thin, pale face, a stiff yellow mustache and small, pointy eyes full of cold-blooded murder. I remember how I slammed my fist into that face, and couldn't hold back a strange bellow, like a wild ox. After that everything spun around me and in me, spun around fast and hot, and I was having a great time.

I don't know how long it lasted. My anger and my enjoyment grew at the same rate that my strength met resistance and overcame it. At the same time, a kind of chirpy, unyielding voice reached me from somewhere far away, like the buzzing of a mosquito, along with disjointed words in Russian: "Don't have to . . . don't have to . . . tie him up! Tie him up!" The resistance started to grow quickly, more quickly than my strength, from all sides, from above, from below, until it suddenly froze around my entire body, like a stone skin. The joy disappeared, and the anger, the pure hellish anger, scorched my breast and choked my throat. Little by little it cooled, froze and then settled in my heart, like a heavy shard of ice. I came to my senses.

I was lying on the ground tied up, almost entirely wrapped up in rope, hurt, bloody, and the little goy with the pointy eyes was dancing around right near me, but with a really bloody and rearranged face. I also noticed blood on the faces of the other guys standing around me.

They picked me up off the ground like a full gunnysack, and tied me to the footboard of my mother's bed.

My mother! Only now I remembered about her. She had jumped off the bed, apparently to help me, but now someone had dragged her back onto the bed where I was tied up.

I almost didn't recognize her in her shift. Wide, thin bones. Wildly disheveled gray hair and sparkling eyes. Her teeth tightly clamped together and silent. They had thrown her into the bed, across from me.

6

Just imagine:

What's a hair, one single gray hair, pulled out of a head? Nothing, nothing at all. And two hairs? And a clump, ripped out all at once? And many clumps of long, gray hair? Pssh! Absolutely nothing.

Sure, when you break bones they crack. But if you break little sticks, dry wood, and—who knows what else?—they crack too; that's a "natural occurrence."

Just imagine:

What are two old, shriveled breasts? Flesh. Matter. They consist of certain "elements"—just go ask a chemist. Even when they're your mother's breasts. Two modest breasts that nursed you, and that you've never, not even once, seen uncovered since you were a little kid. Even if they're torn into tiny pieces by filthy fingers right in front of your eyes?

Tell me, I ask you:

What does nature, *the world,* know about filth and shame? There's no such thing as filth or shame in nature.

Yes, it's true: never, never was a human body, the glorious body of man and woman, so degraded and debased! But—why should I care? Because—you should know: there's no such thing as filth and shame in nature.

A year or two pass by, and ten, and a hundred, and two hundred. How is this possible? How is it possible that I can live so long? Can a man live so long?

Mama: scream, oh scream! Damn you! What do you think, it's one of those times when you used to hit me so wickedly and you kept so quiet! Just one scream, just a groan! Oh, God! . . .

Years and years . . .

Do you see that bloody face over there? That's the first human face I ever saw in my life. A harsh, gloomy face, but also the first I ever saw in my life. The woman with that face used to beat me, and I hated her. And I still hate her even now, and even more than before, and my hate sticks in my throat and chokes me. Because why then, if not out of hate, do I stare with such intensity at how the face changes from minute to minute? Why don't I close my eyes? Why do they bulge out of my head, with such pain and such burning curiosity? Good, dear people: tear out my eyes. Why should it trouble you at all? One slice with a knife, they'll fall right out—these two watery bubbles, these—these—two cursed watery bubbles, which, I swear, I don't need any more. You laugh! You're merry people, very merry, but tear them out, why should it trouble you at all?

Years and years.

7

The little goy said:

—The old bitch still won't scream. Just let me at her.

A little while passed, and then I heard a sound. It was a groan, a cry, a scream all at once, and there were words in the scream, and though the voice was hoarse and wildly changed, the words rang in my ears loud and clear, like slow, distinct chimes of a bell:

—Oh, my son!

For the first time in her life.

Sweat poured like rain off my forehead and filled my eyes. I gave a jerk with all my might, and the rope cut deeper into my body. God was merciful for the moment: my head spun, and I lost consciousness. But I did manage to hear the laughter all around me.

Later I came to for a minute, and the little goy was talking again:

—Enough. Let her kick the bucket little by little right before his eyes. And I'm gonna cross him up, to save his kike soul from hell.

I felt two deep cuts on my forehead, one across the other, and heard laughter again. A small warm stream ran down my forehead, over my nose, and into my mouth.

I lost consciousness for a second time.

8

Absolute darkness. Absolute silence. Not a single external impression, and no firm internal point. Only everywhere an uneasiness, a heavy uneasiness and a huge effort to find some sort of point.

A single word wandered about in this world of darkness and void, a tiny word: "What?" And three times: "What?" "What?" "What?" And twenty times "What?" The word grows and it spreads and it increases and out of this it becomes: "What is here? What is around? What is me and what is outside of me?" Suddenly a sharp brilliance and a strong pain are in my head. Three words stick in my brain like a thin, long needle that is stuck in one ear and going out the other: "Oh, my son!"

In a moment I regain consciousness.

Night. The lamp has gone out, or *they* have extinguished it before leaving. I stand tied to the bed, and I feel, on my forehead, a wound burning, burning sharp and making me forget all the other wounds. From the city different sounds reach the room: the city screams in the middle of the night, muted screams with occasional sharp outbreaks like a distant fire. Not far from me, on the bed, something quivers in the darkness.

—Mama!

Silence.

—Mama!

No answer. My voice doesn't make it there, in the world of torment, where her harsh, rough spirit is flying around. "Oh, my son!" she called me. Yes, her son, since every drop of blood which she has now spilled flows into my veins through unknown paths and lights a hellish fire there. "Oh, my son!" A heavy hammer is raised slowly and unceasingly up and down. Every time it lands on my head whole worlds collapse in ruins.

9

—What's that on your forehead?

—That's something to save my soul from the torments of Hell, I answer.

They shake their heads and begin to walk away. I become uneasy.

—Wait, I say. I'll explain it to you.

They shake their heads and disappear.

"I am the Lord your God, who has taken you out of the Land of Egypt!"

"Thou shalt have no other gods before me!"

"I am a zealous and vengeful God—and I demand of you: be something!"

The breath of the storm spreads out over the shaken camp. The servile bodies tremble, as if under the lash, but the dark, thin faces and the dark feverish eyes are lit with the red fire that wreathes the mountaintop.

"Oh, my son!" she said. In those very words: "Oh, my son!"

Daylight.

My head is empty and swollen like a barrel. I had to get away from there. Yes, get away, but—ah, the rope. I had to find a way. There has to be some kind of way. Some kind, some kind of way.

I struggle to collect my thoughts as much as I can.

There's an iron nail. In the footboard I'm tied to, a wide-headed nail is pounded in and half-bent. What's a nail doing here? That's not important. But with a nail you can—what can you do with a nail?

I tossed and turned for a long time until I had managed to snag one end of the rope onto the nail. Then I started rubbing the rope over the sharp iron head.

Hours passed. I became confused and hardly knew what I was doing, but I have, apparently, continued my work with the exactness and the stubbornness of a machine. Then the moment came, and the rope gave a little. A little more effort, a little more—and at my feet lay tattered, frayed rope; at my feet there lay the shattered shards of gods.

10

I bent over the bed. There was definitely something there. It was feverish and had no resemblance to a human being, but the groans had already become so quiet, my ear could hardly catch them. I spoke quietly: "Mama . . ." My breath reached the wound that was formerly a face, and I said once more: "Mama!"

Movement took place over the wound, and something opened. I looked at it closely. This had been an eye. An eye—the other had leaked out. The eye was soaked with blood, but despite that it sparkled, like a glowing coal.

Did it recognize me? I don't know. It seemed to me it did, and that it looked at me with a question and a harsh demand. "Yes, yes, it's going to be fine!" I said loudly and seriously, not knowing for certain what I was talking about.

Afterwards I looked around the room. A table leg lay among the other pieces of smashed furniture. It was round, thick, and well-shaped. It would do.

I raised the table leg and with all my might I brought it down on the glowing eye. The bloodied something gave a single twitch and then lay there like a stone. The glowing eye was no more.

A short sigh and a kind of strange, quickly stifled roar reached my ear. But this was against my will, I assure you. The voice was so strange, that I wasn't sure whether or not it was mine.

When I went out onto the street the sun was about to set. That old sun, that had spun its gold here a thousand years ago. Who was it that said that a thousand years was more than a day? I was a thousand years old.

11

And so began the darkest day of my life.

The city had survived a sort of fever. Arson, murder, bloody beatings and shooting in the streets. A self-defense unit had indeed been organized while already under the fire of the pogrom.

What did I do then? I don't know. First I found myself among the ranks of the self-defense corps, and then in the masses of the pogromists. I felt like a leaf carried along by a storm. On my forehead, the cross burned. In my ears, "Oh, my son!" rang.

If I'm not mistaken, I once encountered *my goy*—the goy who, by all accounts, belonged to me alone. I had the feeling that if I wanted to, I could take him and put him right in my pocket. He grew pale, and, apparently, couldn't move. I didn't take him, though. He awakened nothing in me. I just gave him a friendly smack across the shoulders and winked at him merrily with one eye. I didn't notice whether this inspired more courage in him.

A second scene has remained in my memory.

An old Jew is running across the street, and after him a young goy about sixteen, an axe in hand. The goy catches up to the old man and with one blow splits his head open. When the old man falls, the goy presses down on his split head with his boot.

At that moment a young Jewish man runs over with a revolver in his hand. A pale young man, a thin face. Glasses.

They run, and I follow. The young Jew shoots and misses. The goy abandons the wide open street and ducks into a courtyard. I trip on something and fall.

When I got to the courtyard, the goy was standing in a corner with his back leaning against a fence. His almost childlike face had turned green, his gray eyes were huge and round, and his fine teeth were chattering quickly.

The young Jew stood right up close to him with the revolver in his raised hand, but his face was even paler than before. He looked at the wild fear of the young flesh and blood, looked for a moment, and then he placed the revolver to his own head and fired.

The last remnant of sanity vanished from the goy's eyes. He sat down next to the body that was twitching near his feet, stood up again and with a mad cry jumped over the corpse and ran out of the courtyard.

A loud laugh tore out of me. My foot raised of its own accord and gave a kick to the bloodied corpse that was writhing on the ground, like a trampled worm.

12

This went on for days and nights. I don't know how many. One evening I stood at a door and knocked on it in a certain way. It was a sign that one of us was coming. What sort of signal was that? What purpose did it serve and how did I come to know it? I never asked these questions, the same way you don't ask those kind of questions in a dream. The door opened and I saw Mina.

Lightning flared in my brain, and for a moment I was overwhelmed by terror. I understood where I was and what I was going to do. And at that moment I grew calm.

She didn't recognize me right away, and then she gave a little shudder. She grabbed me by the hand and pulled me into the room. I let her sit me down on a chair.

She looked at my head and at my forehead where the cross burned, and was silent. Afterwards, she said with a muted voice:

—Tell me.

I told her. I told everything gladly, slowly. In detail. The agonies of my mother and the shameful details. On her face the colors kept changing: red, white, green and yellow. When I finished, I bowed to her with a pleasant smile. She hardly noticed and buried her face in both her hands. Afterwards she uncovered her face, which was stained with real tears. I swear to you: wet, soft, and so warm. She got down on her knees in front of me and took my hand. My smile grew wider. This time she saw it, and quickly got up from the ground, and started to go back and forth across the room, casting nervous glances in my direction. I just sat there and smiled, as it seemed to me, very pleasantly.

Finally she decided to try something which she, apparently, supposed was very clever. She sat down once more on the chair across from me and asked quietly:

—And your decision?

My decision? What decision? Wait a minute. Yes, years ago, many years ago, I had made some sort of decision, a very important decision, but—about what? Suddenly I remembered.

I laughed right in her face. Then I immediately grew serious and looked her right in the eyes. She turned white, like linen, and jumped out of her chair. Slowly and calmly I also stood up.

I raped her.

She defended herself, like my mother. But what good were her powers against the man with the cross on his head? Flaming redness and a corpse's paleness played frighteningly across her face. She didn't scream. She bit her lower lip, chewed it and swallowed the blood. And I did my work. With all of the attendant degradations. It lasted a long time.

Afterwards I strangled her. I did it fast and thunderously. I sank my fingers, my long, bony fingers, into her white throat. She turned red, blue, and then black. The end came quickly.

I threw myself down onto a chair and immediately fell asleep, as if I had sunk into deep water. Dreamless.

13

When I woke up I noticed that the candle on the table had hardly shrunk at all. I had probably slept no more than fifteen minutes. But I was refreshed, lively and calm. The exclamation: "Oh, my son!" hasn't left me to this very day, but it has become softer, more maternal. My mother's soul had found its peace.

Our underground cell was arranged comfortably, almost elegantly, so as to eliminate any suspicion. I went into the bathroom and washed my face and my hands thoroughly. The mirror showed me that my hair had turned gray. I finally saw the cross that I had only felt this whole time. The wound didn't hurt any more, it only stung a little.

At first, I wanted to take a knife, cut a slice out of my forehead and erase the cross. Afterwards I reconsidered. It should stay. "They shall be frontlets between your eyes . . . " Ha! Were these the sort of "frontlets" our dear, old God had meant?

14

I didn't owe anything to anyone and I didn't want to pay for anything.

That very same night I left our city. A few days later I crossed the German border and set sail for America.

The sea greeted me with endless vastness, with raw winds, and sharp, salty breath. It spoke to me of wondrous things, both out loud and silently. I listened to it with joy and with astonishment. I will not tell you in words what it related to me.

Almost immediately after my arrival in America I began to wander across the land. The prairie began to explain in its own language what the sea had meant with its speech. Ah, the prairie! Her nights, her days!

It has been three years that I have wandered. And I, newborn child, feel, that I have become strong enough. Soon I shall return to civilization.

And then—

I looked over in his direction, but he didn't say anything else. He had, apparently, forgotten all about me.

And I, a man who hadn't been shocked by anything for years, thought:

There will come a generation of men of iron. And they will build that which we have let lie in ruins.

1909 (translated by Jeremy Dauber)

1

True, it had been a terrible storm. Yet when you are nine years old you quickly forget even the most violent tempest. And Meyerl had turned nine a few weeks before Passover. However, it was also true that winds were always blowing through their house: biting, icy gusts which cut into him and reminded him of that storm. In fact Meyerl spent more time in the wild streets of New York than in the house. Tartilov—and then New York. New York had flooded over Tartilov and washed it out of his memory. The only thing he still remembered was a dream from that time. And besides, when you are nine years old you quickly forget any storm. But even if it was just a dream it was still terrifying!

At that time they had been studying at kheyder. They were really just going through the motions, because at the end of term, on the Days of Repentance leading up to Rosh Hashana, the rebbe relaxed a little. So while they were sitting learning, suddenly from the street came the sound of doors banging, and through the windows of the kheyder they saw Jews running around as if they had gone mad. They were jerking and spinning about, just like leaves in a whirlwind, when a witch rises up from the earth in a pillar of dust and spins through the street, so swift and unexpected that a shiver goes though your body. Seeing the people running around in the street, the rebbe collapsed onto his chair, as white as a corpse, his lower lip trembling uncontrollably.

Meyerl never saw him again. Afterwards people said that the rebbe had been murdered. Meyerl was not pleased to hear this even though the rebbe used to beat the pupils brutally. But he also wasn't sorry about it either. He just didn't really understand what had happened. What did that mean: "murdered?" And so the whole puzzling question completely disappeared from his mind, together with the rebbe.

Afterwards the real terror began. For two days, together with some older people, he and some boys hid in the bathhouse without food, drink, or their parents. The adults wouldn't allow him to go home, and once, when he started screaming, they almost smothered him. He carried on sobbing and shaking, unable to stop crying immediately. A few times he dozed off, and when he woke with a start, nothing had changed. In the midst of all the horror, he only heard one word—"goyim"—which conjured up in his mind an image of something really terrible. The rest of it was very confused. In fact he did not actually witness anything directly. Later, when it was all over, no one came to look for him, and he was taken to his home by a stranger. Neither his father nor his mother said anything to him, but acted as if he had just come back from kheyder as usual.

Everything in the house was destroyed. His father's arm had been dislocated and his face beaten up. His mother was lying on the bed with her blonde hair tousled, her eyes puffy as if she had overslept, her face pale and dirty. Her whole body looked untidy, like a heavy, crumpled featherbed. Meyerl's father silently paced about the house, not looking at anyone, his bandaged arm hanging in a white sling around his neck. Meyerl suddenly sensed some kind of hidden horror and burst out sobbing. His father merely looked at him with a bleak, morose expression and continued pacing about the room without saying a word.

Three weeks later they sailed for America. During the voyage the sea was very rough, and Meyerl's mother lay below on her bunk vomiting violently. Meyerl was fine. His father however kept on pacing backwards and forwards on the deck, even in the heaviest rain, until one of the ship's crew came and drove him below deck.

Meyerl didn't know exactly what happened, but at one point a goy on board annoyed his father—laughing at him, or something like that—and his father drew himself up and gave him a look. It was only a look, but the goy was frightened. He retreated and started crossing himself while spitting and muttering inaudibly. When Meyerl saw the way his father twisted up his mouth and ground his teeth, with his eyes protruding out of their sockets, he was also scared. Meyerl had never seen him looking like that. But soon his father started pacing the deck again with his head buried in his turned-up collar, his hands in his sleeves, and his back hunched.

When they landed in New York, Meyerl's head began to spin, and pretty soon Tartilov had turned into a dream.

2

It was the beginning of winter, and soon masses of fresh, white snow began to fall. Meyerl had become a "boy." Like all boys, he went to school, he learned to throw snowballs, whiz down slides, and light fires in the middle of the street—and no one was upset. He lived mostly on the streets and would come home only to grab some food or sleep.

Cold, biting draughts penetrated the house, making it seem strange and eerie. Meyerl's father, a thin, large-boned man with a dark-skinned face and a black beard, had always been quiet and only occasionally spoke to say things to his wife like: "Listen to me, Tsipe . . . " Now he was completely silent and it was really frightening. Mother, on the other hand, had always been lively and talkative, constantly bustling around with her "Shloyme" this and "Shloyme" that and telling lots of stories. But now all this had changed completely. Father constantly paced around the room while Mother followed him with her eyes like a child, as if she was desperate to say something but did not dare to. And there was something different about her expression. What was it, exactly? It reminded Meyerl of the eyes of the dog Mishka that he loved to play with back there, in the shtetl that had become a dream.

Sometimes, waking up suddenly in the middle of the night, Meyerl heard his mother sobbing. At those times his father, in the other bed, would be smoking his cigar, drawing on it fiercely. It was frightening to see the glow flaring up as if of its own accord as it hovered over his father's dark head. As sleep overcame Meyerl, his mother, the glowing cigar and the whole room would jumble together in his head and then fade away.

Twice that winter his mother was ill. The first time it lasted for two days and the second time for four, but both times it seemed very serious. Her face was fiery-red, and she bit her lower lip so hard with her sharp white teeth that it bled, but, despite that, wild groans revealed her dreadful pain. She vomited frequently as she had during the sea voyage. The vomiting was so violent that it seemed as if her intestines were going to come up.

At these times she did not look at Meyerl's father pleadingly. No, this was something different . . . this was like . . . what was it like? . . . Oh yes! It was like the time when Mishka had a sharp thorn stuck deep in his paw, and he squealed and howled with furious rage while chewing his paw as if to devour it and the thorn together.

Father also was different during those periods. He didn't just pace but ran about the room with the smoking cigar crackling ceaselessly between his teeth. Instead of the one cloud which perpetually hovered motionless over his brow, now cloud after cloud chased each other, twisting into the deep broad furrows. From time to time it was as if flashes of lightning passed over and then were immediately extinguished again. He did not look at his wife, and neither of them paid any attention to Meyerl, who felt altogether lost and lonely.

It was strange, but it was at those times that Meyerl felt drawn to stay at home. In the street everything was just as usual, whereas at home. . . . There, it was rather like the atmosphere in the synagogue during the Days of Awe when the shofar was blown as tall fathers with prayer-shawls over their heads stood holding their breath, and from far away the note of the *tkiye* reverberated over the congregation—a solitary, powerful, long-drawn-out sound: to-to-u-uuuuuuuuu!

Both times after his mother recovered a dark shadow would descend on the house. Father became even gloomier, and Mother's expression, as she followed him with her eyes, was even more submissive and dejected. Meyerl in turn would run out of the house and into the noisy street.

3

The white snows had become less frequent and soon they departed altogether like birds leaving the nest. It felt as if something new was in the air. What it actually was, Meyerl couldn't really say. But in any case, it must be something good, something very good, because all the people in the street were very happy about it. You could see that in their brighter and friendlier faces.

On the morning of the Eve of Passover the sky also cleared a little at home. It was as if the outdoors and the indoors were clasping hands through the window, which had been opened for the first time. This friendliness made Meyerl feel happier.

Father and Mother made preparations for Passover. They were, however, meager preparations: there was no festive, noisy matzo-bakery so they instead bought a package of cold, ready-baked matzos. There was no barrel of borscht standing in the corner covered with coarse unbleached linen. There were no dusty Passover dishes to get down from the attic where they had been kept for years. Instead, father bought cheap unmatched odds and ends of crockery from a street peddler. But all the same, there was a still a slightly festive atmosphere that warmed Meyerl's heart. Once or twice, back in Tartilov, Meyerl had lain in bed at night with his eyes open, his heart petrified with fear, listening to the dark stillness. It seemed as if the whole world—his whole family—had died. But the sudden simple crowing of a cockerel was enough to fill his heart again with a warm stream of joy and homely comfort.

Father's face brightened a little. When he was wiping the glasses for Passover, although his eyes still stared rather distractedly, his lips looked as if they might just break into a smile at any moment. Mother appeared almost cheerful as she bustled around in the kitchen, preparing the first of the matzo-pancakes, which were sizzling and chattering in the pan, when a neighbor came in to borrow a pot. Meyerl was standing beside his mother. The neighbor took her pot, and the women started exchanging a few words about the forthcoming festival. Then the neighbor said: "And there'll soon be something else to celebrate in your house, won't there?" pointing at mother with a smile and a wink. It was then that Meyerl suddenly noticed for the first time that his mother's figure had become rounder and fuller. But he had no time to think about it, for he heard the crash of breaking glass from the other room. His mother stood as if she had been struck dumb, and his father appeared in the doorway.

"Get out!"

His voice made the windowpanes rattle, as though a heavy wagon was riding over the cobblestones.

With a clumsy movement, the terrified neighbor turned round and left.

4

Father and mother looked awkward in their festive clothes, with their faces like mourners at a funeral. In fact the whole "seder" seemed awkward. The atmosphere was more like the last evening meal before the fast of Tisha B'av. When Meyerl began chanting the Four Questions in an expressionless voice, like someone hired for the job, he felt his heart aching; around him all was strangely silent, like in the synagogue when an orphan is reciting his first kaddish . . .

Mother's lips were moving without any sound at all. From time to time she wet her finger and turned over the pages, one after the other, and a large, heavy, shining teardrop slowly rolled down her beautiful but unhappy face, falling on the siddur, on the white tablecloth, or on her clothes. Father did not look at her. Did he see her weeping? And how strangely he recited the Haggadah! He chanted a little bit of it with a melody, with long-drawn-out tones, and then suddenly his voice would break down with a choking sound, as if a hand was squeezing his throat. Then he would look at the Haggadah again, or his unfocused eyes would stray around the room. He would start to recite again, until his voice broke down once more . . .

They hardly ate anything and each of them said the grace privately and silently. Suddenly father said: "Meyer, open the door."

Rather nervously, full of vague fear of the prophet Elijah, Meyerl pulled the door open.

"*Shfoykh khamoskho al-hagoyim, asher loy yedo'ukho*—Pour out Thy wrath upon the nations that know Thee not!"

A slight shudder ran down Meyerl's spine. A voice that was completely strange to him resounded from one corner of the room to the other, shot up to the ceiling, flung itself downwards again and began to ricochet off the four walls, like a caged bird going berserk. Meyerl turned to look at his father, and his hair stood on end with terror. A wild figure in a long snow-white robe, as straight as a taut violin string, with a black beard and a thin, dark-skinned face stood by the table. Its eyes were burning with a dark, eerie fire. It grated its teeth and its voice turned into the wild howling of an animal roaring for quivering flesh and warm blood. Mother sprang out of her chair, shaking in every limb. She looked at Father for an instant and then threw herself down at his feet, clutching the hem of his long white robe with both hands and letting out a wail.

"Shloyme, Shloyme. Please kill me, Shloyme! Put an end to me! Oh, the agony, the agony!"

Meyerl felt all his insides turning over, as if a large hand had dug into them with long talons and twisted them with one tearing movement. His mouth opened wide, and the scream of a terrified child burst out of his throat. Tartilov suddenly whirled in front of his eyes. Terrified Jews were rushing about in the street like leaves in a storm. The pale rebbe was sitting on his chair, his lower lip trembling. Mother was lying on the bed, all screwed up like a crumpled featherbed. Meyerl sensed as clearly as if it had been written there in front of his eyes, that all that was not over, that it was just beginning, that the real, enormous calamity was coming and was about to fall on their house, on their heads, like a thunderclap. Once again a scream of wild helpless terror burst out of his throat.

A few Italian neighbors were standing in the corridor, staring at this incomprehensible scene and whispering fearfully to each other. In the room the terrible curse still resounded; one instant ringing out in strong steel-like tones, and in the next, in the rasping, persistent death rattle of a slaughtered man:

Mighty God! Pour out
Thy great wrath upon the nations
Who have no God in their hearts!

Thy great wrath upon the kingdoms,
That know not Thy name!
My body they have devoured, devoured—
My house they have laid waste, laid waste!
Let Thy wrathful anger pursue them!
Pursue them—and overtake them,
Overtake them—and destroy them utterly
From under the heavens!

1908 (translated by Heather Valencia)

◆ ◆ ◆ *In the Dead Town*

1

A certain soft and peaceful quiet always reigns in the town of the dead.

All the former people whose tents are to be found there, even the happiest among them, never enjoyed, down below in the town of the living, such joyful peace, such mild stillness as they do now. Throwing off their heavy bodies like tight, bulky clothes and leaving them under the tombstones, they, the freed, lightened souls go out of the graves and soar over the holy place of their eternal rest; they examine their kingdom and gaze far beyond it.

Whatever their eye sees glancing northward, stretches before them as white shimmering corn fields under the golden rays of the golden sun. Westward, on the other side of the wide, dusty road, they see two or three sleepy peasant huts and behind them—again the hot shimmering cornfields. Eastward, under their feet, at the bottom of the sharply severed clayish hill, flow the yellowish waters of a wide river, and on its opposite bank, trees, branches and willows curve higher and higher until they support the sky there, in the distance, like a dark-blue mountain pass. Only southward do the souls throw an involuntary and unhappy glance and quickly avert their eyes. There in the valley, under the gray fog, lies the town of the living, their former abode.

Long rows of huts of primitive yet varied architecture with high and low tombstones mark the cemetery on all sides: newly laid graves as well as long overgrown earthen mounds are arranged symmetrically in some places, scattered with a free hand in others. Ink trees and "tomb pears" reach out of the green-grassed carpet that is richly sprinkled with flowers, flowers and more flowers. Carefree, fearless of the sun and the shine of day, the light souls soar over the wide graveyard from one end of the fence to the other. Many, the boldest among them, take the liberty of flying over the fence into the open field to flap their wings frivolously over the heads of the sleeping corn husks and return quickly with subdued laughing whispers. Still and peaceful in the dead town; still and peaceful.

Occasionally, a living person looks into the dead town or someone approaches too near the fence; then all the souls disappear like a dream. Only by the horror that seizes his soul does the passerby realize that someone was here and that something occurred. Even when old Dan, the caretaker of the place of rest, strides through the "field" with his shovel in hand and the tassels of his undergarment running on ahead—the souls take refuge among the tombstones, peer out impatiently from every crack and wait: when will he go and leave the place free for them?

Only one living person has access to them. When nine-year-old Beylke, old Dan's granddaughter, appears among the graves, the purified souls fuse with the sun's rays and the free field winds and together they embrace her, play with her curly black hair, pursue her, catch her, release her and pursue her again. Beylke runs among the tombstones, jumps and dances, claps her hands and babbles something. Her laughter rings in the dead stillness like a thin, happy bell in a deserted snow-ridden steppe. Hearing her voice, old Dan looks out the window and calls out to her:

"Beylke . . . Beylenyu! Who are you talking to there, daughter?"

She doesn't hear him and disappears among the graves. Her grandfather watches her with dark, worried eyes, utters a quiet sigh and his lips murmur with embitterment and pain:

"Daughter, dearest daughter . . . what'll become of you?"

2

He on the threshold of death, she on the threshold of life, and together they guard the dead town.

For thirty years old Dan has been living in the small cottage with the blind windows. For thirty long years he has been silently opening the old ash colored gate under the overgrown roof and has admitted the endless line of stretchers. To this day he cannot overcome the quiet and gentle excitement that strikes him every time a new member joins the dead community. Once again someone has died! Of course it cannot be otherwise for God created the world in this way. . . . And while the assistants pour earth into the grave, while the orphans recite the kaddish and the crowd looks and listens, Dan's expression is serious and meaningful. An important event has occurred. A man has gone to account for his deeds. A mound of earth sprouts forth and the crowd disperses. Only then does the old man approach the grave, examine it carefully, observe its neighbors and begin to calm down. Somewhat later when a headstone grows out of the fresh mound, Dan enters it in the register. Only a name remains of the person. Before the old man's eyes stretches a long straight row, similar epitaphs, no telling one from the other.

Once the old man had many children—daughters and sons, their husbands and wives—it was a large family. Like water it dissolved: one died, one left for America, one for somewhere else. The Missus was still alive not too long ago and then the small cottage with the little windows was much homier. But as soon as Beylke was brought here three years ago after the "incident," the Missus began to expire like a light. Two months sufficed for the old woman to move from the cottage to the foot of the old pear tree that stands over there, not far from the fence, facing the South. Even now when the old man's heart is heavy—every man has moments such as these—he visits the tree secretly, to avoid Beylke's eye, and reads, as if for the first time, the inscription on the stone: "The woman Malka daughter of Reb Tanhum Solomon." He sits down and stares. His head is confused not with thoughts but with . . . nonsense. It pulls at the heart a little. Sometimes he imagines a wonderful place near his Malka, a quiet secluded corner. It's no use—his resting place will be elsewhere, among the males.

Before leaving he has a habit of feeling the lettering on the tomb with his fingers, almost haphazardly it seems. Then he drags himself away thoughtfully and slowly . . .

. . . And lives with Beylke. For the first period after her arrival she walked around as if in a daze but, children being what they are, her laughter now resounds over the entire burial ground. Curly black hair, a full, rounded face and pale blue, the palest of pale blue eyes. "A noblewoman," thinks grandfather as he looks at her. He feels a strange sensation in her presence, like an old, faithful servant who has the honor of educating a princess. The old man himself has gray, hard and angry eyes, a grayish and similarly angry moustache. Sometimes he tries to make an angry face but the little one knows his heart and laughs—laughs in such a way that Dan begins to blink his eyes, hums and lets his fingers caress her hair—pure silk!

He suffers enough on her account, however. Firstly, how can a child have no fear whatsoever of earthly things? She climbs trees, jumps down from the fence to the ground, and when she runs wild among the tombs, even a man on horseback could not catch up with her. No fence was constructed on the far side of the cemetery. There the "field" drops directly down to the river like a wall. While Dan is afraid of even approaching the spot, she descends, climbs back up, bathes in the river and swims.

Secondly, she seems too closely related to "them." She appears to converse with someone, to laugh and sing. Does she really see anything? It's not a good sign when a living person becomes a buddy of "theirs." What can it be? They really should have no power whatsoever over a child who has never sinned. Isn't that so? Whom then does she speak to?

The old man fears something else in Beylke even more. Her singing, jumping and dancing seem all right. Sometimes, though, very seldom, she sinks into thought. Then her smooth white forehead wrinkles up, wrinkles up just like an old man's. A deep ridge protrudes between her thick black eyebrows and casts a cloud over her face. With that, her moist light-blue eyes become extinguished and dark, almost black. Then they become bottomless as the river under the hill when it clouds over on the verge of anger. The old man is struck with fear. He sees instinctively that she is struggling to remember something. Her face pales, ages and she becomes her mother, her mother, may she rest in peace, in every detail. For hours it continues in this way.

"Beylke," Dan calls out with uncertainty. "Would you like something to eat, daughter?"

She doesn't answer.

3

Over the graveyard stand several pear trees on which grow small, hard, round pears. Beylke prefers to eat these sandy, very sour pears. Or better yet—to jump up as high as possible, to grab a branch and shake it, shake it . . . The pears jump over the earth, dance on Beylke's head like hail, and if one of them has the urge it disappears into the grass, somewhere very close by, almost at her feet; and search for it, if you will, for days on end, you still won't find it. But best of all is climbing the oldest pear tree that stands near grandmother's grave, way up to the top, picking the fruit from the thickly populated branches and throwing them down one by one, here and there. How strange the world looks when seen from the tip of the tree! The ends of the sky diverge slightly. The earth gets bigger and the graveyard—smaller. The town in the distance emerges somewhat clearer, like an old garment with many green, red, white and plain old dirty patches. The river burns under the sun in a heavy stupor. If grandfather just happens by underneath the tree, waddling so ridiculously, small, agile, one foot forward, one foot back and he fumbling in the middle, he hears a ringing laugh overhead, shudders and jerks his head upward. He doesn't always succeed in convincing Beylke to climb down for fear she might fall off.

On the edge of the graveyard, where the ground drops down to the river, grows a willow. Crooked it stands and hangs over the precipice. To compensate, it dug its roots deep into the guts of the clay, stretched its long thin fingers, entangled them, sharpened one with the other and now stands securely. From time to time the wind shakes it, fondles its light, straight almost priestly braids and the willow creaks quietly and dreamily—and remains standing.

Beylke likes to sit in the willow and look at the river. A little lower downstream stands the dark green dock. Lorries, boats and rafts rock on both sides. A steamer passes, puffs tobacco smoke and slaps the water with its wheels. Beylke anxiously observes the deck. A peasant woman in a red kerchief with heavy boots on her feet; a fellow in a jockey cap with binoculars at his eyes—how strange! There are so many different people in the world: green, red, with kerchiefs, with glasses at their eyes. These are not real little men of course, only toys. Wouldn't it be worth it to break one of them open and see what's going on inside? There ought to be wheels and spools and teeth, just like in grandpa's old clock that fell to the floor once and has been coughing ever since. Hm . . . strange creatures are these little men and these clocks.

And when Beylke feels very light, she likes to let go of the trunk of the willow, to grab hold of a branch and remain hanging only by her hands. The willow sways and says something—one could swear it says something—and Beylke's feet hover free in the air. Throwing a glance below, she sees the river swaying towards her: up and down, up and down. Dan saw her once in this position and the hair on his head began to prickle.

This is the way she grew up in the cemetery.

Juices rose directly out of the earth, flowed through her veins, penetrated her soft bones and invigorated her. The sun filled and colored her cheeks as it fills and colors the fruit on the tree. Flowers blossomed, butterflies fluttered in the air and the souls, the pure peaceful souls of the once troubled people encircled her at every step, hovered over her head and murmured into her ear:

"Little child, little girl, little girl, little child . . ."

4

In Elul, when the first signs of weariness appeared on the burning, exposed face of the summer, life in the lower town boiled stronger, rose like a spring flood, whose crests rolled up to the hill, splashed apart and stormily inundated the dead town.

From dawn till the dead of night, crowds of wives, men, children, walkers and wagons stretched over the dusty way from the graveyard and to the graveyard.

The gray gate under the rotting roof opened wide, and through it life burst into the field with all its confusion: with its hidden wounds exposed, with shrieking beggary and with prosperous bare-faced thievery. On the road, on both sides of the gate, stood beggars in two rows, cripples, old men tripled up, women with red, tearful eyes—they stretched out their hands, moaned, mumbled and fought among themselves. At the entrance proper, at two long tables, sat Jews with plates, bowls, books and notes, who wrote and received, received and wrote. And from all sides, among the gravestones, from the farthest most hidden corners of the field rose prayers, cries, shouts, long and drawn out, pained, dispirited and broken like the people who uttered them. The agitated, frightened souls who were ordered from above not to set foot outside the cemetery for the duration of the month, hid in their graves and listened with discontent to all the complaints, the hardships that were laid down before them, the well-known hardships that they had long since abandoned. On the very ground, on the graves, on the grass, on the people, stiffly lay an awkward mixture of sun-gold and man-groan.

Just as Dan could not accommodate himself to death, so Beylke could not comprehend life. Since her arrival here, she had been to town perhaps three times, no more, and each time she returned in confusion. Whenever a corpse was brought, Beylke hid herself among the graves and attentively, somewhat wildly, considered the attendants— they appeared as strange and remote to her as those passengers on the steamers that she often observed from atop the willow. It still seemed to her that they were mere play-people, not Beylkes. They made believe that they walked, talked, did things but—it was not real. Grandfather, though, was another case. He was—grampa, her grampa. She knew him the way he really was, try as he might to appear angry when he was gay or pretend to be happy when his heart was heavy. After all, grandfather was almost a Beylke and all the other people—were not.

But come the month of Elul, Beylke could find no place for herself. For the whole month life boiled, foamed, moaned and shook before her eyes, as in a fit. For a whole month on end, the cogs inside the toys grated and turned feverishly and the little men cried, argued, talked about something or other, and cried again. It often happened that the wheels inside one of the little men got jumbled and stopped with a bang. Then the little man emitted a broken, choked moan and fell silently face down on any random tombstone . . . Beylke sensed a growing awareness within herself. They awakened something within her, forgotten pictures, muffled sounds, or what? There was no hiding from them. They were everywhere—in every corner or hill, and wherever they came they chased the souls underground and brought into the place of eternal rest their eternal unrest. With each day something grew and was nourished. Beylke sensed a hidden horror. Only after the month ended and the Days of Awe passed and the human stream gradually abated into the valley, did Beylke draw a deep breath.

Then the liberated souls would leave the cemetery for a while, would rise to heaven and leave behind them a deep longing. The autumn that comes is like her grandfather: gray and gruff, but basically good hearted and very sad. A melancholy moves into the "field," the trees look meager, the willow speaks, but of something else entirely, something other. Rain and wind. Wind and rain. No more sky. So it continues until . . .

5

"Grampa, Grampa! The souls have flown in!" shouts Beylke, looking through the window into the field. She runs out of the cottage.

Truly: the souls have flown in. Light, white. Tiny, they come from all sides of the sky, dance in the air, attack Beylke like white butterflies, alight on her brows, her cheeks, whisper a secret into her ear and disappear like an affable smile. Others replace them—as numerous as the stars in the sky, as the sand on the riverbank. Beylke prances over the field as if drunk. In the milky white air she throws back her head and lets her face catch the white flowers that fall from the sky. The snowflakes keep falling, coloring the field gray-light-white. Soon they spread out over the earth in a blanket that covers its breast in silky soft folds. They babble and murmur from below softly and affably like doves in a nest.

But most important—the river! Day in, day out Beylke looks at the river and shares in its life. Between white banks it speeds along the almost black waters, fierce and angry, foreseeing dark days . . . From the North a cold wind blows, penetrates everywhere, passes through flesh as if through a vacuum and hovers over the river for a day or two or three. The river turns blue, dark blue from the cold, trembles and contracts, wrestles with the deadening sleep that attacks its powerful limbs—keeps wrestling, but slower and heavier, heavier and lazier, lazier and drowsier. Out of somewhere comes a formless yellowish dirty piece of ice and swims quietly by, stealthily, meaning no harm of course . . . Another ice floe passes by and another, and a few at a time and a whole pack already stretch downstream and it seems—like heads peering out of the water or clowns frolicking among the crests, turning over and causing a commotion in the river. Blows and knocking sounds resound with greater frequency. The river is already completely covered with floes. A large one pushes its way through the smaller ones broadly, with aristocratic impudence and the smaller ones give way to it, grinding their teeth and crawling over each other, fighting among themselves like wolves over a corpse.

Seeing the agonizing death of the huge river, the people scatter, the boats, logs and lorries disappear and the surroundings become waste and wildness as before Creation. Gradually, the floe comes to a halt, turning in the same spot, colliding with the banks until it stops altogether. Awkward and ugly, on all sides monstrously large spiked noses protrude; smooth, sheer and white heads, crooked knees and backs—a battlefield covered with naked corpses and dried up skeletons. Then the white little souls come flying in again and alight with great compassion on the carcasses to hide their shame. A few more snows, a few more frosts and no sign remains of the river. Gray, short days reveal their pale uncertain smile to the world, but soon become discouraged and are extinguished. They are replaced by endlessly long sad nights when the wind whistles its melancholy tune, when from the forest that darkens on the opposite bank, hungry, frozen wolves emerge and congregate on the grave of the river, wailing wildly and bitterly for hours, and snap their teeth and sparkle with their green glowing eyes into the womb of the night.

6

The winter drags on, so long that summer happens almost like a fiction: maybe it took place, maybe it didn't. And Beylke is amazed that the river is gone, completely gone. How it can be? There were days when the heart of the river hung in pieces on the tombs and even in the quiet nights a murmur reached here from below the hill, seemingly out of a dream. And now sleds fly by, people stroll, secure and thoughtless, as if this is the way it ought to be. But will it stay this way?

No. Unnoticed by anyone, the long-lasting north wind starts breathing from the south, a moist, lazy and adhesive wind. The smooth white path on the river gets dirty, dark and creased; the strollers lose their nerve, move with deliberation, tap the ground with sticks and listen for something. The carriages move capriciously, make strange zigzags, avoid most spots and still produce an occasional sob or spurt beneath them. Meanwhile the south wind blows obstinately. Days become somewhat larger and nights—somewhat smaller and the river begins claiming its first victims: a man falls in, a carriage breaks down, suspicious holes, ditches and wells appear. Gradually the people disperse: the fear of rebirth is no less than the fear of death's agony.

Then comes a night when Beylke awakens suddenly and asks fearfully: "Grampa, what is this?"

Dan has been up for a long while.

"Nothing, daughter, nothing . . . the river's moving."

He lights up his pipe in the dark, smokes, coughs, spits and grumbles.

"What?" asks Beylke again.

"Hmmm . . . nothing, nothing." In a short while he grumbles again, but Beylke senses that he is not displeased, yet the cause of his joy is unknown to them both. Meanwhile the river thunders, making the entire cottage shake and the window panes grate. The whole night Beylke stares out into the darkness and holds her breath. She imagines that she sees what she hears.

Barely awaiting daybreak, she jumps out of the cottage and falls right into the arms of a warm wind that smells like a summer rain. She closes her eyes for an instant, opens them, runs over to the willow and looks down.

The ice is rumbling. Beylke sees instinctively that underneath the ice stands someone large, huge, on hands and feet, trying to lift the hard heavy cover on his back. The ice bends, cracks in spots and settles down again heavily. The captive down below becomes more restless and excited: he pants, rumbles, exerts himself even more. The ice, cracking wider, wrestles despairingly for its power, and cracks nonetheless. Individual pieces collide, shake and overturn like tremendous dead fish with their white bellies upward. Water spurts from all the wounds, floods the ice, rinses it, cleanses it and eats it. Suddenly the entire mass trembles and moves from its place.

Several days in a row, like an army in the wake of a terrible defeat, the floe races downstream in haste and fear. Abandoning the plans and fortifications for which they labored the whole winter, entire corps, divisions and regiments run ahead; after them, helter-skelter, smaller divisions and single soldiers fly by, whom the army lost in flight and who are now trying to catch up. Many of them perish en route. The sun rises higher with each day and its arrows grow hotter and sharper. At times a piece of ice catches on a corner of the jutting bank and expires slowly and painfully, eyeing his brothers with anguish as they run past energetically. Once the last piece of ice has disappeared, waters still pour in from above and swallow the left lower bank and burst into the side valleys. At night, from below the hill, one can hear something gurgling short and deep, as if the river were choking from containing its laughter and were breaking away from strong tickling hands. Life opened its radiant eyes once again.

7

There was a person—only one—whom Beylke tried to befriend. The person was the seven-year-old son of Phillip Karpenko, who lived on the opposite side of the road, in one of the cottages over there. Yashke had a low forehead, gray eyes, a broad clayish face and wore broad heavy slacks. He always went without a cap and his white flaxen hair fell over his eyes and face. He held his mouth open and the little finger of his right hand often stuck into one of his nostrils. He was usually bewildered.

Once Yashke stood near the fence of the cemetery, looked in at the green pears that grew on "Grandma's Tree" and, befuddled as usual, he swallowed his spittle. This type of pear did not grow in his father's garden. Beylke walked by and stopped next to the fence on the inside. Yashke was astonished and Beylke laughed.

"White hair," she said laughingly, pointing at him with her finger.

"How?" asked Yashke and glanced back, looking for what she was pointing at.

"You have white, I have black . . ." said Beylke, approaching the fence and ruffling her black locks with her hand.

Yashke stretched out his hand and felt her hair, not knowing exactly what was wanted of him. Beylke laughed again and he quickly withdrew his hand with great embarrassment. The children looked at each other for a while.

"Give pears," Yashke uttered suddenly and stood bewildered. From the glance that he threw at the tree, Beylke understood what he wanted and at the bat of an eye was up in the tree. Yashke hesitated for a second, then he too climbed over the fence and up the tree.

In this way they got acquainted.

For a while Dan did not know about this childish friendship. He was surprised once to hear Yashke and Beylke in the cemetery. Yashke fled. Dan reddened.

"Who is this brat?"

Beylke answered calmly: "Yashke."

"Yashke? Who's Yashke? What do you mean? For shame, with a goy, yet!"

Beylke was surprised.

"Why?"

"Why?" repeated Dan. "What do you mean? You are a Jewish child. What does he have to do with you?"

"But it's Yashke!" Beylke's bewilderment grew.

"Listen. You are a Jewish child and he is a Gentile. Don't you understand?"

She understood nothing, and when Yashke approached the fence stealthily the next day, she played with him as before. She showed more masculinity than he: she called the cards, invented new tricks and explained important life issues to him. Yashke, on the contrary, was very lazy, phlegmatic, moved little and heeded Beylke in everything. His greatest pleasure was to draw his feet under him, with a finger in his nose and stare, free of any thought, for no rhyme or reason, stare as long as possible. It happened once that he drowsed off in this position and was startled when Beylke awoke him with her happy shout.

Everyday he came to pick pears, to play and talk. They conducted strange discussions in a strange language:

"Do you have a *stari dir*, an old grampa?" Beylke was curious to know.

Yashke, not removing his finger from his nose, shook his head from left to right.

"No. I have a mom and a dad and a small brother and two small sisters . . ."

"And do you have *hrushki*, pears in the garden?"

"Yes, *bila malina, i korova*, and white berries and a cow."

"*Korova?*" asked Beylke uncertainly, not knowing what kind of plant it was.

"*Nu da*, of course. *Korova* Mooooo!" explained Yashke and with his hands made a pair of horns over his head.

It lasted a few weeks. The children lived in a special world. A small creature, however, destroyed their little world and lost its own life in the process.

A butterfly flew by between the children while the two of them sat on the grass and Yashke caught it. He held it by its wing and the butterfly wrestled despairingly, buzzed and created a wind between Yashke's fingers. Astonished, Yashke observed it with a great eagerness. Beylke was struck with fear.

"Let go, let go of the little creature!" she barely uttered with anxiety.

"What?" Yashke did not understand and ripped a wing off the butterfly.

Beylke caught him by the hand. Yashke suddenly became angry.

"Leggo!" he shouted, pulling his hand away.

Beylke did not let go.

"Oh hell!" He squashed the butterfly, threw it away and pushed Beylke with his free hand.

In an instant Beylke jumped up from her place. Her face became deathly pale, her blue eyes—dark and deep and between her half-opened lips sparkled two rows of sharp, white, gritted teeth. Suddenly she bit deeply into Yashke's hand.

Yashke's eyes and mouth opened wide and he began to scream like a calf being slaughtered. When Beylke let him go, he ran home with a frightened, helpless wail. She glanced after him with sparkling eyes and pressed lips.

After this incident, Beylke went around confused for several days, and no matter what her grandfather asked her, he could not discover what was wrong. Dan was frightened and he prayed quietly:

"Lord of the universe. Have pity on my age and on her young years. Cure her wounds. Oh, my daughter, my daughter."

A week later Yashke returned. He had forgotten the whole incident and his wide face smiled softly and good-naturedly, as always. When Beylke explained clearly and precisely that she did not want to play with him ever again, he took his leave very sadly. He could not understand at all what he had done wrong and his unaccustomed head labored in vain over the riddle that Beylke had presented.

8

Years streamed over the cemetery. Four times the river passed away and four times the spring brought it back to life. Four times "Grandma's Tree" evicted its hard, round pears and strewed them over the field. Meanwhile the older trees withered somewhat, grimaced and began to creak, while the young ones, in contrast, stretched, straightened up and their strengthened, slender limbs trembled youthfully and vigorously. Four times the white clear snowflakes and the colorful childish flowers embellished the earth, one following the other.

Meanwhile, Dan's gray beard whitened and his compact but straight figure became slightly twisted, shabby, somewhat bent. Now he visited the tree over Malka's grave with greater regularity; he sat there lost in thought for longer periods and when, on leaving, he caressed the letters on the tombstone, his fingers trembled lightly and his lips moved silently. The words "The woman Malka daughter of Reb Tanhum Solomon" had worn off slightly, but for the old man they grew sharper and clearer. Beneath the words a face emerged, good-natured and round, somewhat aged, with a quiet smile and with friendly, familiar eyes that stared straight at him, at Dan, just like they used to once, many years ago . . .

And Beylke grew. Her little face broadened, her large eyes looked dreamily into the wide world as if she were listening to something. It was difficult to say whether she was listening to the sounds of the outer world, to the eternal voices of heaven and earth, to the quiver of life and death, or whether in her very self, in the depths of her childish heart, she heard an oracle calling and calling—still undefined and unclear, like a song from afar; or like the rumble of thunder about to be born, or like the breath of a storm on the verge of escaping the Stronghold of the Winds . . .

Once Dan caught sight of her on the river's edge on a hot summer day: completely naked, with uplifted hands joined above her head, she planned to throw herself into the grayish-yellow deeply drowsing water. The old man started in fright. He imagined that he saw a creature from another world, with white skin and naked limbs over which hovered a barely discernible slender tremble, as over a tautly tuned string. And when this dazzling half of her childish body sparkled in the air and penetrated the river like an arrow—Dan fled, confused, frightened, not knowing the reason why. He sat at the cottage window greatly disturbed and waited for his grandchild. In his heart he thought: "Beylke is no more. Not this Beylke. What will she say when she returns?" A half hour later she appeared on the narrow path that meandered from the precipice at the river to the small cottage. With free flowing, freshly wetted hair, her face slightly flushed and with a tired gaze, she walked on the grass barefoot, slowly and gracefully, like a princess. Meeting her grandfather's uncertain look, she replied with a hearty, childish smile. Dan suddenly livened.

"You went bathing? Ha, ha," he laughed for no apparent reason. "It's really quite hot, may the Lord protect us. Ha ha!"

9

The heat in July was unparalleled. For days the sun stared openly and sharply at the earth: whoever cannot countenance my face should quit the world! It seemed as if the languid earth would to the last seed be transformed into white dust. The world was petrified in deathly fear.

Finally a day arrived.

The sky inhaled a dirty green breath. With difficulty, living creatures swallowed the air, like thick warm oil. The sun looked angry and bloody.

Since morning, Beylke had gone around uneasily. Between her brows the wrinkle appeared, her wrinkle. In the evening, when the sun set in hell fire, Beylke's face no longer clouded over. But at night, lying in the darkness on her cot and hearing the wailing of the wind between the graves—all her limbs began to tremble. What's happening outside? Whose anguish trembled in the air? Who was being tortured out there? Whose patience burst—completely, entirely, for ever and ever?

"Grampa, are you asleep grampa? They're calling me, do you hear? No, I'm not going! I'm not going . . ."

The door opened quietly and a small white figure left the house.

The cemetery revived.

On that night a black, wild witch took over the world. Her dark gray disheveled hair writhed, whipped over the sky and covered it completely. Her eyes shot occasional pale green sparks. She ground her teeth and roared, still dull and restrained, and her heavy breath shook the air.

On that night the dead remembered their lives down below, in the town of the living, everything they had endured and had left behind. While the town of the living seemed to have died out and no flame from there emitted its living flicker, here, in the town of the dead, no blade of grass was quiet. A frightened rustle traveled across the ground. Higher in the air where the bloated heads of the trees darkened, choked moans and a sharp murmur severed the night, and among the graves, like wounded birds they wrestled with death, quivered and slapped the tombstones with weakened wings.

As swift as an arrow Beylke cut through the cemetery and flew over to the willow that veered silently and sullenly from the abyss to the sky. Impudently the wind tore and lifted Beylke's blouse from her flesh and with wild desire it wrapped itself around her white flesh and pressed itself to her burning skin. She jumped up onto the willow and grasping the shaking branches with all her might she shot her glance into the abyss.

Dark. At times it sparkled below like a whitish foam and evaporated immediately like a snowflake in water. A rebellion down below, a great rebellion. Fighting, gurgling, wild and bloody roaring. Familiar sounds. Familiar sounds.

Once. Once. What? When?

Then Beylke uttered two short, abrupt cries:

"Mama! Mama!"

For the first time since she came to her grandfather's house.

Suddenly someone ripped off the heavy veil that weighed upon her head for so many years. She saw what she saw . . .

10

A small, shabby room. A troubled young man looks out the window— her silent father. Behind him—a shining woman's face—her beloved mother. Outside—horrible cries, wailing, banging, roaring—like the present storm. In the room—a stubborn quiet.

The voices approach. Father pales. With drunken steps mother goes over to the bed and sits down. The door cracks and shatters. Father grabs a chair and mother's eyes grow fearfully large and black.

A frenzied noise and a whistle. Red faces, fat hands, axes, hammers and clubs. Father hits a red face with a chair. A fat hand swings a hammer at father's head. He falls. Someone lies down on top of him and bangs the hammer onto his head. Clear, separate strokes: tap, tap, tap . . . Beylke's back shivers and bristles. Her teeth press together and her lips open of themselves. She sits on the ground and stares.

Mother grimaces and her face turns sickly green. A huge goy with a red, hard moustache makes his way to the bed and gags her mouth with his hand. Beylke sees feet in large boots stamping near the bed—and the frost in her bones grows sharper. Mother emits a muffled cry: "Chaim," but from the corner, the soft but clear strokes on father's head can no longer be heard: tap, tap, tap. Then mother rasps: "Bey-le-nyu!"

A hot stream streams through Beylke's back. Her limbs soften, feel freer. She still looks at the feet in the big boots and starts sharpening her teeth. She slides to the bed, moving from side to side, still grinding her teeth. When the boot seems near enough she sends her teeth into one of them with eyes closed and loses herself in wild intoxicating joy.

A short cry. The boot lifts Beylke. Then all is dark and still. Dark and still.

11

The storm reached its height.

It wasn't the wind that blew anymore but the whole atmosphere reeling and turning in a wild frenzy around the frightened earth. The trees tore the hair from their heads. The souls threw themselves upon their tombs, shook them, tore and broke them, as if wanting to erase the dead town entirely from the face of the earth. It looked as if the world were turning back to primordial chaos from which it had come and had hardly departed.

A quiet lament tore from the willow over the abyss:

"Mama—mama—mama . . ."

The tiny play-people finally opened up and showed all their little wheels! Suddenly and unexpectedly the wheels revealed themselves, all at once, in their entanglement, their confusion and their distortion. The little man falls silent and embittered face down on the tombs of his loved ones—and strikes softly and muffled with a hammer on father's head and rips the clothes off mother's flesh. The little man shuns pain and shame, fears pain and shame—torturing, tormenting, raping, humiliating with endless rapture, passionately, selflessly, with the heat of true devotion. The wheels turn and turn, the teeth catch and tear—and the little man dances. Dances!

Hey, puppet-people, fish and birds—
Come here and join the dance.
Hand-in-hand, round and round
God has made the world.

Men and wives he molds with clay,
A cat, a moon, a cock,
Oh wolves and sheep and snakes and doves—
The dance begins without delay.

God in a striped and spotted robe
And trousers—half yellow, half red.
He's playing a comb and blowing a flute—
And Life goes on dancing with Death.

He beats out the beat with his sticks,
He leers and he grins and does tricks;
A God in a clown's cap with bells—
Ho-ho—has created the world.

1910 (translated by David G. Roskies)

Reb Shakhne's hands and feet were shaking and there was an unbearably bitter taste in his mouth. He was sitting on a chair, hearing the wild cries from the street, the whistling and cracking of breaking windows. It seemed to him that all the shattering, crying and ringing were inside his head.

The pogrom had started so suddenly that he hadn't even had the time to lock up his store. He had run home immediately. The house was empty. Sarah and the children had hidden somewhere, apparently, abandoning the house with its bit of silver and cash to God's mercy. He himself hadn't thought about hiding; he hadn't thought about anything at all. He had just listened to the shouts for help from the street and to the bitter taste in his mouth.

The noise of the pogrom would get nearer, then farther, like a fire in the neighborhood. Suddenly, it surrounded the house from all four sides. The windows began to crack, several stones flew into the dining room, and all at once, through the doors and windows, goyim began to crawl in, mostly young toughs, with sticks, knives and red drunken faces. Reb Shakhne felt he had to do something. He raised himself from his chair with great difficulty and right in front of the pogromists' eyes, began to crawl under the couch. The crowd began to laugh.

"Vot durok!" one of them said and grabbed him by a foot. *"Eh, ty, vstovoy!"*

He suddenly got his wits about him and burst out crying like a small child.

"Children," he begged, "I'll show you where the money is myself, the silver and everything. Just don't kill me. Why should you kill me? I have a wife and children . . ."

None of it helped. They took everything and they started beating him, hitting him in the mouth, the sides, and the stomach, with murderous violence. He cried and begged, and they beat him. He knew one of the toughs and he turned to him for mercy:

"Vasilenko, you know me. Your father worked in my house. Tell me: did I ever not pay him? He did good work for me. Vasilenko. Vasilenko . . . Help! Help! Sav—"

A blow to the solar plexus cut off his plea. Two toughs sat down on him and started pressing his belly with their knees. Vasilenko, a small, thin tough with a crooked face and little gray eyes, smiled arrogantly and said:

"To shtsho? You paid, what else? Father worked, you paid. I would've liked to see you *not* pay him."

Still, he had liked the way Reb Shakhne turned to him for help, and he said to the others:

"Well, *rebyata,* enough, let the corpse live. Just look—he's barely breathing . . . "

Little by little they tore themselves away from their victim and started to leave the house, breaking all the furniture that had managed to remain intact.

"Well, Shakhne, you can thank me for the fact you're still alive," Vasilenko said to Reb Shakhne, who was standing in front of him with a lowered head and bruised face, breathing heavily. The crowd would've taken care of you pretty quickly if I hadn't . . . "

He started to leave, but suddenly he had an idea.

"Here," he stretched his hand out to Reb Shakhne, "kiss it . . . "

Reb Shakhne raised his bloodshot eyes and gave him a confused look. He didn't understand.

Vasilenko's face clouded.

"You didn't hear, *shto ly?* Kiss, I'm telling you!"

Two of the toughs had remained standing in the doorway, interested in what was going on. Reb Shakhne looked at Vasilenko and remained quiet, and Vasilenko turned red.

"Ah, you and your damned kike face!" He gritted his teeth and gave Reb Shakhne a full-handed slap to the face. "You're still hesitating? . . . Eh, you guys, come here!"

The two toughs came nearer.

"Well, start working him over again. If he's such a big shot, then he's going to have to kiss my foot. If not . . . "

He sat down on a chair. The toughs grabbed Reb Shakhne and threw him down at Vasilenko's feet.

"Pull them off!" Vasilenko ordered, kicking his boots into Reb Shakhne's teeth.

Reb Shakhne slowly pulled the boot off the tough's foot.

"Kiss it!"

They faced each other: a red, filthy foot, reeking of sweat, and a bruised face with a long, distinguished dark beard. By remarkable chance, the crowd hadn't spent much time on the beard, and the hairs had been plucked out only in a few spots; the glory of a grown Jew and a respectable householder still lay on his face. Vasilenko's red, crooked face with the gray eyes looked down on him from above.

"Kiss it, I tell you!"

Another kick in the teeth accompanied the order.

For a moment everyone in the room was silent and motionless. Then Reb Shakhne bent his head, and Vasilenko let out a sharp, terrible shriek. All of his toes and a good part of his foot had disappeared in Reb Shakhne's mouth, and two rows of teeth had buried themselves deep in the filthy, sweaty flesh.

What happened after that was as savage and horrific as an oppressive and evil dream.

The toughs beat Reb Shakhne in the sides with their boots with such force that every blow rang loud and hollow, like hitting a barrel. They pulled his beard in clumps, stuck their fingers in his eyes and tore them out, looked for the most sensitive places on his body and ripped chunks out of his flesh. The body trembled, shook feverishly, tossed and turned about, and the two rows of teeth pressed together even more convulsively and went even deeper. Something cracked inside the foot: the teeth, the bones, or both of them together. The whole time Vasilenko screamed, madly, nonsensically, like a stuck pig.

The two toughs didn't have any sense of how long it all lasted, and they only came to themselves when they noticed that Reb Shakhne's body wasn't twitching any more. Looking at his face, they both shuddered from head to toe.

The ripped out eyes dangled near the bloody sockets, large, round, and sticky. There was no face to see. The beard had been shoved together in wet bloody locks, and the dead teeth were fixed with the piece of foot between them, like a slain wolf. Vasilenko was still thrashing about—not on the chair any more, but on the ground. His body twisted around like a snake, and hoarse, drawn out cries tore from his throat. His little gray eyes grew large, dull, and glassy. He was, apparently, out of his mind.

With a terrified *"Haspodi pamiloy nas!"* the two toughs ran out of the house.

In the street the angry pogrom raged, and among the overlapping voices no one noticed the broken screams of the living man who was slowly expiring in the teeth of the dead man.

1907 (translated by Jeremy Dauber)

1

One day a neighbor broke the leg of a stray dog with a heavy stone, and when Vasil saw the sharp edge of the bone piercing the skin he cried. The tears streamed from his eyes, his mouth and his nose; the towhead on his short neck shrank deeper between his shoulders; his entire face became distorted and shriveled, and he did not utter a sound. He was then about seven years old.

Soon he learned not to cry. His family drank, fought with neighbors, with one another, beat the women, the horse, the cow and sometimes, in special rages, their own heads against the wall. They were a large family with a tiny piece of land, they toiled hard and clumsily, and all of them lived in one hut—men, women and children slept pell-mell on the floor. The village was small and poor, at some distance from a town; and the town to which they occasionally went for the fair seemed big and rich to Vasil.

In the town there were Jews—people who wore strange clothes, sat in stores, ate white challah and had sold Christ. The last point was not quite clear: who was Christ, why did the Jews sell him, who bought him and for what purpose?—it was all as though in a fog. White challah, that was something else again: Vasil saw it a few times with his own eyes, and more than that—he once stole a piece and ate it, whereupon he stood for a time in a daze, an expression of wonder on his face. He did not understand it all, but respect for white challah stayed with him.

He was half an inch too short, but he was drafted, owing to his broad, slightly hunched shoulders and thick short neck. Here in the army beatings were again the order of the day: the corporal, the sergeant, and the officers beat the privates, and the privates beat one another, all of them. He could not learn the service regulations: he did not understand and did not think. Nor was he a good talker; when hard pressed he usually could not utter a sound, but his face grew tense, and his low forehead was covered with wrinkles. Kasha and borscht, however, were plentiful. There were a few Jews in his regiment—Jews who had sold Christ—but in their army uniforms and without white challah they looked almost like everybody else.

2

They traveled in trains, they marched, they rode again and then again moved on foot; they camped in the open or were quartered in houses; and this went on so long that Vasil became completely confused. He no longer remembered when it had begun, where he had been before, or who he had been; it was as though all his life had been spent moving from town to town, with tens or hundreds of thousands of other soldiers, through foreign places inhabited by strange people who spoke an incomprehensible language and who looked frightened or angry. Nothing particularly new had happened, but fighting had become the very essence of life; everyone was fighting now, and this time it was no longer just beating, but fighting in earnest: they fired at people, cut them to pieces, bayoneted them, and sometimes even bit them with their teeth. He too fought, more and more savagely, and with greater relish. Now food did not come regularly, they slept little, they marched and fought a great deal, and all this made him restless. He kept missing something, longing for something, and at moments of great strain he howled like a tormented dog because he could not say what he wanted.

They advanced over steadily higher ground; chains of giant mountains seamed the country in all directions, and winter ruled over them harshly and without respite. They inched their way through valleys, knee-deep in dry powdery snow, and icy winds raked their faces and hands like grating irons, but the officers were cheerful and kindlier than before, and spoke of victory; and food, though not always served on time, was plentiful. At night they were sometimes permitted to build fires on the snow; then monstrous shadows moved noiselessly between the mountains, and the soldiers sang. Vasil too tried to sing, but he could only howl. They slept like the dead, without dreams or nightmares, and time and again during the day the mountains reverberated with the thunder of cannon, and men again climbed up and down the slopes.

3

A mounted messenger galloped madly through the camp; an advance cavalry unit returned suddenly and occupied positions on the flank; two batteries were moved from the left to the right. The surrounding mountains split open like freshly erupting volcanoes, and a deluge of fire, lead and iron came down upon the world.

The barrage kept up for a long time. Piotr Kudlo was torn to pieces; the handsome Kruvenko, the best singer of the company, lay with his face in a puddle of blood; Lieutenant Somov, the one with girlish features, lost a leg, and the giant Neumann, the blond Estonian, had his whole face torn off. The pockmarked Gavrilov was dead; a single shell killed the two Bulgach brothers; killed, too, were Chaim Ostrovsky, Jan Zatyka, Staszek Pieprz and the little Latvian whose name Vasil could not pronounce. Now whole ranks were mowed down, and it was impossible to hold on. Then Nahum Rachek, a tall slender young man who had always been silent, jumped up and without any order ran forward. This gave new spirit to the dazed men, who rushed the jagged hill to the left and practically with their bare hands conquered the batteries that led the enemy artillery, strangling the defenders like cats, down to the last man. Later it was found that of the entire company only Vasil and Nahum Rachek remained. After the battle Rachek lay on the ground vomiting green gall, and next to him lay his rifle with its butt smeared with blood and brains. He was not wounded, and when Vasil asked what was the matter he did not answer.

After sunset the conquered position was abandoned, and the army fell back. How and why this happened Vasil did not know; but from that moment the army began to roll down the mountains like an avalanche of stones. The farther they went, the hastier and less orderly was the retreat, and in the end they ran—ran without stopping, day and night. Vasil did not recognize the country, each place was new to him, and he knew only from hearsay that they were moving back. Mountains and winter had long been left behind; around them stretched a broad, endless plain; spring was in full bloom; but the army ran and ran. The officers became savage, they beat the soldiers without reason and without pity. A few times they stopped for a while; the cannon roared, a rain of fire whipped the earth, and men fell like flies—and then they ran again.

4

Someone said that all this was the fault of the Jews. Again the Jews! They sold Christ, they eat white challah and on top of it all they are to blame for everything. What was "everything?" Vasil wrinkled his forehead and was angry at the Jews and at someone else. Leaflets appeared, printed leaflets that a man distributed among the troops, and in the camps groups gathered round those who could read. They stood listening in silence—they were silent in a strange way, unlike people who just do not talk. Someone handed a leaflet to Vasil too; he examined it, fingered it, put it in his pocket, and joined a group to hear what was being read. He did not understand a word, except that it was about Jews. So the Jews must know, he thought, and he turned to Nahum Rachek.

"Here, read it," he said.

Rachek cast a glance at the leaflet, then another curious glance at Vasil; but he said nothing and seemed about to throw the leaflet away.

"Don't! It's not yours!" Vasil said. He took back the leaflet, stuck it in his pocket, and paced back and forth in agitation. Then he turned to Rachek. "What does it say? It's about you, isn't it?"

At this point Nahum flared up. "Yes, about me. It says I'm a traitor, see? That I've betrayed us—that I'm a spy. Like that German who was caught and shot. See?"

Vasil was scared. His forehead began to sweat. He left Nahum, fingering his leaflet in bewilderment. This Nahum, he thought, must be a wicked man—so angry, and a spy besides, he said so himself, but something doesn't fit here, it's puzzling, it doesn't fit, my head is splitting.

After a long forced march they stopped somewhere. They had not seen the enemy for several days and had not heard any firing. They dug trenches and made ready. A week later it all began anew. It turned out that the enemy was somewhere nearby; he too was in trenches, and these trenches were moving closer and closer each day, and occasionally one could see a head showing above the parapet. They ate very little, they slept even less, they fired in the direction the bullets came from, bullets that kept hitting the earth wall, humming overhead and occasionally boring into human bodies. Next to Vasil, at his left, always lay Nahum Rachek. He never spoke, only kept loading his rifle and firing, mechanically, unhurriedly. Vasil could not bear the sight of him and occasionally was seized with a desire to stab him with his bayonet.

One day, when the firing was particularly violent, Vasil suddenly felt strangely restless. He cast a glance sidewise at Rachek and saw him lying in the same posture as before, on his stomach, with his rifle in his hand; but there was a hole in his head. Something broke in Vasil; in blind anger he kicked the dead body, pushing it aside, and then began to fire wildly, exposing his head to the dense shower of lead that was pouring all around him.

That night he could not sleep for a long time; he tossed and turned, muttering curses. At one point he jumped up angrily and began to run straight ahead, but then he recalled that Rachek was dead and dejectedly returned to his pallet. The Jews ... traitors ... sold Christ ... traded him away for a song!

He ground his teeth and clawed at himself in his sleep.

5

At daybreak Vasil suddenly sat up on his hard pallet. His body was covered with cold sweat, his teeth were chattering, and his eyes, round and wide open, tried greedily to pierce the darkness. Who has been here? Who has been here?

It was pitch-dark and fearfully quiet, but he still could hear the rustle of the giant wings and feel the cold hem of the black cloak that had grazed his face. Someone had passed over the camp like an icy wind, and the camp was silent and frozen—an open grave with thousands of bodies, struck while asleep, and pierced in the heart. Who has been here? Who has been here?

During the day Lieutenant Muratov of the fourth battalion of the Yeniesey regiment was found dead—Muratov, a violent, cruel man with a face the color of parchment. The bullet that pierced him between the eyes had been fired by someone from his own battalion. When the men were questioned no one betrayed the culprit. Threatened with punishment, they still refused to answer, and they remained silent when they were ordered to surrender their arms. The other regimental units were drawn up against the battalion, but when they were ordered to fire, all of them to a man lowered their rifles to the ground. Another regiment was summoned, and in ten minutes not a man of the mutinous battalion remained alive.

Next day two officers were hacked to pieces. Three days later, following a dispute between two cavalrymen, the entire regiment split into two camps. They fought each other until only a few were left unscathed.

Then men in mufti appeared and, encouraged by the officers, began to distribute leaflets among the troops. This time they did not make long speeches, but kept repeating one thing: the Jews have betrayed us, everything is their fault.

Once again someone handed a leaflet to Vasil, but he did not take it. He drew out of his pocket, with love and respect, as though it were a precious medallion, a crumpled piece of paper frayed at the edges and stained with blood, and showed it—he had it, and remembered it. The man with the leaflets, a slim little fellow with a sand-colored beard, half

closed one of his little eyes and took stock of the squat broad-shouldered private with the short thick neck and bulging gray watery eyes.
He gave Vasil a friendly pat on the back and left with a strange smile on
his lips.

The Jewish privates had vanished: they had been quietly gathered together and sent away, no one knew where. Everyone felt freer and more
comfortable, and although there were several nationalities represented
among them, they were all of one mind about it: the alien was no
longer in their midst.

And then someone launched a new slogan—"The Jewish government."

6

This was their last stand, and when they were again defeated they no
longer stopped anywhere but ran like stampeding animals fleeing a
steppe fire, in groups or individually, without commanders and without order, in deadly fear, rushing through every passage left open by the
enemy. Not all of them had weapons, no one had his full outfit of clothing, and their shirts were like second skins on their unwashed bodies.
The summer sun beat down on them mercilessly, and they ate only
what they could forage. Now their native tongue was spoken in the
towns, and their native fields lay around them, but the fields were un-
recognizable, for last year's crops were rotting, trampled into the earth,
and the land lay dry and gray and riddled, like the carcass of an ox dis-
emboweled by wolves.

And while the armies crawled over the earth like swarms of gray
worms, flocks of ravens soared overhead, calling with a dry rattling
sound—the sound of tearing canvas—and swooped and slanted in in-
tricate spirals, waiting for what would be theirs.

Between Kolov and Zhaditsa the starved and crazed legions caught
up with large groups of Jews who had been ordered out of border
towns, with their women, children, invalids and bundles. A voice said,
"Get them!" The words sounded like the distant boom of a gun. At first
Vasil held back, but the loud screams of the women and children and
the repulsive, terrified faces of the men with their long earlocks and

caftans blowing in the wind drove him to a frenzy, and he cut into the Jews like a maddened bull. They were destroyed with merciful speed: the army trampled over them like a herd of galloping horses.

Then, once again, someone said in a shrill little voice, "The Jewish government!"

The words suddenly soared high and like a peal of thunder rolled over the wild legions, spreading to villages and cities and reaching the remotest corners of the land. The retreating troops struck out at the region with fire and sword. By night burning cities lighted their path, and by day the smoke obscured the sun and the sky and rolled in cottony masses over the earth, and suffocated ravens occasionally fell to the ground. They burned the towns of Zykov, Potapno, Kholodno, Stary Yug, Sheliuba; Ostrogorie, Sava, Rika, Beloye Krilo and Stupnik were wiped from the face of the earth; the Jewish weaving town of Belopriazha went up in smoke, and the Vinokur Forest, where thirty thousand Jews had sought refuge, blazed like a bonfire, and for three days in succession agonized cries, like poisonous gases, rose from the woods and spread over the land. The swift, narrow Sinevodka River was entirely choked with human bodies a little below Lutsin and overflowed into the fields. On the ruins of Dobroslawa sat a madman, the sole survivor of the town, who howled like a dog.

The hosts grew larger. The peasant left his village and the city dweller his city; priests with icons and crosses in their hands led processions through villages, devoutly and enthusiastically blessing the people, and the slogan was, "The Jewish government." The Jews themselves realized that their last hour had struck—the very last; and those who remained alive set out to die among Jews in Maliassy, the oldest and largest Jewish center in the land, a seat of learning since the fourteenth century, a city of ancient synagogues and great yeshivas, with rabbis and modern scholars, with an aristocracy of learning and of trade. Here, in Maliassy, the Jews fasted and prayed, confessing their sins to God, begging forgiveness of friend and enemy. Aged men recited Psalms and Lamentations, younger men burned stocks of grain and clothing, demolished furniture, broke and destroyed everything that might be of use to the approaching army. And this army came, it came from all directions, and set fire to the city from all sides, and poured into the streets. Young men tried to resist and went out with revolvers in their hands. The revolvers sounded like pop guns. The soldiers answered with thundering laughter, and drew out the young men's veins one by one, and broke their bones into little pieces. Then they went from house to house, slaying the men wherever they were found and dragging the women to the marketplace.

7

One short blow with his fist smashed the lock, and the door opened.

For two days now Vasil had not eaten or slept. His skin smarted in the dry heat, his bones seemed disjointed, his eyes were bloodshot, and his face and neck were covered with blond stubble.

"Food!" he said hoarsely.

No one answered him. At the table stood a tall Jew in a black caftan, with a black beard and earlocks and gloomy eyes. He tightened his lips and remained stubbornly silent. Vasil stepped forward angrily and said again, "Food!"

But this time he spoke less harshly. Near the window he had caught sight of another figure—a young woman in white, with a head of black hair. Two large eyes—he had never before seen such large eyes—were looking at him and through him, and the look of these eyes was such that Vasil lifted his arm to cover his own eyes. His knees were trembling, he felt as if he were melting. What kind of woman is that? What kind of people? God! Why, why, did they have to sell Christ? And on top of it all, responsible for everything! Even Rachek admitted it. And they just kept quiet, looking through you. Goddamn it, what are they after? He took his head in his hands.

He felt something and looked about him. The Jew stood there, deathly pale, hatred in his eyes. For a moment Vasil stared dully. Suddenly he grabbed the black beard and pulled at it savagely.

A white figure stepped between them. Rage made Vasil dizzy and scalded his throat. He tugged at the white figure with one hand. A long strip tore from the dress and hung at the hem. His eyes were dazzled, almost blinded. Half a breast, a beautiful shoulder, a full, rounded hip—everything dazzling white and soft, like white challah. Damn it—

these Jews are made of white challah! A searing flame leaped through his body, his arm flew up like a spring and shot into the gaping dress.

A hand gripped his neck. He turned his head slowly and looked at the Jew for a moment with narrowed eyes and bared teeth, without shaking free of the weak fingers that were clutching at his flesh. Then he raised his shoulders, bent forward, took the Jew by the ankles, lifted him in the air, and smashed him against the table. He flung him down like a broken stick.

The man groaned weakly; the woman screamed. But he was already on top of her. He pressed her to the floor and tore her dress together with her flesh. Now she was repulsive, her face blotchy, the tip of her nose red, her hair disheveled and falling over her eyes. "Witch," he said through his teeth. He twisted her nose like a screw. She uttered a shrill cry—short, mechanical, unnaturally high, like the whistle of an engine. The cry penetrating his brain maddened him completely. He seized her neck and strangled her.

A white shoulder was quivering before his eyes; a full, round drop of fresh blood lay glistening on it. His nostrils fluttered like wings. His teeth were grinding; suddenly they opened and bit into the white flesh.

White challah has the taste of a firm juicy orange. Warm and hot, and the more one sucks it the more burning the thirst. Sharp and thick, and strangely spiced.

Like rushing down a steep hill in a sled. Like drowning in sharp, burning spirits.

In a circle, in a circle, the juices of life went from body to body, from the first to the second, from the second to the first—in a circle.

Pillars of smoke and pillars of flame rose to the sky from the entire city. Beautiful was the fire on the great altar. The cries of the victims—long-drawn-out, endless cries—were sweet in the ears of a god as eternal as the Eternal God. And the tender parts, the thighs and the breasts, were the portion of the priest.

1919 (translated by Norbert Guterman)

1

The wide oak door leading to the women's section of the synagogue is always closed. In the center, at eye level, a small opening has been cut out. It is slightly larger than a human face, arched at the top and straight at the bottom. The piece of wood which has been cut out of the broad oak surface forms a little door hanging on two hinges.

At the moment it is open, revealing a young woman's face framed by a white silk kerchief. The face is rather long and plump like a plum, a little pale after the fast, but with a pallor which is translucent and fresh. A wanton lock of hair, thick and curly, the color of light Turkish tobacco, has escaped from under the scarf, and two large blue eyes look with curiosity at the men in the synagogue.

This is forbidden.

Menachem the rabbi's son stands beside the Holy Ark and his father, with his elbows on his reading desk and his head in his hands. His brand new tallis with bands of silver embroidery covers his eyes, yet he can still see. And he sees.

The air in the synagogue is full of sanctity and pure spirituality. The burning wax candles have a heavy, pungent and spicy scent. From the lock of blond hair a fine thread of sinfulness spins out and floats through the whole synagogue, wrapping itself like a spider's web round Menachem's heart and causing some confusion in his thoughts. He closes his eyes, opens his mouth, and breathes slowly and deeply.

2

At the Blessing of the Moon, the sky was clear and cool and the Jews wished each other that their names should be sealed in the Book of Life for the coming year. Unconscious of the calm, gentle smiles on their faces, they all went slowly and pensively back home.

Wrapped in his dressing gown, the rabbi sat in the parlor with a religious tome in his hand, drinking a glass of tea and waiting for his daughter-in-law Ettel and the cook Sloveh to prepare the meal. His wife, heavy and bloated like a lump of dough, sat opposite him on the wide, old-fashioned couch. An illness had robbed her of her speech and twisted her mouth. When she wanted something, all she could say was "meh." Menachem was standing at a window. From time to time he stroked his little black beard; he did not look at Ettel. The young woman prepared the meal and did not look at him.

They washed and sat down at table, eating with moderation and talking quietly about the sukkah, which was to be built the next day. When Ettel was serving out the soup, she stared at the plates, while Menachem hurriedly told his father what a certain scholar had said on the subject of the Temple Service in Jerusalem. Between eating and talking, the rabbi looked in his book. His wife, sitting in an old armchair, could clearly see that the two young people were avoiding each other's eyes, and one corner of her mouth twisted itself up even more. This was her way of smiling.

The Jewish town lay in the valley, while the houses of the Gentiles were scattered all over the surrounding hills. From there, shouting, laughter and singing could be heard at night. The singing was sometimes sad, sometimes wanton, but it always had sweetness and depth. In the dark, silent parlor the old wall-clock mumbled in its sleep: t-tick . . . tock.

3

Time passed and night lay on the world, slowly extinguishing all the more audible sounds, until there spread over the earth only a rustle, a whisper, a sigh as faint as a breath. And then there was stillness. Once more, from somewhere far away, a piercing yell of fear and pain was heard, perhaps a living creature's last scream, but night cut it off as if with a knife and the stillness hardly stirred as it hung delicately poised over the town. Then the houses came together on the market-square, looked at each other with sightless eyes, swayed and rocked like shadows and whispered together for a long time in dumb excitement about various matters until a cock crowed, and a light spurted out of a window, red and unexpected. The assembly was startled and dispersed. The houses stood in their places again and the windows on the western side of the market were illuminated by a dull, watery glow.

The candle was lit in the kitchen of the rabbi's house. Sloveh the cook had washed herself. While she was reciting the blessing, she had already begun her work.

The kitchen seemed cramped around the old woman. Sloveh was tall and bent and she consisted mainly of large bones and dark, parchment-like skin. Her eyebrows were like a thatched roof, her eyes small dark holes, and she had a sharp nose and long angular hands. She walked with a flatfooted, shuffling gait. Her head jerked frequently from side to side and the black holes did not simply look out but bored into people searchingly.

She was supposed to be the cook, but in fact she also cleaned the rooms, washed and scoured the pots and pans, did the household sewing, looked after the rabbi's wife, managed the accounts, served the food and even poked her nose into the rabbi's business by expressing her opinion on questions of religious ritual. She did everything within the house and outside the house. Not very fast, not very well, rather badly in fact, but to remove anything from her jurisdiction would have been impossible.

The old woman had a lot of children, twelve or perhaps fifteen, scattered around the world. She gave them just about as much thought as they gave her. The rabbi's household possessed her—possessed her absolutely.

While kneading the dough for the challah, she would mutter: "They say, it seems, that four times in a row . . . " Later, raking aside the glowing coals in the oven, she would assert: "In any case, I don't want to . . . " but the end of the sentence came out as a mumble. She seldom spoke with other people and said little when she did, but she talked to herself a great deal. Sometimes her words had some connection with her work or her immediate surroundings, but more often it was impossible to know what regions she was inhabiting.

The challah was already in the oven. The old woman gazed out of the window. The sky grew pale and shimmered like mother-of-pearl. She raised a hand and opened her mouth, but hearing steps at the door of the dining room she turned her head and said without preamble:

"Don't be too long: There'll be a fresh bun with the coffee."

Menachem, with his tallis-bag under his arm, muttered "Good-morning" and went past her to the front door. His chest expanded as he breathed in the fresh early morning air. The window of the young couple's room still stood open and silent from the night before, and as he passed it, he gave a quick sideways glance toward it, then shut his eyes for a while and opened them again.

In the kitchen, old Sloveh was still standing with her hand in the air. She had forgotten why.

4

The rabbi went through the parlor to lie down in his room. Menachem was playing checkers with Gershon the shoykhet at a little table by the window on the left.

"What's this? You're playing during the days of Sukkes!" the rabbi said in a tone of reproach, which quickly faded into indifference.

"Harrrrrr!" Gershon's whinnying laugh rang out. "It is merely a harmless diversion," he said pompously. "What does it matter? Harrrrrrrr!"

With the outspread fingers of his left hand he pushed his yarmulke from the back of his neck to the crown of his head. With an expansive gesture of his right hand he moved a piece. It was one of the bad moves he was famous for.

"You're a hopeless case!" Menachem said jokingly and then punished him mercilessly for his false step.

"Harrrrrr! So they tell me. So they tell me. But you just think you're smarter than everyone else? Harrrrrrr!"

Gershon didn't take it to heart. In fact, the devastation which his opponent was inflicting on him seemed to amuse him greatly. He made whinnying noises, jumping from one side of the board to the other and his moves went from bad to worse. This was the way he played checkers.

He was a tall, bony, clumsy man with a fiery red beard sticking out in all directions, small piercing eyes and a bluish nose. He really looked like a savage, an impression which was only intensified by his whinnying laugh and his disjointed speech.

The shoykhet was certainly not an erudite man. He liked a bit of fun, a drop of liquor, and a tasty morsel. He was an expert with the slaughterer's knife, and it was said in the town that besides slaughtering an ox in the conventional manner, he was capable of killing it with his bare hands.

From time to time he would come into the rabbi's house to play checkers with Menachem and to have a chat with him on a "philosophical" theme. It did not seem that he was any more of an expert at philosophical speculation than he was at checkers. "What's the news in the paper? And what's the latest about that saintly fellow, that friend of the Jews—what's his name again—the count? He's a real count, eh? Harrrrr! The things a goy can do! . . . And what about that 'fiery chariot'? What a thing it is—that's what I call a machine—not half!—Let's see: if, for instance . . . " Although he did not always understand what Menachem told him, he always expressed noisy appreciation by opening his mouth and whinnying with delight.

A girlish figure slipped out of the couple's room and cut across the corner of the parlor. Her head and even her arms were completely covered by a black silken shawl. Menachem became even more engrossed in the checkerboard. Gershon the shoykhet took the end of his beard in the fingers of his left hand and looked after the figure with an intense and embarrassed expression on his face. The fact was that once, purely by chance and without her realizing it, he had seen her taking a bath. Seen everything! From head to foot, harrrr! Her skin and—especially—that body of hers—the body of a virgin, yes, of a virgin—had inflamed him.

He cracked the fingers of both hands noisily and ground his strong white teeth.

5

During the day the air in the synagogue vibrated and trembled under the rolling waves of sound. Menachem the rabbi's son sat alone at a table by the western wall, studying aloud.

The rabbi spoke little. For him, thought was like a broad avenue, but the pathways of speech seemed to be dark and narrow. After a sentence or two about the essence of a religious question he usually tired of it and fell into a reverie. With time this even affected his hearing.

His son, on the other hand, loved sound, every kind of sound, but especially musical tones. More than once he had listened with mixed feelings of joy and embarrassment to the ringing bells of the Polish and Russian churches which stood facing each other on the hill on the outskirts of the town.

He also liked hearing his own voice. His speech was smooth, well-rounded and fluent. He even sang a little in a baritone, slightly sweet but surprisingly strong for someone of his small stature. Above all he loved the melody used for studying the Talmud, which lent itself to the subtle expression of the words, to triumphant tones at the end of a section and to the smooth transition from speech to song. Menachem loved embellishing his singing with trills and ornaments, and did this frequently.

He read aloud and the synagogue responded. The ancient walls which enclosed the wide, high interior reacted to even the smallest sound, like thin slivers of dry wood. The sounds echoed, re-echoed, multiplied and rose and fell like the swelling and ebbing of the sea on a calm day. They cascaded like foaming spray across the synagogue and out through the open windows. And when at last Menachem felt tired and got up from the table, an unconscious smile of pleasure hovered around his face, his eyes had a faint dreamy shimmer and his body swayed and stretched with a gentle fatigue as if he had been swimming in the surging waves of sound.

The door closed behind him. His footsteps, soft and muffled as though he had been wearing slippers, receded and faded away. The synagogue remained alone.

Then both the doors of the Holy Ark swung slowly and silently on their hinges and opened wide, all on their own.

From the high southwest window a strip of golden light shines into the synagogue, slanting diagonally downward. Its edges are sharp and straight, as if cut with a knife. It is a barrier, a dead, absolutely impassible barrier, between a world of innumerable gilded somethings hurriedly crowding together, and a world of pale transparent nothingness. The strip of light falls somewhere by the door, in the opposite corner.

Stillness.

A sparrow flew in with the rays of sunlight and alighted on the windowsill. He turned his head this way and that, and his little eyes darted swiftly and inquisitively around the whole synagogue and he gave a chirp. The echo suddenly awoke, seized the short, staccato chirp and shattered it into a thousand droplets. Frightened, the sparrow flew off, fluttering frantically. The echo sank back into the corners, the ceiling, the floor. All is still.

Very still. And as the minutes, or the hours, or the years, pass and are gone, the stillness becomes deeper, denser, more taut, until it begins to tremble like a stretched violin string and bursts with a single thin metallic sound which pierces the whole space, penetrating into the farthest corners.

Was it real or a dream? The sound was like a steel needle, sharp and real, but the old echo remained undisturbed.

The reading desks stretch in long rows across the synagogue. Gradually their straight edges become blurred, their sharp corners rounded, their immobile limbs and forms appear in stiff but flexible relief. A crowd is standing there in mute expectation with raised shoulders and bowed heads, the reading desks turned to face the east. In the darkness of the open Ark, faintly colored shadows shimmer with a calm silver gleam, and over the Holy Ark hover two long hands with outspread fingers. They rest high and motionless above the still crowd. Then within the depths of the Ark a sound is born and increases and spreads through the whole synagogue. It is the long ascending note of the shofar, harsh, bitter and strong, like the breath of frost itself: T-e-r-u-a-h!

6

It happened about three weeks after Sukkes, beginning on a market-day. On the third day everything became quiet again. At midday a few shops even opened, but around three they shut again as the whole of Krivodov gathered in the great synagogue. The oak door was thrown open, and the two sections became one: men, women and children all came together. It was clear that all the adults had been fasting that day, without the rabbi having ordered it.

The rabbi stood in front of the cantor's desk and recited some penitential prayers suitable for the occasion. He recited *"Shema koleynu,"* hear our voices, and "Hardships have surrounded me," the lament over the destruction of the communities of the Rhine. Then he went over to the bima. The rabbi's wife had already been brought in to sit on the bench at the very back of the synagogue. The corner of her mouth was twisted up even more, one eye was swollen and bloodshot, and she stared with the other.

The congregation huddled together round the bima. Among those at the back stood a girlish figure hiding her head and face with a black shawl. It was the rabbi's daughter-in-law.

Gershon the shoykhet was pacing about the synagogue with his bandaged right arm in a sling. Sloveh, who was mumbling inaudibly, had retreated into the empty corner by the western wall.

During the memorial prayer for the dead, a woman suddenly let out a long wavering cry from somewhere at the side of the synagogue. The rabbi raised his tallis from his head, revealing a pale, calm face, and said sternly: "Sha!"

"It's Khone the porter's . . . widow," someone whispered.

The rabbi stood silently for a while and then he said more gently:

"We must not weep."

The woman's voice broke off abruptly with a thin screeching sound like the twisting of a rusty hinge, and then she was silent.

Ink and a goose-quill were brought out and Shmaye the scribe began to set down the events of the previous three days in the community's record-book. It was a lamentation and a chronicle written in a mixture of Hebrew and Yiddish and composed by various people. The rabbi started and others continued. It read thus:

"*Re'ey Adonoy me hoyo lonu*—See, O Lord, what has befallen us. We have been led like sheep to the slaughter and they have plundered our possessions and have disgraced Thy Name among all the nations . . ."

Suddenly they stopped. A wind rushed through the synagogue, and an open window slammed shut with a bang. The broken windowpanes could be heard shattering on the ground outside. When the rabbi saw that everyone's eyes had turned toward the door, he looked there and immediately leaned his hand on the desk to support himself. His wife tried to get up from her bench but did not manage it and fell back heavily.

During the whole of the three days nobody had seen Menachem, the rabbi's son, and everybody had assumed that he was lying murdered somewhere. He stood for a moment in the doorway and then walked over to the bima.

His clothes were crumpled, but undamaged, and there were no signs of violence on him. His face was unwashed and he looked unslept, but his eyes looked quite normal. So normal that a cold fear passed over the people in the synagogue. He was smoking a cigarette.

The rabbi opened his mouth and shut it again. Menachem remarked calmly:

"You are praying again? Praying, praying! You were always a nation of prayer-babblers, men and women both."

The congregation started uneasily. The rabbi looked at his son. The synagogue was very silent.

"Well, why have you all gone quiet?" Menachem noticed the record-book and burst out laughing. "You've forgotten something, Shmaye. You mustn't forget to enter the names of the Holy Ones: Khone the porter died for the Sanctification of the Name, so did Berl the thief, and

Gitl the soldiers' whore had eight goyim on top of her. All for the Sanctification of the Name!"

The tone of his voice became as coarse as his words and acted like a whiplash on the congregation, who backed away from him, confused and bewildered.

Suddenly the rabbi regained his power of speech. With a grating, screeching voice he uttered confused words:

"Is that so! And who created the world, and the sea, and the seven heavens. You, perhaps, eh? You, perhaps, eh?"

His shrunken figure in its torn gabardine bobbed up and down, up and down, looking like a little cockerel with wet bedraggled feathers.

Menachem gnashed his teeth.

"And who created the bath and the woman who bathes in it? I, perhaps, eh? And who created bean tsimes and scrawny beards and Grandma Trayne's cotton bloomers? I, perhaps, eh? *Reboyne shel oylem,* Lord of the Universe, thou mighty Creator of Trayne's bloomers, take under Thy wings the souls of these Holy Ones who have been tortured for the honor and glory of Thy Holy Name—Yahweh!"

"He has gone mad!" someone screamed with a shaking voice.

The rabbi, who had not heard his son's words, continued:

"And who brought the Children of Israel out of the land of Egypt and led them for forty years through the desert and brought them to the land which He promised to Abraham, Isaac and Jacob? You perhaps, eh?"

"Aha! Still calling in that old debt, is he? We've suffered thousands of Egypts since then, been through thousands of deserts, and remained in slavery until this very moment. Yet that old usurer is still calling in his debt! And he hasn't even compensated us for the bad liquor he sold us!"

At last the congregation was stirred to anger. Voices were heard:

"It's because of our sins, because of heretics like you, that God is punishing us!"

"For *your* sins, ha ha ha! Little chicks like you have sinned! Oh dear, someone missed out a word when he was reciting a section of the Mishnah this year, did he, ha ha ha! Do you think you have the power to sin? Do you think you have the *brains* to sin? Only living human beings can sin and you are carcasses, cadavers, corpses! And what a creature that God of yours is! He boasts of being a jealous and vengeful God, and what he means is: vengeful against *you!* Against *them* he's completely powerless. He's a father who punishes his own child with savage ferocity and will not defend him when he is attacked—oh no! Oh holy congregation! Your rabbi, the judge and leader of your community—if only you could have seen with your own eyes how a stinking goy beat him and uncovered his private parts and other secret parts of his body. How they tortured and humiliated him."

Menachem broke off abruptly and a sudden change came over him which horrified the congregation. He pursed his lips like a pious woman and spoke with a nasal voice in a cloying, yet venomous tone:

"*Their* God really is a God, you see! *He's* a God of Love who wouldn't hurt a fly on the wall. And look what he can do! Look how he runs his world—*his* world, it's *his* world. A God, my dear Jews, has to be worth something. A God, my brothers and sisters, has to be able to *achieve* something. When it comes to achieving *nothing,* then you too are gods."

The rabbi, who had been shrieking almost continuously, suddenly fell silent. He straightened up and looked at his son as if he were a stranger. He pressed his pale, thin lips together and his dark eyes stared coldly and alertly.

Gershon the shoykhet was standing a little to one side twisting his fiery beard in the fingers of his left hand. He was grimacing and looking at Menachem. It was impossible to judge whether he was about to laugh or was full of rage.

And then a girlish figure pushed its way to the bima. Her shawl fell back from her head, revealing a face covered with pale blotches, as if it had been smeared with white clay.

"Menachem!" she said. "Menachem!"

The young man opened his mouth wide like a suffocating fish.

"Get away from me!" he gasped.

His eyes became round and protruded from under his brows. He put his hands to his head and shrieked:

"Get away from me, you—you defiled creature! You'd really like to have been a whore and run to the blond-haired goy of your own accord!"

Someone caught the young woman as she fell to the floor, and carried her over to a bench.

Menachem suddenly seemed to calm down and turned to face the congregation with coldness:

"Listen to me. I'm not embarrassed in front of the likes of you. It's almost a year since we got married and I haven't even touched her yet. I haven't even seen her body. I loved her like Jacob loved Laban's younger daughter. But I was shy. And now this *goy* comes and digs into her like a pig into a pile of dung." He wiped the sweat from his forehead. "Oh well, that's what they are like—that's *their* work. But the whole time— are you listening to me?—the whole time I was lying hidden in the yard. Lying—in a corner—of the yard—watching. *That*—is their work. And *this* is *your* work. Your Torah, your worm-eaten life, your business. It's deadly poison. I swear to you by my misfortune that I will use all my strength to exterminate you from the face of the earth!"

"Harrrr!" whinnied Gershon the shoykhet.

The rabbi approached his son, pointed to the door and said quietly: "Go."

The son replied with a look of hatred and a gnashing of his teeth. His firm, measured steps resounded through the synagogue. The rabbi turned his face to the eastern wall and quietly but clearly began reciting the Kaddish:

"*Yisgadal veyiskadash shmey rabo*—Magnified and sanctified be His great Name . . ."

The silence was broken by muffled blows coming from one corner of the synagogue. It was Khone the porter's widow mutely beating her face against her lectern.

The rabbi's wife twisted her eyes toward the door and said: "Meh." Then she died.

7

For weeks the rain soaked and ravaged the earth, and then one night a wind carried away the clouds. When the sun rose, the land lay in the bony arms of a bitter frost, and the rough surface of the frozen earth sounded like cast iron underfoot. In the evening a snowstorm came from distant places and whistled the whole night through the chimneys, danced in the marketplace, and disappeared at daybreak to travel to other distant places. The cold let up for a while before returning to bite into the helpless earth with its sharp pointed teeth. Whirlwind upon whirlwind galloped in brutal triumph around the town. Overhead low gray clouds gave way to pale frozen skies, and pale frozen skies in turn gave way to low-hanging clouds. And then the hard arms relaxed their grip and the half-suffocated earth fell backward and drew a deep, warm breath. Her paralyzed limbs started to revive again, juices coursed through her weak, shivering body, scents floated through the air, and from time to time indistinct sounds, a cross between a sob and a soft laugh, darted out from somewhere and then bashfully hid again. Vegetation sprouted from the earth and spread out like a flood taking on a deeper darker color. The summer had come. He arrived in rich colorful clothing, vivacious and familiar, becoming ever more insistent and passionate, until the tormented and intoxicated earth succumbed to spasm after spasm of wild abandon. For a long while she shuddered in hot oblivion and at last lay in a gold-red glow, exhausted from her ecstasy of conceiving and giving birth. And again white winter came, and again red summer followed, and year after year rolled over the town. Sometimes they were noisy and stormy like a train rushing through, sometimes smooth and calm like the water of a stream.

Life in the town flowed on drearily through the winters and summers. Relations between Jews and Gentiles were difficult and complex. The Jews both looked forward to and feared the fairs and market-days. Bad news reached them from other towns: decrees, persecutions and pogroms were increasing and multiplying. They were approaching from all sides. People's brows clouded over, their eyes were full of astonishment, and they angrily announced that there was no sense to all this, no sense at all!

Silence reigned over the rabbi's house. His daughter-in-law had gone back to where she had come from and Sloveh was in sole charge of the household. The old woman had hardly changed, though she had become slightly deaf and talked to herself ceaselessly. The rabbi had become even smaller and more shrunken and his face, with its thin pale lips, looked gaunt and bird-like. Throughout the night he lay on his bed with his eyes open while his old clock wheezed and stuttered like an old dotard, coughing and choking from time to time in its attempt to announce to the world what time of night it was.

Occasionally Gershon the shoykhet came to chat with the rabbi. His arm had healed. It was rumored that those who had broken it had got more than they bargained for. He whinnied now less frequently and with less pleasure, and usually in situations where it was inappropriate.

These were strange almost wordless conversations. The rabbi now found it difficult to utter a single word, and Gershon's speech had always been disjointed, coming out in short bursts. Since it did not seem proper to discuss "philosophy" with the rabbi, the shoykhet squirmed and shifted about and eventually came up with the concrete theme of "the Jewish people." "So what is the meaning of 'the Jewish people'? What if, for instance, a Jew is captured by heathens? I, uh, mean to say, is the law for the individual the same as the law for the whole people, eh?" He sweated from the effort of formulating his nebulous ideas and paced back and forth in the unlit room. The floorboards creaked nervously under his feet with a tone which was strangely high-pitched, like Gershon's speech. The rabbi always looked in some other direction, toward the window or the ceiling, but somehow or other he understood Gershon and occasionally put in an appropriate word. The long pauses were usually filled by the distant but audible mutterings of Sloveh alone in the kitchen.

8

Lately, unusual things had begun happening to Gershon the shoykhet, the master of the knife. He had begun to bungle the work, making the meat treyf. He didn't slit the throat properly or he cut it too deeply. The women were surprised and angry, but initially each one kept it to herself and did not know the others felt the same way. That is until his own wife, Genesye, a complaining harridan who bit off everyone's noses, started clamoring: "He's gone mad, my fine shoykhet of a husband! For months now he's been refusing to eat meat or anything with meat in it. At first he said he was ill, but now he says that he hates meat—

hates it, did you ever hear the like? And now it has all come out: he doesn't want to slaughter any more! He says he will not shed blood. Help me, everyone, why don't you say something!"

The Jews laughed and did not believe it. But on Thursday morning the butchers stormed Gershon's house. The man who had the official concession for kosher meat came out sweating and shrugging his shoulders. The butchers raged that they would tie Gershon up. But when they realized that a bound shoykhet would do no good for any of them, they started begging, then threatening, then pleading. All to no avail.

The people were astounded. Had he lost his mind, or what? Whoever heard of such a thing? It was absolutely ridiculous! The warden of the synagogue told the rabbi about it. The rabbi raised his eyebrows and said "Eh? What's that?" He repeated the story. The rabbi was silent, and the warden shifted from one foot to the other, not knowing how to proceed. At last the rabbi told him to send Gershon. But the shoykhet had hidden and was nowhere to be found. That Sabbath the community had no meat.

On the evening of Sabbath finally Gershon came to the rabbi of his own accord. Instead of giving the customary greeting *"gut vokh"* as he entered, he started whinnying in his finest tones, and peered with great interest into the corner of the room where there was nothing to see.

The rabbi turned his eyes toward Gershon and eventually pulled himself together and said:

"What's the meaning of this?"

Gershon replied with another resounding whinny.

The rabbi pursued the point: "Well?"

"*Ve'es hadom loy soykhlu*—ye shall not partake of the blood!" Gershon exclaimed with a conviction which was not entirely convincing.

"*Loy sokheylu*," said the rabbi, correcting his grammar.

Gershon instantly lost his faith in his biblical verses; with a verse you could easily get lost.

Nevertheless he tried again, this time with clear uncertainty in his voice. "*Ki hadom hu hanofesh*," he recited, "for the blood is the life."

"Yes, but three verses later it says: *vehabosor toykhel*—and you shall eat the flesh! How do you reconcile that?" But the rabbi suddenly lost patience and carried on:

"And in any case—what is all this nonsense? Who do you think you are?"

Gershon was silent. The rabbi became uneasy. It was a complex issue which he never devoted any thought to. Gershon still remained silent. Why didn't he speak?

As the shoykhet was leaving, the rabbi called after him:

"You did not create the world."

Gershon admitted that this was true. He had not created it. Gershon went home and sent a message to the warden that he should find another shoykhet.

The warden in his anger had already done so. But when the new shoykhet arrived, the people thought that Gershon should be paid some compensation money for surrendering the title. But his wife Genesye started creating another fuss. She went to the warden's house:

"He's refusing to take it. He says he won't take any compensation payment. He'd rather I and the children went begging from door to door. Well, I'm going to get a divorce and that will be the end of it. For twenty years I've put up with that crook, that murderer . . . that . . . that . . . That's it! I can't take any more!"

The warden tried to calm her down: They would give the money to her personally, and she could open a little shop, or something like that. But the old witch cursed him from head to toe. Did he think she was going to take compensation money? Her enemies and ill-wishers shouldn't live to see that day. How could she have the right to the money? She wasn't the shoykhet, but the shoykhet's wife. And he was still alive, though God willing he shouldn't live another year, that murderer who had been sucking her blood for the past twenty years.

In the end she absolutely refused to take it.

The whole community was at a loss. A pack of lunatics. How were they to solve this dreadful problem? The neighbors were already reporting that Gershon's family was starving. All right—they would find a position for him as a teacher of Jewish law.

They tried that, but it emerged that the man was not much of a scholar. The older boys learned nothing from him, and gradually the older pupils melted away, and younger ones—together with a few girls—took their place. Thus Gershon became a melamed, or teacher, but he was still known as "Gershon the shoykhet."

9

Before Passover Gershon appeared at the rabbi's in the middle of the day. He had a strange expression of triumph on his face. He had brought the newspaper with him. It was all in there! The rabbi looked at it and for the first time in years a vague smile hovered over his thin lips. Gershon whinnied in sympathy: harrrrr!

"And an apostate, what's more!" he exclaimed, and stood there with an open mouth. The rabbi turned very pale and his face seemed to stretch like elastic. Gershon left and the rabbi stared for a long time at the window.

The Jewish public didn't understand the news at first. They had already heard of the "mad apostate"—a kind of monk—a converted Jew, whom people had been talking about recently. He was apparently a tremendously powerful orator. His voice, his gestures, his facial expressions were all startling and bizarre, and his listeners, mainly simple peasants, were seized by frenzied excitement. His latest theme was "The Jews."

The Jews shrugged their shoulders. Blood—matzos—Passover . . . It was just babbling. Who would believe him? Mind you, the subject was not unknown. Blood for Passover—"the blood libel," wasn't it called? It brought to mind the Middle Ages. And names like Gonta and Chmielnicki, and the "Haidamacks," half-forgotten but yet familiar names, a kind of strange inheritance which, because it was part of them, Jews did not, perhaps, really want to relinquish. Their interest in this man became more intense, more fearful, more filled with bitterness. The lost end of the thread had been found again. Life was suddenly full of terror and splendor like a mighty conflagration in the depths of the night.

10

In time the storm about the blood-libel abated. Its consequences were inscribed in the record-books of many Jewish communities. And before the writing had begun to fade, the war had started.

11

In the daytime nothing could be heard, but darkness brought a distant rumbling from the west: sometimes a short boom, at others a long-drawn-out sound like rolling thunder. Day and night, past the town and along the main highway through the long narrow district of Golorov, poured crowds of Jews who had been driven out of the towns along the front. Jews were now said to be spies who were betraying the country to the enemy. At one point the highway went round a nearby hill which faced the town, and from Krivodov could be seen the endless slow stream of people on foot, with here and there a heavily laden wagon, usually pulled by oxen, and occasionally someone mounted on a skinny nag. At night the drunken red eyes of torches danced around. There spread out all over the country, accompanied by the bombardment which was increasing daily, a screeching of axles, a whinnying of horses, a lowing of oxen, and the muffled, confused noise of the human stream.

Many of the wanderers came into the town asking for food or water. Briefly and apathetically they described the situation in other towns and then trickled back into the stream. They said that it would soon reach Krivodov and that people should take precautions. But they failed to do anything, and in any case, what sort of precautions could they take? No one was buying anything. A few people offered their homes and goods for sale to wealthy peasants of the town, but their answer was: "Why should we pay good money for them?"

The highway was clearly visible from the windows of the rabbi's parlor, and for days on end and late into the night he sat and looked out. His hair had become completely gray, his forehead white and almost transparent, and his gaze as cool and clear as crystal. He sat and thought about what he saw: about things related to it and about things that were distant from it in both time and place.

The rabbi looked back over his whole life and many things became clear to him, while others remained incomprehensible. He did not worry about these, however. When his glance happened to fall on Sloveh, a faint shimmer of interest lit up in his eyes.

The old woman was still keeping the house, but she did things without rhyme or reason and with a certain absentminded haste. She talked to herself constantly, even in the presence of strangers, in fragmented utterances. If there was any chain of reasoning in her thoughts the links were known to her alone. In all other respects she did not show her age. On the contrary, her figure had become more wiry and her movements more energetic. She was as taut as a spring, but without its rounded form. To a stranger's eyes she could seem a little confused, but the rabbi did not view her like that, although he could not form any clear idea of her thoughts. Her words gave no sign that she was aware of what was happening in the world, or to the Jews. She coped with the details of her own immediate surroundings, but God knows what she was talking or thinking about.

At last Krivodov's turn came. The police commissioner, official forms, Cossacks. The Jews were given three days, but the first two passed in preparations which were made and then cancelled again, and at dawn on the third day the stream on the Golorov highway absorbed a new tributary. The community was broken up. Each person was fending for himself and the confusion was great, but nevertheless they went on in a state of stunned apathy. Only babies at the breast cried now and then; older children thought it was all great fun.

The younger and middle-aged Gentiles were still in the town. There were no old people to be seen. The locals paid little attention to the departing mass of Jews, taken up as they were with their own affairs. At one point a fight broke out over a house which had belonged to the richest Jew of the town. During the brawl a few young lads started throwing stones until a gray, squarish head with shaggy eyebrows poked out of a window of one of the huts and shouted at them in a lugubrious but brusque tone. The boys disappeared. It was a long day during the month of Tammuz, but until late into the night the road to the hill was still black with human beings.

And so the important Jewish town of Krivodov, which had paid interest with its blood long after the days of Chmielnicki, ceased to exist.

12

The main stream pouring along the highway was dense and slow-moving. Relentlessly, it ground down and absorbed the tributaries, so that families found it almost impossible to stay together. Mounted Cossacks rode along on both sides, occasionally encouraging the stragglers in their own manner. From somewhere the thin, soft weeping of a woman could be heard.

The rabbi walked slowly with his tallis-bag under his arm, with Sloveh beside him. The night was hot, but in the open field it was bearable. When they came round the hill, the wide, unknown world spread out before them. Toward the west distant fires raged and long shadows flitted across the land. In places large faint patches suddenly emerged from the darkness and then disappeared again. The thunder of cannons rolled with ease from horizon to horizon. The bombardment, which for the most part had come from the west, seemed to change direction and come closer, from the southwest. There the sky was blood-red, and the redness fluttered like a flag, not resting for a single moment. Light winds carried the faint but acrid and pungent scent of burning wood and other materials, which quickly dissipated. High overhead, stars peeped out from the blotchy sky. They were white and faint or yellow with the dull gleam of polished brass. Low in the eastern sky a little star blinked its eye uncomprehendingly.

Throughout the night the endless caravan became ever denser. Its ranks were swollen by the Jewish populations of Polorot, Balnik, Maravan and Tshernopolye, of Bakhtsha, the only Jewish farmers' colony in the province, and of the few tiny shtetlekh which formed the remote police district of Roslov. The air became denser, and when day arrived the distant red glow in the sky disappeared. A thin mist, mingled with smoke, covered the nearby faces with a gray melancholy haze. The movement of the people became even slower, and all the new arrivals soon adopted the monotonous pace, walking mechanically and sleepily as if on an eternal march. The few wagons squeaked softly and forlornly, and the oxen swayed onward, their heads drooping and their eyes half-shut. Only occasionally did an ox raise an eyelid, revealing a dull glassy eyeball, and then lower it again. Some of the wagons belonged to Gentiles who had hired them out for very high prices, but now the owners were swaying on their seats with as much apathy as if they too belonged to this mass of banished people. On one of the wagons a Gentile with a thin youthful face kept blinking his eyes, and then suddenly broke into a long, sad song, full of nasal tones, pensive and forlorn, as if he were all alone on a remote and silent road. A Jewish wagoner who was traveling directly behind him opened his mouth and stared at him for a while. Then he dropped his head onto his chest again. The hours dripped like drops of molten pitch.

People started to fall by the wayside. At first the Cossacks drove them on with curses and whiplashes, but as the number of the stragglers grew, the Cossacks, with angry faces, began to turn a blind eye. In any case, where were they going? Nobody really knew. The Cossacks had unclear and contradictory orders, given either without any logic or with some secret intent—or both. Many of the people had already consumed the small amount of food which they had managed to bring with them, and children were crying. But even worse was the thirst, and at a place where the flat, muddy river Lelitsh came close to the road, the congestion lasted for hours, as ever more crowds of people surged from behind like an avalanche.

Jews from Karavay came out to meet them with bread and water. But before this meager aid could be distributed, the congestion in the valley beside the town became so great that everything came to a standstill. People were being crushed together, forming an impenetrable wall. Women were fainting or screaming about their children. Several horses took fright and pranced around in their harness, kicking into the dense throng. From afar the shouts and curses of the Cossacks could be heard, the whistling of their whips, and the screams of pain and terror. A few minutes later the whole mass shuddered and tore apart like ice on a thawing river. The rift came suddenly and with enormous momentum. From various sides there was at once a thrusting and a twisting into arcs and circles. In one single moment hundreds of people were trampled to death, and thousands of families were separated as their desperate hands stretched out toward faces which were being swept away forever. Some of them were struggling wildly and hopelessly while others were staring with a dumb apathetic gaze. The disaster came like an explosion—instantaneous and irrevocable.

The rabbi of Krivodov's chest was being crushed in the great congestion. The old man was suspended, unable to breathe, as if tightly wrapped up in a human ball of wool. He thought he was about to die and so his thoughts became jumbled. Then he was carried along like a little piece of driftwood, and in the narrowest part of the valley, where the stream of humanity surged wildly and beat up against its banks, he was thrown out onto a little hillock while the stream flowed on. When he came around a little, he was lying on the earth. The stream was still tearing on, beating in foaming waves up against its banks, often coming close to where he was. The rabbi was in great danger of being trampled by the feet of the fleeing people, so he tried to stand up, but only fell down again. He opened his eyes a little wider and strained his ears as if he were listening to something inside himself. He shook his head. Why not? It was high time. He managed to gather his strength and slowly, inch by inch, he clambered up the hillside. He leaned his head against a rock and stretched out his small, old body. He felt no pain but his weakness was increasing from moment to moment.

A broad vista opened out for miles around. The cause of the congestion became clear to him.

At Karavay a broad soft dirt road joined the Golorov highway. It came from the southwest, from the Gorni-Palyetz district, and carried a stream of emigrants from around the town of Palyetz. At the same place a high-lying narrow paved road joined the highway at a sharp angle, and in the distance a long string of oxen with provisions for the military could be seen, heading for the railway in the southwest. The stream of people coming from the dirt road fed into the main stream, almost doubling the mass of people, who were then jammed into the valley. The paved road was supposed to have been kept free for the military commissary, but the escort of Cossacks had lost control. At first they had begun to drive the crowd in both directions along the highway and the paved road. But then they thought better of it and drove them back off the paved road and onto the highway. After that some Cossacks rushed back with an order to halt the stream somewhere before Karavay, in order to allow the supply-train to get through. The confusion grew into a catastrophe.

The rabbi lay on the hillside and breathed deeply. His body had fallen to the ground, flat and sagging like an empty sack, while his eyes roved slowly and calmly over the panicking crowd, the open plain, the misty horizon. The fields had been left to grow wild that year and formed a sea of yellowed, withered grass and pale dry hay flattened to the ground. In one isolated spot there was, strangely, a square patch of fresh green and gold: one single cultivated piece of land in the middle of the abandoned steppe. To the east, some miles further, the earth had broken up revealing a subsoil of yellow clay mixed with huge brown boulders. This was the beginning of the famous ravines: clefts in the earth's surface, hundreds of feet deep and zigzagging capriciously for miles and miles. Alongside the cultivated field ran a narrow whitish village path. Not a single sign of life was to be seen on it. Lonely and peaceful, it stretched through the grasses—stretched and stretched on to somewhere very far away, becoming ever narrower until the eye could no longer distinguish the thin whitish thread from the surrounding steppe. Where, the rabbi wondered, did that path lead?

13

In the crush at Karavay, Gershon the shoykhet lost his hat and his family.

He managed at last to fight his way out of the stream and ran along it for several miles, waving his hands and shouting and screaming until he became hoarse and his cries came out as something between a croak and a shriek. Gradually he quieted down. He dragged himself along, dejected and bewildered, his head hanging down, and he did not hear the rumor which spread among the crowd that there was trouble at Masliyanitsi.

The highway cut right through the middle of this large industrial village where there were large brickworks, a great many small smithies which produced handmade nails, and a samovar factory. The workers gathered around the highway, laughing and throwing stones. The Cossacks pretended to be angry, but the attackers, mainly young Gentile boys, saw through this and became bolder and bolder. At the beginning and end of the village some people were being beaten up and robbed.

It took Gershon a long time to realize what was going on. He was about twenty yards away from the highway. When he saw what was happening he gave a start, and slowly, as if unintentionally, began to draw nearer to the crowd. A young lad, noticing him, laughed and pulled on his friend's sleeve. Gershon glanced sideways and started moving away from the highway, as if he were looking for something. Out of the corner of his eye he saw that the two lads were following him. His knees were shaking and he quickly turned back, approaching the crowd again at an angle. A third young lad was coming toward him. He darted forward again, but by this time he was cut off from the crowd, like a sheep from its flock and, just like that stray sheep, he ran off senselessly, further and further into the field.

The hunt proceeded at a leisurely pace. The three Gentile boys spread out, but not too far from each other, and circled round Gershon in a broad arc. They gestured gaily to each other as if something was extremely funny.

The highway receded further and further into the distance. Gershon's nerves could not stand it any more and he suddenly started running as fast as he could. The boys behind him burst out into raucous laughter: with his little yarmulke on his head, his coattails flapping, and his long legs running with hasty, awkward strides, he looked like some kind of weird comical bird. He saw a small hill, ran round it and stopped, petrified, at the very edge of a ravine. One of the boys was coming toward him. A second one appeared at the top of the hill. Without looking round, Gershon knew that the third one was behind his back.

The hunt was proceeding exactly as the boys wanted: the tall clumsy figure had landed at a bend of one of the great ravines. The lads gnashed their young white teeth, obviously enjoying themselves.

Gershon threw a sidelong glance into the ravine. It was very deep, and from where he was standing the bottom was not visible. The cliff went down like a wall, broken here and there by a jagged protruding stone. In one place a consumptive-looking willow tree sprouted out crookedly from the wall. On the opposite side, about twenty or thirty feet further on, there were a few inverted terraces like upside-down steps.

Gershon felt cold, his throat was dry, and when he opened his mouth to speak nothing could be heard. For a while the boys looked with curiosity at the mute movements of his lips. Then one of them, a boy with a good-natured, round, feminine-looking face, burst out laughing and with a slap of his hand knocked Gershon's yarmulke off his head. One of the others said "No" and placed it very carefully on Gershon's head, a bit too far forward. He really did look very funny.

"*Davay haroshi*—give us money," said the one who had replaced Gershon's yarmulke.

Gershon cleared his throat with a cough and answered: "*Ni*—no." He really meant that he had none, but he knew only a few broken words of their language.

The boy narrowed his eyes:

"*Ni?*"

He went up to Gershon and started to search him.

"He hasn't any," he said to the other two. Suddenly he made a vicious degrading attack on Gershon which left him writhing in pain.

Gershon let out a groan and grabbed him by the hand. The boy stood still for a second, and then he twisted his hand free from Gershon's, leaned on the latter's chest with both hands and started to push him backward, slowly, very slowly, looking into his eyes the whole time with a mild and friendly expression. The other two boys were smiling.

Gershon's hair stood on end. "*Zhinka*—a wife . . . ," he gasped and went on "*Dite*—children . . ."

"*Nitshoho*—that doesn't matter," the boy said in a gentle reassuring voice and continued pushing.

Gershon began to weep, quietly at first and then more loudly. His mouth twisted, his chin stuck out, and his voice quavered. It was a thin, despairing, bitter wailing like that of a child. The boys on either side of him did not move. In unison they clenched their teeth, their lips drawn back and their eyes staring out, large and glittering.

The two wrestled at the very edge of the ravine, each of them locked in the arms of the other. Gradually Gershon's weeping abated until it was completely stifled by the compression of his chest. Huge drops of sweat appeared on his brow. Something slid away under his foot and tumbled downward. The drops of sweat became larger and fell more thickly, a couple of them rolling into his mouth. He arched his back like a cat's and started to push his chest forward, slowly, with pauses, but always pushing forward, forward, never allowing himself to be pushed backward.

His opponent's face lost its venomous mildness. It grew longer, tensed and darkened as his eyes widened and became even larger than before. The boy opened his mouth, but no words came out. His mouth remained open because at that moment Gershon released his grip for a short instant and then locked his arms around the boy's chest. The Gentile's body became limp and began to sink down to the earth, but Gershon did not let him fall. He lifted him, turned in a circle, and when he was facing the ravine, opened his arms. The figure with hanging arms, protruding eyes and twisted legs, hovered for an instant over the ravine, level with the edge, then suddenly plunged downward and was, without a sound, lost to view.

The two other boys blinked. In twirling round, Gershon had been thrown a little away from the edge. His fiery beard stuck out on all sides and his eyes were bloodshot. He laughed.

At the sound of this laugh one of the boys stopped blinking, sprang over the hillock, and ran away. Gershon's hand descended like a block of wood on the other one's girlish face. The boy fell with a groan, and Gershon jumped on top of him with the whole weight of his body and laid his bony hand with curling fingers on the boy's face. One of his fingers went into the boy's eye and he let out a terrible scream.

"Stop screaming," Gershon said and bored the fingers even deeper.

The screams grew longer and more piercing, and one of the boy's hands grabbed Gershon's, seizing Gershon's fingers between his own.

"Stop screaming!"

Gershon gnashed his teeth and twisted his fingers. The boy's hand slipped away from Gershon's like a dead man's. The screams became more piercing and stabbed into Gershon's head.

"Will you not shut up?"

With a hard, gnarled fist he rained blows on the boy's side and ribs, which resounded like an empty barrel. The voice stopped its piercing screaming and became hoarse and muffled. But the last glimmer of reason had disappeared from Gershon's eyes. They burned with a green fire and rolled into his head. His gaze wandered around, unfocused. He lay down flat on the boy and fastened his teeth onto something soft and slippery. His hands wandered over the twitching body and his fingers sought tender places, tearing flesh and bone with the hard unyielding grip of iron tongs. At one point he inflicted such excruciating pain on the tortured body that the ruined voice rediscovered high-pitched, nonhuman screams. But Gershon did not let go of what he was holding until his gripping fingers almost came together in a closed fist. All sorts of noises were coming from his own throat: he croaked, whinnied, squealed like a puppy, and from time to time he giggled like someone being tickled. The sweat was pouring from his skin as if through a sieve. All his organs were erupting in raging activity, spreading a pungent odor around him. This great construction of bones, flesh and blood throbbed feverishly in the grip of a deep, blind life force.

Later, much later, he realized that he was meeting no resistance and in that same moment all the strength ebbed from his body. He rolled off his victim, turned over, and lay face-up, enervated and glowing, as if after a hot bath. His breathing was deep but slow and weak. His mouth gaped open and his eyes were red and misty.

He sat up and looked into the distance. Then his troubled and uncertain gaze fell upon something nearby. But Gershon turned his eyes away, sniffed the air with his nose and fumbled about in the grass around him. A wild flower came into his hand, a yellow dandelion, slightly withered. He looked at it, but unseeingly. His left hand moved to his chest, feeling for something. He came upon a button from his coat and started twisting the button round and round, from left to right, from right to left, round and round. Without turning his head he glanced sideways to his right, but the tip of his own nose got in the way, and he squinted at it with interest for a while. And then suddenly he turned his head sharply and looked directly at the body beside him.

The broken body was jerking and shuddering. One leg was bent at the knee and the fingers of its left hand had dug themselves into the earth. There was blood on the grass beside it, but not much.

Gershon sat and looked. The mist began to clear from his eyes, but they remained bloodshot. He covered them with his left hand, propping his elbow on his knee.

He sat like this for a long time; an hour or more. When at last he raised his head, the blood had drained from his face. His eyes were calm and distant, his chin and lower lip hung down like those of a corpse. The body beside him was no longer moving, but he did not look at and did not see it.

The air became clearer and the sun, huge and red, hung low in the west. In the distance the sounds of the caravan could still be heard, faint and indistinct, but here everything was still. Somewhere nearby a grasshopper chirped as if lost in thought. A little breeze came to life and immediately faded back into the earth.

Gershon looked behind him: he was sitting with his back very close to the ravine. He made a feeble attempt to stand up, but immediately sank back lethargically and carried on sitting motionless. Then he slowly lay down on his back. His head and shoulders were hanging over the edge of the ravine—but not far enough. He pushed both hands into the grass and shoved himself forward. His legs rose into the air, slowly at first, then faster.

14

From Karavay, old Sloveh was carried along through the countryside on the crest of the human wave.

The defeated army was retreating and on the way it vented its rage on the "nation of spies." Gradually a large part of the population became inflamed, and the hunt went on: from east to west, from south to north.

Sloveh was present at almost all the great massacres which took place during this expulsion. In Grayev a soldier almost strangled her, squeezing her neck until she stopped twitching, but when he went away she started breathing again. Between Sokol and Byelizne she picked up a lost child, a little girl about two years old, with blue eyes and soft cheeks. She looked after the child for almost three weeks, until in the pogrom of Verkhovensk a Gentile woman murdered her while she was in Sloveh's arms. In Salovar she hid for twenty-four hours under the bridge, up to her knees in water. She was one of those who were thrown into the River Hlubotsh at the Vinokur forest fire. She was caught in the machine-gun fire at Stavishtsh. Shortly after that, in a small village near Stavishtsh, a peasant beat her with a lump of wood and left her lying unconscious on the ground. Three days later she was gnawing a lump of bread rubbed with garlic in the house of a Swedish colonist. And finally she found herself in a carriage of a train which was traveling across one of the central provinces. This was the famous "lost train."

If there originally had been the ghost of a plan or system in the dispersion of the migrants around the country, this had now vanished. Whoever had any power did whatever occurred to him and everyone was simply trying to get rid of any responsibility. A great many of the fugitives from the southwestern region had gathered in a sleepy central town that had previously permitted Jews only for a few weeks in the year during the great annual market. They were now dying of hunger in the streets. The local authority equipped the train and sent it on its way.

During the previous sixteen hours the train had been diverted three times onto a different line and twice changed direction. No one wanted to let the migrants in, and furthermore the train was not timetabled and was disrupting the rail traffic. Now for the second time it was rolling toward the southeast, between close-cropped yellow fields. Here and there a strip of violet passed, and between the stiff sparse stalks of the harvested buckwheat the gray, meager earth showed through. The sun was low in the sky and slanted in from behind through the windows on the right. The carriage was lit up with a red glow.

A man with a shaven head and sunken cheeks came in through the front door and walked through the carriage toward the rear door. He had already got to the exit when out of the corner of his eye he noticed an old woman sitting at a window. He stopped, turned, looked in her direction, started walking again and then stopped once more. He went up to the old woman and silently stared at her. Then he said: "Sloveh."

She did not hear him, but kept on moving her lips, her head bent. The man repeated: "Sloveh!"

She raised her eyes to his face.

"Sloveh, do you not recognize me?"

"Why wouldn't I recognize you? You're Sheyne the widow's son, Khayim Dovid, eh?"

The man stood silently for a while, looking at her.

"I'm not Sheyne's son," he answered gently.

"Where have you been? Your mother has been complaining about you. You didn't even remember to write a letter—that's all the thanks you get for slaving away for your children."

She spoke severely, her sunken eyes peering searchingly at him. He stood in front of her, rubbing his chin absentmindedly with the fingers of his left hand.

"I am not Sheyne's son," he repeated.

She had already forgotten him and was looking past him, muttering something.

He rubbed his forehead and went up closer to her.

"Sloveh, how is the rabbi's wife?—the rabbi's wife?—the rabbi's wife?"

She raised her head. In her eyes there appeared a sudden glimmer of recognition.

"The rabbi's wife—" she repeated in confusion.

"Yes, the rabbi's wife—how is she? Where is she? Where is she now? Is she—is she still alive?"

Sloveh got out of her seat and started looking round at the other passengers. He glanced hastily around too.

"She isn't here, Sloveh. Where did you leave her?"

She spread out her hands helplessly. He went out through the rear door into the other carriages. Soon he came back but Sloveh was again sunk in her own thoughts and her fragmentary monologues. He sat down beside her.

He took off his little cap. The skin of his shaved head was gray and bloodless and the hollows in his cheeks were deep, but his movements suggested self-restraint rather than feebleness. He wore a short jacket, dark and threadbare, and trousers of the same material.

The shaven-headed man looked intently and coldly at the people around them. There was not much talk in the carriage—Jews had of late lost the habit of talking. Occasionally two people exchanged a word or two, but for the most part the passengers looked silently out of the windows at the steppe rushing by. Two children were playing on the floor.

The shadows of the train on the eastern side slowly lengthened as night fell. A conductor brought in a little piece of candle, stuck it into the lantern hanging from the ceiling, and lit it. The darkness became even more gloomy. The conductor had an unfriendly expression and muttered something under his breath. Before he left the carriage he scolded the children.

The train went straight through two stations and stopped at the third for one minute. Some passengers jumped off into the station for hot water, among them the shaven-headed man. As he was coming back with the tea and an old tin dipper which he had bought in the buffet, he heard the stationmaster talking with the two conductors and the engineer from the train:

"You've certainly taken on something here, I can tell you that. He sends me a telegram saying that I've to detain you. What does he mean—detain you? Where am I to put the train? But he'll not let you in—just wait and see."

The engineer cursed someone, but the shaven-headed man did not hear any more. He took a glass of tea to Sloveh. She sipped it, scalded her mouth, blew, and hardly took any notice of him.

The silence in the carriage deepened. The passengers fell asleep in their seats. Some curled up on the floor. The occasional sound of someone sobbing in their sleep accentuated the stillness.

The train creaked and groaned as it went along. Night passed. The shaven-headed man was sitting in a corner beside the sleeping Sloveh.

Strange ugly grimaces danced over his hollow cheeks in the fluttering darkness of the flickering candle.

After midnight the train arrived at Razyezd, but before it had even come to a halt the shaven-headed man heard the stationmaster of this important station running around the platform in a rage. "They're sending trains all over the place! What about the timetable? Who cares about the timetable? They don't even ask if the line is clear, or if there aren't any more important priorities than those Yids!" What was he to do, for example, with this train? Swallow it, perhaps? He couldn't possibly let it through and yet he couldn't send it back. Soon the regiment from Yenisey was due to come through, and on the other line an express train was to come by in half an hour, and—and—spare tracks, eh? There weren't any spare tracks! He hadn't prepared any spare track for them! All his spare tracks were taken up. Where was he to get spare tracks? For the last two weeks his spare tracks had been totally occupied by supply-trains and the goods had just about gone rotten and no one remembered anything about it. And now they were sending him plagues and pestilences from all over the place!

He cursed and coughed and spat, glaring at the conductors and not allowing them to get a word in sideways. The engineer looked down from his locomotive in phlegmatic silence, his pipe stuck in his mouth. Behind him the fireman shone in the red glow of the open furnace as he fed it with coal.

The boss ran off into his office and the conductors followed him. After a quarter of an hour they came back, and the train moved off. Soon the characteristic clattering under the wheels showed that they were crossing onto different rails. The train moved on slowly for a while, and then stopped. Something was going on in the distance. Then the train moved off again, and once more there was a clattering under the wheels, first from one side and then from the other. This time the carriages moved in the opposite direction, picking up speed, until the shaven-headed man realized that they were going "back" somewhere. He shrugged his shoulders. Back is back. What did it matter where to? He bent his head onto his chest, and his body swayed back and forward.

15

Suddenly he raised his head and opened his eyes wide. In the carriage it was dark. The candle had gone out and the train had stopped. It was very still, and he realized that he had dozed off and that the train had been motionless for a long time. Around him the passengers were in a deep sleep. Through the open window came a fresh breeze, and he sensed that it was late in the night.

He stuck his head out of the window. Darkness. He could not see ten paces in front of him, but it was clear that they were not at a station. He left the carriage, climbed down onto the track, and made his way along to the locomotive. His eyes gradually got used to the gloom, and it became obvious that they were in the middle of fields. Here was the locomotive; there was nobody around and the fire under the boiler had gone out. The engineer, the fireman, the conductors—they had all disappeared. He gave a short, angry laugh and went on along the track. A hundred paces further on the line stopped. The earth round about was dug up and the embankment was rough and unfinished, crumbling underfoot. On both sides of the track, a few steps further on, there were rows of some kind of dark piles that turned out to be railway-sleepers. The shaven-headed man shook his head: "So that's how it is."

He smoked a cigarette and began to pace back and forth along the track. In the east the border of the sky began to grow pale.

Soon sleepy Jews began to emerge from the carriages. What's happened? Why are we not moving? Where are the conductors? Nobody answered, but the situation immediately became clear to everyone. One woman started crying. An elderly woman asked her: "What's the matter, auntie? Have you got important business waiting for you?" She was ashamed and fell silent. The people were not frightened, just slightly bewildered.

Someone appeared in the field approaching the tracks. From his movements it was clear that he was hurrying, but he didn't make very fast progress. At last he got to them. He was a middle-aged peasant with a wooden leg, walking with a stick.

Well, yes, certainly. He's the watchman, of course. He had just popped over to the village. Who would have expected this to happen? Because of the war, they stopped building the line before it was finished. They tell him to guard it, so he guards it. Is this his problem?

He blinked his watery eyes and looked frightened: a crowd of hundreds of people was surrounding him. Foreign, strange-looking people. Jews were not often seen in this part of the world.

It turned out that there was a village very close, a few hundred paces from the line, but since it was low-lying, nobody had noticed it. Villagers started appearing, and by the time the sun came out a whole crowd of peasants was mingling with the Jews: older men and women, flaxen-haired boys, and girls with red ribbons in their hair.

The older peasants spoke in a slow and measured way and took their time answering questions: "Milk? No, there isn't any milk. Well, there is a little. Very little. There's no milk to speak of. Bread? We can't complain. We also have a few garden vegetables—we could sell you some. What we need we keep for ourselves, but the rest is for sale—why not? Bread, thank God, we have. For the meantime we still have bread. Bread we have, yes."

Loaves of black bread, onions, cucumbers and apples appeared. A girl brought along some dried sunflower heads in her apron—bright and as big as cartwheels, full to bursting with black and white seeds. People looked at them with interest, but nobody bought any, and the girl stood there in embarrassment with her apron spread out, not knowing what to do. Some Jews brought wood and kettles of water from the village and then made fires and boiled the water. Some had tea and others had a little sugar. The sun was already quite high in the sky and very hot. Someone suddenly burst out laughing merrily.

To one side, a boy and girl were sitting on the railway sleepers. She was still almost a child, about sixteen or seventeen years old, with amber eyes and long dark eyelashes. He was a couple of years older, slim, gaunt, restless, with red hair, gray eyes and a freckled face. They were exchanging their life-stories and their plans, speaking in short, impatient sentences. He was an orphan and had wanted to set out for Siberia: his uncle who was out in the east had written: "Come!" She had heard that her mother, whom she had lost along the way, was in Tshernovodsk. The boy could not sit still for a moment: he danced around, sat down, stood up again, shaved slivers of wood off one of the sleepers and started carving something with a penknife.

"You know what?" he said suddenly, boldly raising his pointed nose toward her: "I'm going to go to Tshernovodsk too. Tshernovodsk is a town worth seeing. Where is it written that I have to go to Siberia?"

The long eyelashes lowered over the amber eyes.

The shaven-headed man wandered among the crowd, watching with raised eyebrows and a wrinkled brow. At one carriage a group of people had gathered and he went up to see what was going on. A Jew had dragged a wooden box out of the carriage, an ordinary traveling trunk, with tin bands and brass nails, and had opened up a shop. There were combs, mirrors, penknives, kerchiefs, colored ribbons, and even an old pair of binoculars. The peasants standing around were looking on respectfully. The women were jostling each other with their elbows and giggling, while the trader gave his patter and demonstrated his wares. His face, which was still very young, was long and very hairy, and his little eyes peered around with a mixture of cunning and stupidity. The big cap on his head and the left sleeve of his coat seemed to protrude unnaturally. Sticking out of the sleeve there was a black strap which was wound round his arm. Sometimes he spoke out loud in broken Russian, and sometimes he moved his lips as if speaking to himself. The shaven-headed man looked at the "shop," then at the leather strap of the tfilin, back at the trunk and then at the protruding lump in the cap. He paled and murmured two words. Then he went and sat down on the sleepers, a shabby, hunched-up figure. He sat there for a long time with bowed head and half-shut eyes under the red sun of the month of Elul.

The peasants gradually began to disperse and some of the Jews also went off into the village. The day rolled on, hot and sluggish. The air was heavy and the sandy earth around the railway line shimmered dryly in places. Most of the people had sought shade in the carriages and were deep in a heavy daytime sleep. Some were talking to each other, shrugging their shoulders, and wondering what was to come next.

The shaven-headed man wandered alone about the field. Late in the day he dragged himself into the village. He walked along the twisting main street, looking at the jumbled houses with their dilapidated straw roofs, at the sagging fences, at the dry soil in the gardens. The village looked poor and neglected.

At a bend in the street he suddenly came upon a crowd of people. The trader and his shop were in the middle of it, and the shaven-headed man turned back with an expression of animosity on his face, but soon he stopped again. Things looked different now from how they had in the morning.

The trader was red and sweaty and was looking around with a twisted smile. The crowd round him, middle-aged peasants, women and lots of children, were standing close together in silence. Some were holding kerchiefs in their hands, others mirrors. They were examining and fingering the goods, putting some down again without interest while taking up others. It was clear that nobody had any intention of buying. But despite this, everyone pressed closer to the Jew with his little trunk. There were also some Jews from the train, and one of them remarked angrily in Yiddish:

"There was absolutely no reason to bring out his 'shop' here. A typical peddler! Suddenly he wants to do business!"

"What's he babbling about?" a peasant asked angrily and suspiciously.

The trader wiped the sweat from his brow and announced that he was tired and wanted to leave. There was silence.

"It's a hot day, heh-heh" he said, turning from one person to another. "I think I'll just be off."

Someone called out:

"Who's keeping you then? We didn't ask you to come here—not any of you."

Nobody moved from the spot nor returned the objects they were holding. A young lad pushed his way forward and grabbed a penknife. A peasant slapped him and took the knife away from him.

"Don't let me see your face here again, do you hear?" he said calmly. "Go home and drive the pigs into the pen."

And he himself started to examine the penknife, opening the blades one after another.

Another peasant, his eyes popping, stretched out his hand and took the binoculars out of the trunk. The shaven-headed man pushed his way through to him and put his hand heavily on the man's shoulder.

"Put them back!"

The peasant, taken aback, hastily put back the binoculars. He turned fiery red, his eyes protruded even more and he said angrily:

"*A tyevye shto? A ti kto budyesh?* What business is it of yours? Who are you anyway?"

"Spit in his face!" a woman called out. "Let's take whatever we want!"

A moment later the whole trunk was lying upside down on the ground, and all the peasants grabbed whatever they could. The shaven-headed man bared two rows of clenched teeth.

"*Svo-lotsh!* Swine!" he said.

It came out like the crack of a whip—clear, assured, and with the right emphasis. It sounded like the voice of the police authority. Hands were lowered and eyes opened wide. Suddenly the stranger's face changed so that all the onlookers were dumbfounded.

His eyes sank into his head and flashed, small and piercing. He raised his chin, pushed his lips forward and pursed them around a red tongue. Staring right into their faces was something astonishingly like an ugly, dirty-pinkish pig's snout.

The mob trembled with rage at this terrible insult. A deep roar rose from the those at the back. A woman's voice shrieked, her voice cracking:

"Tear him to pieces! To pie-ces!"

Old Sloveh was sitting, half dozing, on the edge of the railway embankment. She heard the buzzing of a gnat in her ear, a sound which changed into a long, sing-song cry which flowed up and down, up and down. She opened her eyes. The sound reminded her of something. The voice was different but yet it reminded her of something. Then from far off came another cry. Sloveh suddenly sprang up like a young woman, and started rushing busily to and fro, searching around for something or other:

"*Oy, vey iz mir!* Oh my Lord. I haven't even put the coffee on yet! He must be starving!"

16

A Jew ran from the village, wiping blood off his face and said:

"They're killing us! The murdering bastards have gone mad. The whole village is on its way here."

The people started whirling around like leaves in the wind. They scattered across the field like a flock of sheep being chased, many of them with children in their arms. Meanwhile a summer storm had blown up: sudden, powerful and majestic. It became almost dark, a tongue of lightning split the sky in two, the earth shook underfoot and in the distance a column of dust and sand whirled in the air. Then the thunder and lightning started raging ceaselessly, and driving rain lashed and beat the earth's body, as if with whips.

The rain was blinding, and the fleeing people fell on the uneven surface of the sodden field. The crowd had become divided into separate groups which lost sight of each other, and nobody knew where they were fleeing to. One group managed to reach a wide dirt road. Its surface was soft and there were some puddles, but it was easier to walk on, and, more important, it had to lead somewhere. The people shouted and called to the other scattered groups.

A Jew with a long beard who was near the front suddenly stopped and turned round to face the group.

"My God! How can such things happen?"

The stragglers at the back gradually caught up, stopped, and stood there silently. A shortsighted young man in glasses came up from one side and exclaimed:

"How can such things happen? *To us* they *do* happen! And they'll keep on happening. What are you thinking of doing about it, my friend?"

The Jew with the beard put his hands to his head.

"Let us curse God and die!"

The crowd was silent. The young man said dryly:

"Curse God as much as you want, but let's keep moving in the meantime."

The Jew's eyes rolled wildly and he repeated as if in a trance:

"Let us curse God and die!"

The young man gestured impatiently.

"Listen here, uncle! If you haven't any deeper wisdom to reveal than this, you'd better keep your thoughts to yourself. Come on, Jews, let's go on!"

"Go on where?"

"Why go on?"

"Go on for how long?"

These questions came from various sides, without haste, without bitterness. Heavy as lead.

"We'll chat about all that later in an inn, over a glass of tea. A nice glass of hot tea with a piece of lemon in it, that wouldn't be bad, eh?" the young man said, smiling, though without complete conviction.

Nobody answered. The rain beat down on their heads and streamed down over their hunched backs. The thunder kept rolling over the world. At the same time there was also a great stillness.

And then an old woman pushed through the crowd and started onward. Her soaked dress clung to her long bony body, her skinny legs strode along woodenly like crutches, her head was slightly bent, and two eyes like holes peered into the semi-darkness. The figure looked weird and ridiculous, like an ancient tattered and disheveled stork.

The Jew with the beard stared open-mouthed after her and then followed her mechanically. The crowd began to move.

Fiery columns danced in the sky, whirled and darted from horizon to horizon. Night was coming. The old woman walked on, gesticulating with her hands and talking to the four winds.

1919 (translated by Heather Valencia)

The Old World

♦ ♦ ♦ *Smoke*

TO THE MEMORY OF I. L. PERETZ

1

At the first puff his face turned deep red, as if he were straining to lift a heavy load. He broke into a violent cough. Still, there must be something to it: the grownups smoked. He grew stubborn—and got used to it.

His father was a poverty-stricken teacher, and besides boys aren't supposed to smoke—so he picked up butts.

Later, studying in the synagogue, he would occasionally have a pack of tobacco. He never denied anyone a cigarette when he had it; he was never ashamed to ask for one when he didn't.

His name was Menasha.

From the synagogue he went as son-in-law to Reb Shoel Marawaner. Reb Shoel himself came to the synagogue with the matchmaker. The imposing Jew with the drooping eyes examined Menasha for a few minutes: a tall youth, broad and sturdy; the half-length frock coat of the Hasidic merchant will fit him perfectly. Reb Shoel peered into the book Menasha was studying, asked a few questions, began a casual conversation, and while glancing sideways listened with pricked-up ears to the youth's modest, somewhat cryptic replies. Rising suddenly from the bench, Reb Shoel ended the conversation with, "Bring your phylacteries."

2

In one of their most intimate moments his young wife asked, "Tell me, what sort of taste do you get from your cigarette? Give me a puff—let me try it."

He took the rolled-up burning cigarette from his mouth and moved it to her lips. Etta's lips closed like two pillows over the cigarette.

"Phew!" she coughed. "It's only smoke."

Menasha smiled. "Smoke—but it's good."

"What's so good about it? It's bitter and gets in your eyes."

He laughed. "But it's good," he repeated, as a whirlwind of shame and shamelessness wrapped the two young people in its folds.

3

He accepted the wealth of his father-in-law's household without betraying any of the pauper's greed. In only one thing did he indulge himself: he used the best tobacco that could be had. Knowing this, the younger people in the synagogue would frequently dip into his tobacco tin.

Once Reb Shoel's older son-in-law, Nehemiah, called Menasha aside. "Why do you let them smoke up your tobacco, those pigs? They themselves buy *mahorka*."

Menasha looked at him quietly. "How can you refuse anyone a cigarette?"

Nehemiah turned and glanced cautiously around the synagogue. One eye closed, the other lit up with wisdom. "Fool, don't you understand? Do as I do—two kinds," he burbled with a little laugh.

Menasha said nothing. But he did not introduce two kinds of tobacco.

He frequented the synagogue, studied at home, strolled about with a stick in his hand. Often he would sit quietly, listening to the business conversations Reb Shoel held with Jewish merchants. Those were the years of journeying to Danzig or Leipzig or Königsberg. Reb Shoel was one of the travelers to Danzig. For his older son-in-law Nehemiah he opened a dry-goods store: "Sit and measure linens." Nehemiah would have preferred to talk about Danzig, but Reb Shoel dismissed him with a wave of the hand. To Menasha he never said a word about business. And Menasha too was silent—until Etta was brought to bed and gave birth to twins, boys.

The evening after the double circumcision the father-in-law called Menasha into his room, handed him a packet of money, and said, "Go."

Menasha was a little frightened. "I don't even know where or what—"

"You'll learn. When you're rid of the money you'll know."

This took place during Chanukah. By Passover, Menasha was back. They celebrated the first two days of the holiday, and Danzig was never mentioned. Only on the evening of the second day did Reb Shoel invite Menasha to his room.

"What's new?"

"I've learned something," said Menasha, blushing.

Reb Shoel nodded.

After Passover, Menasha received another roll of bills and left for Danzig. From then on he would travel regularly for two or three months each year, and often twice a year.

4

With the passage of the years children sprang up in every corner of the house. Some were getting older, others crawled around, new ones were born. Reb Menasha—in time he became "Reb" Menasha—looked on and laughed quietly. Reb Shoel was no more; his business had been taken over by Reb Menasha, as had the old house with the spacious rooms.

During the months Reb Menasha stayed home in Marawan he lived as before: visited the synagogue twice a day, studied in the afternoon, talked business in the evening. The outer world made one change in his habits: he smoked cigars.

"A cigarette is for a youngster," he explained, smiling. "A Jew with a beard, a father of children, has to smoke cigars. The Germans are no fools."

Cigars were not the only thing that the outer world had brought, but of this only Etta knew. That is, she did not know: she sensed. How did he live there, in that outer world? What was it really like? She did not think about this, but it seemed to her that her husband grew steadily broader and taller, and she wondered why the measure of his clothes did not change. He had a habit of smiling with his eyes alone, and this smiling glance wrapped her into itself, carrying her along in a flow that was peaceful, deep, and unceasing, as the river that passed by the town flowed, year in and year out, into the distant world. She was not frightened; on the contrary, she felt secure in this wide stream. And many times she curled up against her husband and even tried to take a puff from his cigar. But this only brought tears to her eyes and spasms of coughing. He would slap her lightly on the back and laugh.

5

There were already a few sizable boys in the house, and a whole flock of half-grown ones and small fry were pushing after them.

Danzig was no longer the Danzig of old. Etta skimped—except for Reb Menasha's cigars, and in this one regard he did not oppose her. It went so far that the family had to leave the old house with its spacious rooms and rent another. At that time Reb Menasha sat down by himself in his room and became engrossed in the problem: what is wrong with Danzig? He sat there, looking through the window, smoking cigars, reflecting. The next day he left for the Don.

For several weeks he wandered about in the tumultuous region between the lower Don and the Caspian Sea, observing, considering, counting, measuring—and at the end he bent a finger of his right hand with his left and said, "Caviar." And he began to connect the Don with Danzig.

He was away for two years, and these were the hardest for the family at home. But after these two years, when he came home to rest for several months, people began to figure according to a new calendar: this or the other incident occurred "at the time Reb Menasha first went to the Don." And when he came home he bought back Reb Shoel's house and life continued as in earlier times.

He would now go to Danzig only once every two or three years, but for that very reason he spent two-thirds of his time on the Don. After caviar, he began to trade in smoked *wobla*—a local kind of sardine he had himself discovered. He earned much and spent much: one child after the other grew up, lived, and studied. In the end the father put each of them on his feet. For the wedding of the youngest he called together all his children. They celebrated in the old style, and at the end of the wedding meal Reb Menasha rose at the head of the table.

"Children, I shall no longer go to the Don. I have enough for myself and the old lady to live out our few years. The rest is for you. Go in good health, and may the Almighty let you live your years no worse than I have mine. You need not worry about us—we will not burden you."

6

Life flowed like a river nearing its mouth: the wider and deeper, the more peacefully and quietly. Menasha's high smooth forehead showed only one narrow crease from temple to temple, his black hair had grayed in only a few places. In the early summer evenings, against the orange glow of the sinking sun, he would stroll, as always, with his stick in hand; and his step remained certain and measured, his back strong and erect. Only his eyes were absorbed, deeply absorbed.

In his middle years he had studied mainly with his eyes. But now, in the quiet afternoon, his voice would rise more frequently through the old synagogue, taking up the mild and sad melody of his youth, taking it quietly, still more quietly, until it sank into the surrounding stillness, like the reverberation of a string—and then rising again until it reached its full strength, sweet and bitter, like the tears of childhood.

He enjoyed spending his time in the synagogue with the younger students, discussing Torah and justice. About the outer world and his life away from home he said little.

"People live and die there just as they do here," he would answer shortly, smiling with his eyes. "A Talmud made in Slavita or in Danzig—what's the difference? Only the printing and the covers. The content on the other hand—" And he would stare at the thread of smoke, taking care that the white ash, which sat like a Cossack's hat on the head of his cigar, should not fall but remain there as long as possible.

Coming home one morning from the synagogue with his prayer shawl and phylacteries under his arm, he found Ziessel, his youngest son. "Ah! I knew you'd come."

The young man's face changed color.

"Now, now," his father soothed him. "I did not mean to shame you. Things don't go well, eh? But first wash, and then we'll eat."

Listening to his son's story, Reb Menasha nodded his head: a fine plan . . . who could have expected that . . .

"I knew you'd come. You're rash and a little hasty, but you'll learn. I put away a small sum for you. Not much, but you'll be able to start again; and keep your eyes open. Here, take it—and don't come for more: there isn't any. We are old, and if I die first your mother must not be left in want. She won't go to you children.

"And another thing—" He called back his son from the door. "Now it's not like the old days. In my time, when a Jew came to Danzig with a thick beard and a high forehead, it was enough; if the corn and wheat were good one sold them at a profit, if not, one had a loss. We didn't run our business, it ran itself. That the world is now different I needn't tell you—you're younger than I. Danzig is no longer Danzig, the beard and the forehead no longer assets. Nowadays business has to be conducted, you understand? Well, go in good health and may good fortune be with you."

7

A summer and a winter passed, and then another summer. Again the winter came, early and bitter, with snows and frosts and wild angry winds. In December, Reb Menasha caught cold, coughed, and spat blood: it was the return of an old inflammation from the early days in Danzig, which was supposed to have left no scars. It spread quickly, and one gray morning, when the thin snowflakes melted in people's eyes and for no reason at all the air smelled different, his children came running from the outer world to stand by their father's bed. A few old friends and the rabbi had remained through the night.

For several hours the cough had not troubled the sick man and his temperature had fallen, but the young doctor did not leave. He sat not far away, at a table, and silently twisted his pencil between his nervous fingers.

Reb Menasha opened his eyes. It was hard to recognize him, but the eyes with their hidden smile had remained the same. He asked for a smoke.

"But Papa—"

The doctor's shrug cut short Ziessel's protest. He turned pale and handed his father a cigar.

"Not that," said the sick man. "Hasn't anyone a cigarette?" And his eyes smiled.

He took a puff from the thin little cigarette and called, "Etta . . ."

She lowered her hands from her eyes and dragged herself out of the corner. In recent years she had become rather fat and short of breath. Now her small round face was drawn together like a child's fist, and her glance seemed helpless and lost: the river, close to its end, threw her upon an unknown shore.

"Menasha, Menasha," she whispered.

"Want a puff?" He laughed. "Smoke . . . but it's good."

A whirlwind seized the old woman. She let out a cry, a laugh, a cough, all at the same time, as if smoke were choking her. Reb Menasha put aside the cigarette and winked to the rabbi, who went over to the bed and began reciting the last prayer with him. After the first few words Reb Menasha lost himself in coughing. The cough never ceased: it froze in the air, and there it remained.

1915 (translated by Irving Howe and Eliezer Greenberg)

◆ ◆ ◆ *Tiger*

1

I was fourteen when I met Tiger. I went to kheyder but I was a very poor learner. Yet I was really good at playing tricks. Well, actually, it wasn't I who played tricks. I was always full of good intentions and wanted to make everyone happy with me, but there was something or other inside me which often played tricks against my will, so that no one was satisfied with me, including myself.

I didn't have a teacher of secular subjects, but, with the help of some friends, I gradually taught myself to read and write Russian. I didn't turn out to be a really diligent student, however, and soon gave up studying. On the other hand I had a tremendous appetite for all types of Russian storybooks and devoured them, as my mother said, like hot noodles. At the time I'm writing about, I was also already reading thick, "serious" novels, travel books and the like. I constantly daydreamed about valiant heroes, cunning hunters, wild animals, robbers, strange lands and dense, mysterious forests. That is why I read something romantic and heroic into my friendship with Tiger, despite the fact that the whole story was as simple as it could possibly be.

One Sabbath afternoon in summer, when the other members of my family had gone to bed to digest their tsholnt, I was strolling outside with my hands in my pockets and with no idea what to do with myself. I didn't have a book with me, and there was nowhere to go. The sun was as hot as it is only on Sabbath. The only things to be seen were the odd peasant woman carrying pails of water, and a few boys riding on a goat or chasing a rooster which was running about the street for dear life. Apart from that nothing moved at all, and a heavy, stifling silence lay on the shtetl.

While I was strolling to and fro in front of our house, looking around for something that would capture my interest, I noticed a dog beside our yard and whistled to him. I just did it for something to do, without any particular intent, but this dog obviously wasn't very bright and thought I was calling him over. He darted toward me, then hesitated a couple of times, doubtlessly considering the matter and suspecting me of having evil intentions. Then he finally ran up to me. Between you and me, I had never been keen on dogs—in fact I was actually afraid of them. But according to my fine literary ideals, my heart had to be as brave as a lion's, so I made myself stroke the dog's head, even though I was trembling inside.

I realize now that the dog had never been used to such gentle treatment, and his doggy heart began to quiver. He squirmed with delight under my touch and tried to lick my hand, sticking out his tongue and panting hard. I really didn't trust him very much, and even though I let him lick my hand, my heart was palpitating madly the whole time. Gradually I felt more and more uncomfortable, and besides, I had sufficiently proved to myself and to the dog that I was not scared of him, so I said as affably and calmly as I could: "Off you go, then! Home! . . ."

He didn't understand, or at least pretended not to, and started springing up at me, trying to reach my hand. This made me uneasy and I shouted more loudly: "Go on! Home!"

The dog sprang to one side and then threw himself on me again, panting hard. Suddenly my fear burst out into the open. I couldn't control myself and yelled in panic: "Get off! Go away! Go away!," kicking at the dog to drive him off. He stood still as if astonished, and then, lowering his head dejectedly, he retreated and moved further off.

As my fear began to abate, I noticed how miserable and abandoned he looked. His coat was a salt and pepper color, and he was scrawny and filthy. His ears drooped, and apart from all that he was limping. I was suddenly overwhelmed by a feeling of pity and remorse, and I whistled to him again. He turned toward me and I began walking toward my house, beckoning him to follow me. I took out some pieces of challah and gave them to him.

And that is how we became acquainted. The dog moved into our yard, and we were nearly inseparable.

At that time we were tenants of Moyshe, Pinye-Leyb's son, who owned the biggest yard in the shtetl. For years he had been planning to build on his yard and every year after Passover he measured its area. This task was always carried out with great pomp and circumstance. First he would position his three sons—whom the townsfolk always called the "the young masters"—holding string and pegs at various points along the fence. Then he would chase them off to different places, then call them back to stand in the original places. He himself, coatless and in his white shirtsleeves, ran all over the place, completely preoccupied and sweating profusely. He was like an engineer and architect rolled into one. Year-round six planks and two wooden beams rotted away beside his house. This was Moyshe's "lumber-yard." Nothing ever came of this project, and the yard stretched out behind the house like an empty steppe, overgrown with grass, with one or two little paths snaking through it to various essential locales. The upstairs rear balcony of the two-story house stuck out into the yard, and under this balcony my dog made his residence.

I was really happy with the fact that I had a dog of my own. The hero of some novel I had read had a dog called Tiger, so that's what I called mine. It didn't bother me that he didn't bear much resemblance to a tiger, which in any case I only knew from pictures in children's reading-books. I soon taught him to respond to his name, and I got great joy from him. As I got used to him, he didn't seem as ugly as he had previously. On the contrary, I noticed that with his intelligent and alert eyes and his rather lugubrious face, he looked altogether like an old philosopher.

2

For as long as possible I concealed my friendship with Tiger from everyone. People found out about it, however, and that was the beginning of a period of persecution for him, and humiliation for me.

"A dog, of all things!" screamed my mother. "What on earth will you think of next? A big shot of fifteen playing with a dog!"

"I ask you, what are you thinking of?" said father reproachfully. "Is that what you really need, a dog? You're not right in the head. It would be a lot better if you put your nose into a holy book, instead of playing around with the devil knows what. Come on, tell me yourself, what's the point of messing around with dogs?"

I didn't answer, because I couldn't think of anything to say. I wasn't really sure myself whether my conduct befitted a fifteen-year-old boy. If Tiger had left me of his own accord, I probably would have regretted the whole business and been pleased to be spared further humiliations, but he didn't. And everyone in our household and the whole street began to persecute him. Initially my father and mother made energetic attempts to chase him from the yard. But mother was a market-trader and father was constantly preoccupied with "business," always going off somewhere or doing something or other. I never did find out exactly what it was he did. Apart from anything else, he really valued his peace and quiet at home, couldn't bear screaming and bawling, and always kept himself absolutely aloof from domestic matters. So because of all that my parents soon gave up and let matters rest.

Then, for two reasons, Moyshe's other tenant, Sholem the Cripple, began to torment Tiger. Firstly because Sholem lived on the ground floor, and Tiger, rubbing himself against one of the windows, had broken a pane. Secondly, the street urchins began calling Sholem "Tiger," because, like the dog, he was lame. I suspect that the second was the main reason for his hatred of Tiger, which burned in his heart like the fires of hell. Whenever Sholem was at home he would pursue the dog round the yard with a stick in his hand, but he could never manage to catch him. Tiger limped away from him, Sholem limped after the dog, and all the boys from the street hung onto the other side of our fence, shouting: "Tiger! Sholem! Tiger! Giddy-up! Hooray!"

The boys themselves never left Tiger in peace, especially Motl, the wagoner's son, a stocky twelve-year-old with a harelip. His father, called Note, was a violent and quarrelsome man who had no time for "stuck-up" folk, and Motl, relying on his father's protection, really tormented me. He had the insolence to beat the dog in my presence, and once he gave him such a kick in the belly that poor Tiger came running to me with heartrending yelps. On that occasion I didn't restrain myself and gave Motl a good thrashing. That evening Note the wagoner made a dreadful scene in our house, cursing my father, searching for me and swearing that he would break my bones. Then he started beating Tiger until the dog, half-dead, managed to break free of him and run away. I heard all this while I was hiding in the attic. My heart almost burst when I heard my dog yelping, as I had to lie there without making a sound. All my heroes flew right out of my mind. The courage I had felt so strongly during my imaginary battles with pirates or Red Indians had completely forsaken me, and all I could do was lie in the attic holding my breath.

Once, when we were alone in the yard, I said to my dog: "They're hunting us, Tiger, they're torturing us, aren't they? Never mind, don't worry, Tiger, I won't let them drive you away!" It was really odd, but when no one was attacking him I felt as brave as all the heroes in my novels, and I was absolutely prepared to protect Tiger from all his enemies, that is, from the whole world. The poor tormented dog gazed at me with his intelligent eyes, and I could have sworn that they were wet with tears. The tribulations only brought us closer together, and I was determined that under no circumstances would I be parted from Tiger.

3

At long last everyone got bored with annoying us. As soon as God had "redeemed us from our enemies," I turned my attention to Tiger's education. The first essential lesson was to teach him to jump over a stick. To my great amazement Tiger showed no aptitude at all for this. In his ABCs he progressed no further than "A," and he seemed to be lacking in all the canine skills. No matter how much I tried to drum it into him, he just didn't understand what I wanted. A couple of times I demonstrated by laying the stick on the ground and jumping over it myself. Then he *did* actually imitate me and in a ridiculous limping manner he jumped over it, but as soon as I lifted up the stick he just stood there again, not knowing what to do. He looked at the stick suspiciously and obviously didn't trust the game. I also tried to teach him to carry something in his mouth. But he didn't fare any better: whenever I pushed something completely inedible into his mouth, he would sniff it and turn his muzzle away distrustfully, as if to say: "What's all this? What's he giving me this for?" When I used edible things, he just calmly and coolly ate up my teaching aids as if that were the whole point of the exercise.

Sometimes I preached at him: "What will become of you, Tiger? You're always going to be an ignorant lout, just like your father was. I can't tell you how much pain you cause me. Just think about it: I took you in. I provide food and drink and a place under the balcony; I always stand up for you and I suffer so much humiliation for your sake—and for what? I want to make something of you—and what do you do? Oh, Tiger! Did your brothers, whom I've read so much about, behave like this??"

The philosopher stared me straight in the face, seemingly wondering why my mouth was moving like that. He would have understood it better if he had seen a bit of bread or meat going into it. I hadn't yet realized that philosophers are useless at things of a practical nature; they *think* about everything under the sun but are not good at *doing* anything. The one thing they actually *do,* namely eat, they don't have to think about at all. So I got really angry and couldn't think what to do about Tiger. I had heard that if you want to train a dog you have to smack him, but I wouldn't raise my hand against Tiger. So I had to be satisfied with the fact that if I called "Tiger!" he would come running up to me, lick my hands and jump up in my face. Making him stop was much more difficult.

Tiger thrived on the bread he stole, and even got fat. Then he got tired of simple food and started fantasizing about a piece of meat. At least I assume he did, because everyone who lived in our yard started to complain that pieces, even complete joints of meat, were going missing, and they pointed the finger at Tiger. On top of all this, he had begun to behave in a very frivolous manner: he had started receiving visitors, relatives presumably, and good friends. These visitors soon felt completely at home and the yard was teeming with dogs. Tiger changed beyond all recognition: he became high-spirited and happy, and seemed years younger. Now he hardly heeded me at all. This upset me a bit and I made some further attempts to lecture him and lead him onto the path of virtue—but with no success whatsoever! Now he didn't even wait to hear me out, but limped around me impatiently and often ran off in the middle of my speech to join the merry crowd with whom he now preferred to spend his time. And they certainly did have a good time! All day they ran around visiting each other's patch, went on "picnics," quarreled and made up. At night they had concerts in our yard and on bright moonlit nights they would yowl till daybreak.

All this resulted in terrible tribulations, much worse than before, and this time they had an unexpected outcome for both Tiger and me.

4

It was our landlady, Moyshe's wife Fat Tsirl, known in the town as "ugly mug" who caused the new heartbreak.

"Dogs! That's the last thing I need!" she screamed. "He's brought a bitch here and now it's trailing all the dogs after it. Soon we won't be able to cross the yard without bumping into them! A plague of dogs, that's what it is. Why did I let in tenants with dogs!"

Fat Tsirl didn't just stop at words. She really laid into the dogs in a big way, driving off the strange dogs. This suited me just fine. However, Tiger kept bringing in new visitors, and the landlady started persecuting him as well. She chased him with sticks, scalded him with hot water, squeezed him in the gate, and so on. I was upset by this and had a big quarrel with her.

"What a fine lad you are!" Tsirl screeched as loudly as she could, so that the whole street heard my humiliation: "Playing with dogs! Wonderful!"

"It's none of your business!" I answered angrily. "I'll play with them if I like and you can't stop me."

"Be quiet, you cheeky brat," said my mother, entering the fray. "Is that the way you speak to your elders?"

"Well then, she shouldn't poke her nose in!"

"Well, I'm not having dogs in *my house!*" yelled Tsirl at the top of her lungs. "Who is the landlady anyway, me or this urchin, this insolent lout? And anyway, look at the dog, what a disgusting, ugly hound!"

Her last words drove me mad and I rudely replied: "Prettier than you, anyway!"

That was the last straw. Tsirl screamed: "That's it. You're to move out this very day. I'm not having you under my roof."

My father, exasperated by her screaming, laid into me.

"You ruffian! What have you got against me? You want me to have enemies wherever I go? Because of you I can't even keep a roof over my head! And you even feed that dog bread-rolls. Is it not enough that I have to give a good-for-nothing like you board and lodging!"

"See if he can get board and lodging with that dog!" said Tsirl venomously.

Father started up his usual litany: "I just don't know what you're thinking of?!" Then he made a gesture of hopelessness and left the room.

And so it went on, day after day. Sholem the Cripple and Motl the wagoner's son revived their old enmity toward Tiger, and started to torment him again. The poor dog really suffered. He became nervous and his eyes had a distrustful, angry expression. His love for me was now expressed in a rather hysterical fashion: he threw himself at me frantically, panting hoarsely, so that sometimes I was a little frightened of him, but I couldn't allow them to drive him away from our yard under any circumstances. "They're going to be the death of him," I thought to myself, and tried to think of a solution.

Deep in my brain a strange thought started to take root. It seemed to me the most honorable way out of this unbearable situation, and finally I was utterly convinced of it: I should kill Tiger.

I wouldn't like to swear to you that my decision was entirely free of the influence of the novels I had read. It's possible that I was unconsciously imitating some event or person. But the fact is that I made the decision to do it, even though my heart was aching at the thought of it.

But how was I to do it? The best thing would be to shoot him, but for that I would need a gun. Hang him? Drown him? It wouldn't work. So—I would have to stab him to death.

One night I took a piece of bread-roll, put a kitchen knife in my pocket, went out into the yard and whistled. Tiger appeared as if by magic and started jumping up on me, licking my hands and generally showing his love for me. My firm resolve began to weaken. I embraced and stroked him and didn't know what to do. The dog almost went mad with joy and actually knocked me off my feet with his affectionate leaps. Nonetheless the realization gradually returned to me that the only way to free Tiger from his torments was to kill him. I felt that if I didn't do it immediately, I would never be able to carry it out. I took the roll out of my pocket and threw it to my dog. "Let him have one last good meal," I thought, and besides, I wanted to stab him suddenly, while he was busy eating. I had kept the knife in my pocket the whole time. I thought that if Tiger saw it, he would realize what I intended to do.

At last the moment arrived: the dog was eating with great relish, standing with his flank toward me. My heart was beating wildly. I was gasping for breath. Stealthily I took the knife out of my pocket, but my hand was trembling and I didn't have the strength to lift it. Tiger had almost finished eating. The thought raced through my head: "Now! This minute! Otherwise it's too late!" and with my last reserves of strength I stabbed the knife into the dog's side . . .

I will never forget that moment. Tiger sprang aside with a yelp and looked at me. It was the look of a sensitive and perceptive creature, and it expressed astonishment, horror, pain and despair—terrible despair! And then, yelping plaintively, he ran away from me, out of the yard.

"Tiger! Tiger! Come back, Tiger! It wasn't me . . . it's not my fault!" I wailed despairingly, stretching out my arms after him. Even while I was stabbing him I had sensed that I didn't have enough strength and that the knife was not suitable for the task; it didn't even have a sharp point. In fact, all Tiger had received from me was a blow. But it was the first time. And the despair and misery in the poor dog's eyes stabbed me like knives . . .

Tiger vanished without a trace.

1904 (translated by Heather Valencia)

1

I was on eating days at that time, and Tuesday was a blank in my schedule.

The full name of the little town was Zagorie-Vitrok (or, Beyond the Windmill Hills), but the Jews had shortened and changed this to Zahoria.

When I came into the street the first afternoon of my arrival, the tiny place lay suffocated under the July sun. Jewish men and women sat dozing in the doorways of their shops. Near the meat market the dogs were lying with their tongues hanging out, their glazed eyes looking upon the world without any interest—not even for the bloody sides of beef that hung in the windows of the little butcher shops. Strewn over the ground of the marketplace and glinting yellowy were loose sheaves of straw left over from the last fair day. The wind, the chief—and sole— sanitary inspector of the town, had not yet swept them away. On the principal street all the shutters were closed—shutters gray, white, green, all kinds of shutters, a long row of them, and all closed. Everything was so still that Zahoria, as I eagerly took in the new scene, looked like a town in a dream.

2

"This yeshiva," the student from Berdichev told me, "was once quite big."

The yeshiva was located over the women's section of the small synagogue; the high-ceilinged House of Prayer was divided into floors toward the back, and this upper floor, with a separate outer staircase, was where we did our studying. It was a long narrow chamber, running the width of the synagogue, with ten windows distributed along the three outer walls. In the fourth, the interior, wall was a tiny window, little more than a slit, facing the Holy Ark. There were two long tables for collective study and a dozen lecterns at which the older boys could study by themselves. Ranged along the walls and at the tables were long benches, and upon these several students, I among them, used to sleep.

Another young student—he came from Stavisk—called me aside, lifted his right index finger impressively, and gave me to understand: "The yeshiva may not look like much now, but it was really big at one time. There used to be a hundred and fifty students here, poring over Holy Writ day and night. In those days the yeshiva was still in the building where the old synagogue is now; and even later, during the first years under Nissel, the assistant rabbi, when he wasn't so hard a drinker, from sixty to eighty students would sit down to study the Talmud with him."

A hundred and fifty . . . eighty . . . sixty . . .

"Now there are twenty-three or twenty-four of us, at all the tables and lecterns," the Stavisker went on. "The yeshiva has been going down for several years; it's falling lower and lower—nobody knows why. The town has no love for us; it has no faith in our studies nor in our fear of God. We're a burden on them, the way a chronic old invalid is to his family; he sinks before their eyes but won't die. The people in the town are not eager to invite us to their tables; whoever can manage to avoid it by contributing a few pennies does so. A great many of us miss one or two eating days—on such days we get seven kopecks for food. When it comes to a place to sleep it's still worse, and getting a clean shirt for the Sabbath is worst of all."

3

The student from Krutogor told me in confidence, "Do you think our yeshiva was always the way you see it now? You should have been here years ago, you would have seen something then."

He too? What was the yeshiva to him? The Krutogorer was a big robust fellow without a sign of beard or mustache on his smooth womanish face. He had great, liquid, bulging eyes and a child's smile on his rosy, fleshy lips—lips like little sausages. He didn't really have a bad head on his shoulders but he had no inclination for study. To make up for that, he excelled in another respect: he could not talk for two minutes without going off into smut. He was an inexhaustible spring of stories, riddles, witticisms, not one of which but concealed under its surface a sexual meaning. His stories somehow were repulsive—deliberate, without warmth, and even without vulgarity, yet always with insinuations, puns and double meanings. If you wanted them to, they had a meaning, but an ugly one; if you weren't after a meaning, there wasn't any at all—they were mere pointless stories. When you persuaded yourself that the fellow was up to no tricks he seemed to be speaking casually—too casually—and the childlike smile on the rosy, moist little sausage lips was somehow too childlike. You felt yourself taken in, mocked; you became angry. But he, the simple fellow, couldn't understand why you were angry since, after all, he hadn't meant any offense, and—

"Sha! You know what? I've got a wonderful story to tell you—"

The Krutogorer had already acquired a disciple, a brilliant lad of fourteen—Ariah Leib's little Chaim. Chaim too had a good head: he was genuinely fond of tackling some abstruse tractate of the Talmud or of joining in some profound discussion on the Talmudic commentators, but the Krutogorer was leading him astray, and the youngster whinnied like a colt at his tutor's stories; now and then he would interpret some passage or homily in a way that turned one's stomach. Both master and disciple made life miserable for the student from Warsaw.

4

The Warshaver did not really hail from Warsaw. He came from a town somewhere in Poland the name of which was almost impossible to remember, and so he had been nicknamed after Warsaw. How he had ever got here from remote Poland no one knew, nor did anyone take any pains to find out. The students were all strangers to one another, and none of them cared to talk about where he had come from or to what family he belonged: most likely there was little worth remembering.

The Warshaver was the oldest student in the yeshiva, well over thirty. He was narrow-boned and spare, lanky rather than tall. His cheeks were pocked with acne; his eyes were black and glowed as if in fever. The nape of his neck was very hairy—the nape of his neck only: his face was beardless—and he wore a tiny Polish cap, the only cap in the whole town with a narrow visor on it. He had a "hard" head: studying did not come easy to him, but he was most diligent and pious. He was forever studying; you never saw him without some tome in his hands, and he generally did his studying aloud, swaying to and fro with closed eyes, which he opened only occasionally to glance at the Gemarah. He went often to the ritual baths. The two days that were blank on his eating schedule he had designated as his permanent fast days; and there were those who held that he mortified his flesh in still other ways.

The Krutogorer made a point of harassing the Warshaver, in which he was abetted by little Chaim. Their scheme was to take a position not far from the lectern of their victim and then proceed to study aloud some tractate from the Talmud—the one on the Sabbath, let us say— with a great show of zeal. The Warshaver tried to stop his ears; but if he did so he could not hear his own chant and consequently was hardly able to understand what he was studying.

"You ugly beasts!" he screamed at them. "Adulterers! Apostates!" He threatened to complain to Reb Zalman, a meat inspector who acted as our dean; he cursed them in his quaint Polish-Yiddish dialect. But they went right on with their beloved studying as though they were in no way at fault, apparently engrossed in the complicated passages of their tractate, until at last the Warshaver fled from the synagogue, his eyes blazing with rage and his lips twisted in pain.

5

Nissel, the assistant rabbi, was giving us a Talmud lesson.

Nissel did not look like a Jew at all. His heavy, massive body, his beetling bushy eyebrows and his red nose with its cross-hatching of tiny blue veins made him look like the coarsest of old peasants—one of those who worked at night on the barges that plied the river. He had a red eczema, quite extensive, on the back of his left hand: when studying, he kept this hand concealed under the Slavita tome of the Talmud. His small skullcap perched close to the nape of his neck, and he wore spectacles.

The yeshiva lads spoke of him under their breath, as though they were perplexed about him. He was a great drunkard—a Jewish drunkard, that is: he did not wallow in the gutter, but he took a drink whether anyone was celebrating or not. He walked around in a daze, wrapped up in himself, as indifferent to his studies as to his pupils. Now and then, when he came to a Talmudic session deeper in his cups than usual, we leaped on our benches with enthusiasm: profound expositions and comments, razor-keen innovations issued from his mouth like fireworks. On the other hand, if once in a great while, God forbid, he put in an appearance altogether sober, it was impossible to stand him: he would curse and revile everyone in angry, vulgar, and barbed words. He had been deprived of his status as an assistant rabbi a long time ago; all he found to do now was to hold the Talmudic sessions in our yeshiva and give a two-hour weekly lesson to the son-in-law of the local Croesus. Because of his sharp tongue he was at odds with the town and the rabbinical court. The overpious Hasidim suspected that he hailed from Lithuania, and the townsmen would shrug their shoulders. "Well, what can you expect from a Litvak!"

Because the yeshiva sessions, except on those rare occasions when he was far gone in drink, held very little interest for him, he finally hit on a new plan: let the students learn by heart. In other yeshivas, now, there were students who could recite hundreds of pages of the Talmud from memory.

"There are scholarly heads for you!" he exclaimed, his small evil eyes looking daggers at his hearers, so that one could not make out whether his words were meant to praise or to damn. Let the students tackle the Baboth tractate, to begin with: it was neither too difficult nor too easy. This would enable him to give a real discourse, to present a new interpretation—whenever he could get around to it and felt so inclined.

6

In the night we used to hear the steamboats paddling down the river, about a mile away. Those of us who slept in the yeshiva could by now recognize the boats that plied our stretch of the river.

"That's the *Imperator*," somebody on one of the farther benches would remark, his cigarette glowing in the darkness. The *Imperator*, its low-pitched whistle wheezing like some substantial householder, was the newest steamboat on the river; it had all the latest improvements and had been built somewhere outside of Russia.

"Fee-fee-ee-ee!" Someone else among us would announce with a laugh that it was the *Pushkin*—a small boat, narrow, long and moving through the water as nimbly as a pen over paper.

A far-flung throaty roar, prolonged and hoarse as that of some beast in agony, meant the approach of the *Dominion*, the oldest and biggest tub, broad-beamed, unwieldy, drowsy and slow.

In the dead of night, after the first siren had made one's ears alert, one could hear the steamboats distinctly as they approached our landing, then slowed down and became quiet. We held our breath and could almost see the boat with all its lights, the people running up and down the gangplank, the strange, gay, animated scene. Within two minutes a second whistle sounded, then a third, and one's ears caught the gasping of the steam, the renewed beat of the paddles, growing stronger, more powerful and impetuous. At a certain point the noise came echoing back from the hills along the riverbanks with special clarity: one could have sworn that the vessel was advancing upon the town. Before long, however, the noise subsided, as though a kettle had been put over it: fainter, more distant. Shh . . . one moment you still heard it, then you didn't. Silence.

The silence lasted quite long—until the Krutogorer started in. "I'm going to ask you a riddle—"

"Stop annoying us!" I would become resentful. "We know every riddle of yours by heart."

"All the same, try to guess this one—"

"Not interested—some other time," I could not help telling him. Sometimes he subsided, sometimes not.

7

My eating days had not come to me easily or all at once. My Sundays and Mondays changed several times: my hosts on these days made no particular impression on me.

The Wednesday meals I had at the house of a butcher known as Buni the Redhead. The rusty, bristly hair on his face grew almost to his eyes—murderous and arrogant eyes—and his voice was gruff. This Jew didn't even know how to pray properly, and there was talk in the town that he beat his wife. Why should he want a yeshiva student? But he himself hailed Reb Zalman, our dean, in the street one day. "Send over one of your shnooks to my house and let him stuff his guts."

For food, Wednesday was my best day. Buni's wife was attractive in a swarthy sort of way, but a sloven. She had apparently never heard of a tablecloth—she put a loaf of bread and a bowl of warm food right on the bare wood: "Eat to your heart's content!" The food itself was heavy, filling—stuffed derma, beet soup with fat meat, baked sheep's head, the roast neck of a kid slithery with grease. And she served meat at both my meals.

The whole family sat down together to the evening meal: Buni, Buni's wife, and their only child, a girl of about sixteen, with her body just emerging from adolescence and a face of piety: white and translucent, somewhat sickly, the nose well shaped, and the eyes large and shiny, like a calf's. But I rarely found Buni home when I came, and either his wife or daughter would serve me my meal.

A totally different sort of household was that of Isser Tabachnik, where I ate on Thursdays. It was situated on the other side of the marketplace, where the principal street began, and had lacquered floors, lace curtains on the windows and potted plants on the window sills. The family lived in grand style, keeping a cook and a country girl for the youngest child. My meal was served at a separate table in the kitchen, while the cook bustled about with her pots and pans, and the time assigned to me was an hour after the family had eaten.

Isser Tabachnik traded on a big scale in grain, timber and beets for the sugar refineries. He was a personable man: tall, broad-shouldered, with a potbelly, smooth skin, and a beautiful, well-groomed dark beard. He wore a fine knee-length overcoat and a soft hat with a deep crease. He had an important air about him, and his word was his bond. A man who knew his own worth.

Shaina Leah, his wife, came of a more aristocratic family than her husband's; she was not so obtrusive as he and seemed to be good-natured. There was also a girl in the house, about twelve, thin, swarthy, ugly, and ill-tempered; at the least provocation she would throw herself on the floor and start kicking the walls or the furniture. Then there was a little boy of three, and somewhere out in the world Isser and his wife had married daughters.

My breakfasts weren't worth talking about. And my two Friday meals I had at Stissy the Widow's.

Stissy was tall, of a dark complexion; she had narrow Tartar eyes, was clever and not much given to talk. The peasants respected her. She ran a dry-goods and notions store, catering chiefly to the womenfolk of the surrounding countryside. The stock consisted of multicolored wool and cotton fabrics, bright ribbons, gimcrack jewelry and strings of beads, headkerchiefs, sashes and kindred items. She wasn't rich, but she did have a fair income and a house of her own on the Rabbi's Street. The house was old and none too big, but well built—that is, it had hardwood floors, a tin roof, and even window shutters. The household was run by her daughter Tsirl, a girl along in years, rather dumpy, not good-looking, with a complexion none too clear or healthy; her dark eyes, however, were quite decent—beautiful, in fact.

I was still shy one eating day though—that same Tuesday.

8

Those were the years when the world crumpled and twisted my soul like a nervous hand impatiently pulling a glove on the other hand. Each day had a flavor all its own. The sun, for instance, shone differently after a meal on the Sabbath than after a meal on a weekday. And merely crossing Rabbi's Street to get back to the marketplace was like making a journey to another town. Just the sight of the rich man's house, its walls painted a roseate hue and a green balcony on the second floor, was as exciting to me as meeting a guest from afar.

There was a chunk of plaster missing on one of the outer walls of the synagogue, and each time I chanced to pass by I looked at the ugly gaping hole with hatred.

On an empty lot not far from the yeshiva four charred girders stuck up out of the ground—all that was left of a house that had burned down. They were an eyesore. Blackened, weather-beaten, gaunt, they mournfully stared at me—at me alone—and frightened me.

Summer, winter, snow, rain, frost, heat—all plucked at me like fiends and pulled me in all directions. At that time other things also piled up on me. Once, at the time of my evening meal in Isser Tabachnik's house, a pan with strudel had been left on the kitchen table, just out of the oven. The aroma of cinnamon and raisins titillated my nostrils. Some liquefied brown sugar had run out at one end of the strudel and formed a glazed jelly. As the pastry cooled it crackled softly and faintly from time to time, as if someone were snapping matchsticks. When the cook left the kitchen for a moment I hurriedly broke off two jagged pieces of the strudel and slipped them in my pocket. After finishing my meal hastily I returned to the synagogue, and in a corner I devoured the cake stealthily. I bit off large chunks, hardly chewing them, so that tears came, and for some time the strudel stuck in my throat.

The whole thing had come upon me so unexpectedly that it seemed to have happened not to myself but to someone else. I was, in other words, a thief and a glutton. A thief? No, not a thief! I had stolen, of course, but then I would never steal again—I wouldn't. A glutton—

yes, I had gobbled the cake down like a glutton, without even enjoying its savor. And the terrific stupidity of it all!

Next Thursday I did not come for my meal at Isser Tabachnik's house. The Thursday after that I hung around his door for several minutes, with my heart palpitating, and then, setting my jaw, opened the door at last. All through the meal it seemed to me that the cook was banging her dishes more than usual. I also had the impression that the good Shaina Leah had met me with a smile in her eyes—a clever and restrained smile—but just the same I dawdled over washing my hands and ate slowly and stubbornly. And within me the turmoil was great.

The incident of the strudel was still fresh in my thoughts when I happened to come upon the scene as Buni and his wife were beating their daughter. This girl with the pious face was run after by all the apprentices in town, to say nothing of a few young men from among the local elite, and even a couple of Gentile boys. She was friendly with all, spending her time with anyone. With the coming of dusk it was impossible to keep her in the house. That day her parents had caught her—not for the first time—with one of the boys, and they were squaring accounts with curses and fists. Through the tears her eyes glistened with a moist brilliance; her fresh lips pouted like a child's as she softly, dejectedly, kept pleading, "What do you want of me? What do you want of me?"

The scene harrowed me. Once, as I was leaving the butcher's house, I came upon the girl in the dark anteroom. I stopped her, stretched out my hand, and touched her—not respectfully. Whereupon she looked at me with her big dismayed eyes and then, lowering them, froze into a mute, sheepish submissiveness. I immediately released her and dashed out. But even then I felt that neither the deep fear of Buni the Redhead nor my dread of the disgrace if I were caught would keep me away from this girl, from the mature face on the half-ripe, tantalizing adolescent body.

I was a low creature—a low creature.

Since such was the case, I locked myself in Stissy the Widow's privy one Saturday afternoon and, rolling a cigarette, had a smoke. When I came out my legs were wobbling. I had never dreamed a cigarette could be so delectable. The savor of the transgression and the pungency of my dissoluteness intoxicated me like strong wine.

The range of my lusts, like the range of my ambitions, was rather small. But the Evil One had swooped down upon me like a tempest, suddenly and from all sides. I was living as if in a fever, my heart in incessant ferment.

9

I did just what the Warshaver had done: I turned my blank Tuesday into a fast day. Of the seven kopecks allowed me for food on that day I squandered two on tobacco and saved five.

On this day I used to study by myself in the synagogue proper. I usually got there when the worshipers had just dispersed after the morning service. Paying little attention to my assigned lesson, I browsed instead through various tomes of Holy Writ, humming as I did so and pausing to meditate between my studies. My stomach was empty and felt hollow; the tobacco smoke was pungent. A strange silence reigned in the high-ceilinged synagogue, where ordinarily the slightest sound gave birth to echoes. Yet on the verge of this silence hovered the dormant sounds and sights of another world: a world not so substantial as the one around me yet hardly less real.

Ruth and Naomi trudged forever through the cornfields on their way to Boaz, under a summer sky—around the fifth hour after noon. Jacob pastured the sheep for Laban—and I saw distinctly the rods of green poplar and hazel and chestnut which Jacob had set before the flocks in the gutters of the watering troughs, that the flocks should conceive when they came to drink: he had peeled white strips in the rods and made the white appear which was in them—and that white was moist from the sap. On a night when the wispy clouds could not hide the light of the moon, Sulamith went about the city in the slumberous streets, knocking on doors and gates, questioning the watchmen that go about the city: "Saw ye him whom my soul loveth?" Esau had just come from his hunting, his hairy garments still redolent of the fragrance of the fields; he sat eating his dearly bought pottage of lentils, and the delicious steam of the lentils blended with the smell of the goatskins upon the luckless Esau. Amid the desert sands the tabernacle curtains of fine twined linen fluttered and bellied in the wind. The ground plan of the tabernacle was not quite clear in my mind, but the "blue, and purple, and scarlet" floated before my eyes; I had a distinct image of the curtains of goat's hair, and of fine twined linens, wrought with cherubs of cunning needlework . . .

The faint hum of a life pattern ancient yet present reached me like a song from afar. And on Tuesdays I rested from myself and my world.

10

As early as the Ten Days of Repentance the skies became overcast; the Day of Atonement was chilly and depressing, and on the Day of Hosannas for the Torah an intermittent drizzle dampened the gala mood of the town. After that the sky remained overcast, the rain came oftener and fell more heavily. At nights the raindrops pattered on the roofs in the same monotonous beat. This went on for ten nights or so, night after night. Before long autumn brought its mud; then the first snow fell, followed by a second snowfall, which blended with the slush and turned it into icy gruel. Melancholy, the great melancholy of autumn, settled in a heavy pall over Zahoria—and over my heart.

On the way to my meals I had to slog through the mire (I would rather not talk about what my shoes were like); but whether I was traversing the marketplace or some other thoroughfare my eyes kept hungrily seeking something, since a great tearfulness pressed on me. Jewish heads—men's heads, women's heads—peeped out of the doorways of the little shops like mice out of their holes. They had a sad, patient, stubborn look about them, these heads. What were they looking for, would you say?

A Jewish crone, all bundled up in shawls, sits near a stall with apples—little apples, frozen apples, all in a heap. She sells them to the children, at a penny an apple. How many children pass by here each day, and how many day after day? How many of them have a penny in their pockets, as well as a lust for her little apples? How much do those little apples cost her, and how much gain can they bring in for her own subsistence? And how many mouths does she have to feed day after day, selling little frozen apples?

At the far end of the marketplace stands an old wooden store; it has all but tumbled down. Its stock consists of a sack of oats and three bundles of hay: just that and nothing more. Zussi, the son of Michlie, huddles in the doorway, staring straight ahead. He is wrapped in a brown coat, with an upturned collar the shade of rusty tin. His face is small, birdlike, hemmed in by a short, stiff, sandy-hued beard, and his small round hen's eyes of the same hue look out upon the world listlessly. No matter when I pass by, Zussi is huddling there in that unvarying position. A mixture of dislike and fear, originating somewhere deep within me, wells up in my throat. A dead man, keeping vigil. They had forgotten to put shards over his glazed eyes: so he huddles there and stares.

The town's pothouse marks the beginning of the Gentiles' quarter. Their principal thoroughfare and side streets engirdle the town.

The Gentiles have a world all their own. A sort of perverse Sambation River, which does not desist from flinging stones even on the Sabbath, and a man—a Jew, that is—cannot cross it except at the risk of his life. Take the Gentiles now: for what earthly reason were they ever put into the world? The way things look, they were created expressly to be a scourge against men—against Jews, that is—like pestilence and famine. On the other hand, during fair days, they pour into town and inundate it like torrential waters—and provide Jews with a livelihood. On such days one can earn something—and on those same days the air is permeated with menace that lurks in ambush like a ravening beast. The Almighty, in other words, has many uses for his creatures. Strange! You take the Gentiles now—it's hard to make them out. There they were, celebrating weddings and holding wakes, worshiping their idols, going to and fro in their fields and their orchards and, in general, following all sorts of callings that had little to do with Jews . . . The whole subject was hazy. A complex enigma indeed.

The steamboats kept getting fewer and fewer on the river. And around the time of Chanukah their whistles and the beat of their churning paddles in the night ceased altogether. In the dead of night, when it was very quiet, one occasionally heard a whistle, high and piercing—but it was the whistle of a locomotive on the railway twelve miles beyond the river. Next summer (word of this had been going around the town for twenty years) the railway would be extended to Zahoria. Meanwhile the locomotive whistle was far off and hard to believe in. I lay on my bench, covered with a few rags, my ears on the alert as they waited in vain for some other sound. From time to time the dead thud of some heavy object against a soft surface came from a courtyard nearby. It was the clumping of Blind Itzi's horse in its stable. Now and then the poor nag let out a whinny: it was afraid of the rats. And then—again the silence.

In the month of January, under the icy breath of two or three cold spells, the mud solidified into clods. Then the cold blew in gusts from the north, sweeping through the town and changing into a three-day blizzard that piled up in drifts reaching to the window sills.

Late one Thursday night I was awakened by the unusual quiet and bitter cold. A green star twinkled in what I could see of the sky through my window, and the bones of the old synagogue crackled softly as it moaned in the arms of a deathly silent and searing frost.

When I came to the marketplace in the morning the world was all new—never had there been such a world! A great reddish-yellow sun was hanging over the hills; pillars of smoke rose like trees from the house chimneys, and fleecy white coats—so white that they were blinding—had been flung in loose folds over the houses, fences, stores, and the whole world, to its very ends. From all the gates heavily loaded peasant sleighs, their bells jingling, were heading for the fair, and wagons, their axle grease frozen, groaned and screeched over the snow. Cows mooed; new earthen pots rang and sang under the taps of testing fingers, and the babel of human voices was so great it jarred the ears, like water pounding one's head after a deep dive. The air was as heady as home-brew and full of fiery needles that quivered in the rays of the sun and pricked one's face. My fingers were numbed from the frost, my ears froze instantly, as though turned into paper, tears came to my eyes from the cold—and from joy at being alive.

Over at Stissy the Widow's they began giving me the big copper ewer. Even before that Tsirl had asked me to come for an additional meal on Friday, about noon. Her mother would still be in her little shop at that time, and it was Tsirl who generally served me. She would spread a snowy white tablecloth and then bring on a fresh loaf and a deliriously browned beef stew. As I ate she went quietly and unobtrusively about her household tasks.

On the eve of the Sabbath, upon my coming from the synagogue, both women acknowledged my "Good Sabbath" greetings most cordially, and I noticed that the beautiful eyes of the daughter's plain face grew bright, as serene and sanctified as the Sabbath candles themselves. An antique silver beaker damascened with black designs and filled with raisin wine stood ready, as always, for the Kiddush prayer, and though mother and daughter washed their hands before the meal in a tin basin, I was given the old two-handled ewer of copper, which, scrubbed and polished, usually lay atop the commode, next to the brass samovar, both flanked by two silver candlesticks. It had roosted there, most likely, ever since the death of Stissy's husband.

When the fish was served the choice bits always went to my plate.

It was warm in the house, and the air was satiated with appetizing odors. I hummed the Sabbath tunes at my ease, and as Tsirl busied herself with washing the dishes between the fish and soup courses, her clever mother sounded me out cautiously.

"So, whose son are you in Tarashcha, did you say?"

I ought to bring my laundry to them, she suggested. They had a peasant woman who did washing for next to nothing, so if I wished . . .

Tsirl very rarely spoke to me, and if she had to ask me something she would address me indirectly, as though speaking to the wall.

I began to bring them my small bundles of wash, and on getting them back I was surprised to find missing buttons sewed on and the holes mended with neat darning or still neater patches. From time to time I found a new shirt in my bundle, or a pair of new socks, or an extra handkerchief.

I felt as if threads were being spun about me. That is, no one really spun them—the spinning came about of itself, as it were, yet I felt, somehow, uneasy.

Later on the widow happened to remark to me, with a smile in her narrow Tartar eyes, "Women, now—you would hardly class them on a par with men, would you? Take the benediction of the outgoing of the Sabbath, for instance. Why, we never even get the chance to hear it. If it isn't too much trouble, perhaps you'll come over on Saturday night, after the last prayer?"

I began going over on Saturdays, after the evening prayers. The commode yielded a small, ancient spice-holder of silver filigree: this container still gave off a faint fragrance, a reminder of the days of antiquity. Tsirl held the twisted white and green candle for the Habdalla prayer for me. She strained like a child and tilted it, the hot wax dripping on her fingers. This made me smile, and yet I was touched.

Inwardly I began to yield a little. Looking at it from another angle—why not? A fine household and good people. They were not without livelihood. The mother was favorably disposed, the daughter liked me. The only drawback was—well, she was not exactly a beauty. And she was such a quiet thing—such a quiet thing!

12

On the eve of Purim the Warshaver was caught with a Gentile girl. That same night he hanged himself with his trouser belt from a chandelier in the women's section of the synagogue. Two fingers of his right hand were caught in the belt noosed about his neck. His trousers had slipped over his thin hips and had bunched up around his feet. The lower half of the body, which men feel so ashamed of and go to such pains to hide from strange eyes, was outlined against the thin, dirty underwear, and the gray-blue stiffening flesh peeped through a rent. As the body was being taken down from its gibbet little Chaim broke into bitter wailing; he sobbed and hiccuped for hours; it was impossible to quiet him.

Aside from us, his fellow students, no one came to the Warshaver's burial. Carrying the coffin on our shoulders, we plowed through the icy slush, and the butcher boys jeered, shouting something after us which we could not make out—nor wished to make out. The dead man was buried as befits a suicide: close to the fence and on the far side of a small ravine.

Ariah Leib's Chaim was taken out of the yeshiva. The Krutogorer quieted down and, before long, disappeared. Nissel, the assistant rabbi, now snarled at everybody like a mad dog. The students began to desert the yeshiva one by one, on the pretext of going home for the holidays but with no intention of coming back. Only fifteen or sixteen of us remained for the next term.

The yeshiva began to disintegrate, as though devoured by maggots. And I was terrified—truly terrified.

13

The spring nonetheless rushed in with the speed of a young colt. The bearers of Purim presents still had to slog along muddy roads, and keep the white napkins protecting their trays from getting spattered; but a little later other Jews, bending under wickerwork baskets that spread the delectable aroma of oven-fresh matzos, could pick out a dry spot here and there to step on. Jews bustled about in the stores with eager faces. And once I chanced to see Zussi, the son of Michlie, chatting with a neighbor—and there was a smile trembling on Zussi's lips—a smile that seemed pitiful, dusty, and insignificant, but a smile just the same. A smile—I saw it with my own eyes!

In the far upper reaches of the Dnieper huge masses of snow thawed; the floodwaters broke up the thick ice all the way down the river and overflowed the Zagorie valley, almost up to the town limits. One could again hear the steamboats whistling on the river; the hills all around turned green again. Sweet, fresh, moist odors spread through the air, and the sun once more gave forth its warmth. Two weeks before the coming of Passover the river reverted to its banks, the mud dried, the lilac was in full bloom—and the sun grew warmer and warmer. By the time the white blossoms had covered the cherry trees in the Gentile quarter we were running each day to the river to bathe. The dust on the highways swirled in pillars; spring galloped on until summer took over the reins with a strong and firm hand.

During a hot spell guests from Cherkassy arrived at Isser Tabachnik's house: a daughter and her baby, which she was still nursing. I heard a strange voice in the living room.

"My mother-in-law said not to wrap the baby in swaddling clothes."

Whereupon a shudder ran down my spine, as if a drop of rain had worked its way inside my shirt collar. It was a rather low voice, throaty, husky, insidious—as if a pane of glass were faintly vibrating within her. And the voice said, "My mother-in-law said not to wrap the baby in swaddling clothes."

I made up my mind not to leave until I had seen the newcomer, and my wish was realized sooner than I expected. Within a few moments she came into the kitchen and, without taking any notice of me, started hunting for something in the cupboard. I had time to catch a glimpse of a towering mass of bright hair and a soft, lithe body in a loose dress of rustling black silk. Suddenly she caught sight of me and her great eyes regarded me in surprise. The food stuck in my throat. She left the room immediately, and although my eyes had been fixed on my plate I had managed to catch a smile lurking in a corner of her beautiful mouth.

I stumbled out of the room.

A mound of red cherries was flaming on a stall in the center of the marketplace and I bought some for a few pennies. At the entrance to the yeshiva I ran into the Stavisker.

"Would you care to pronounce the benediction over the first fruits?" And I held out the cherries to him.

He looked at me in astonishment. "Where did you get those cherries?"

"The mother-in-law said not to wrap the baby in swaddling clothes," I told him.

"What did you say?"

"Not to wrap the baby in swaddling clothes, the mother-in-law said. No swaddling clothes for the baby, said the mother-in-law—"

"You're crazy!" the Stavisker assured me. "Come on—how about a dip in the river?"

"No, I'd rather get back to studying."

I did not study, however. Instead I wandered from the yeshiva to the synagogue, from the synagogue to the rabbi's court, and all the while kept repeating to myself the words of the mother-in-law as if they were a verse from one of King David's Psalms. Such common words! Not in vain does the Talmud say: The voice of a woman is of itself a seduction. Seduction? For shame! Seduction is such an ugly word. On the contrary, such a voice as hers was . . . was as the cooing of a dove. Would the cooing of a dove be deemed unseemly before the Lord? And yet, what a head of hair! Bright yellow, piled high, like a haystack. Woman's hair—there, that was also forbidden, another seduction, a word that was like spitting in someone's face. And the silken rustle of the dress about the body it concealed—a body that rippled like a river under a light wind, like grain in a field when a breeze springs up . . . A slight tremor ran through my body. My God, Thy hand smote me suddenly—and hard!

14

In the evening I could hardly wait for the prayer to end. As soon as it was over I dashed off for my supper. There were no lights in Isser Tabachnik's house to greet me. The tall windows stared blindly at the western sky. A sadness came over me.

The cook was in the kitchen, however; she was alone in the house. She served me without much ceremony. After supper I paced up and down before the house for a long time, but it remained cold and aloof. There was still not a glimmer of light in the windows, and I returned to the yeshiva.

The week dragged on. I lost all zest for studying, and as soon as I opened some Talmudic tome I would slam it shut again. Whoever heard of such stuff? "If one rides astride a cow, and another leads it, and each claims the animal as his"—so? How did that concern me? How did it affect me, a young man from Tarashcha, whose life had so far gone thus and so, and would go on so and thus? But then, indeed, what shape and form would it assume henceforth? What would become of me? What would become of Stissy the Widow's daughter, the decent Tsirl? Of the synagogue . . . the dry-goods store . . . Zussi, the son of Michlie?

The next Tuesday was not of much help to me either. The words from the past, the bygone world, suddenly became remote—very remote indeed; they lost whatever little substance they had retained before. The colors of the past faded away, its odors evaporated. That Tuesday I neither ate nor fasted; it proved to be the worst day of my week.

But the worst thing of all was my having forgotten her face—the face of Isser Tabachnik's daughter, I mean. I had hardly had a good look at her in that fleeting moment in the kitchen. All I could recall was the high-piled hair, the color of straw—that, and the voice with the glassy ring which re-echoed within me, and still another thing which tormented me like a festering thumb. I felt like one who had found something only to lose it the next moment. Several times during that week I prowled around her house in the dark, but in vain. But when Thursday came at last and I showed up for a meal she was not there. The others were at home; there were some visitors too, and the talk revolved around her (or so I thought), but she herself was not there. I ate—ate again, prayed—prayed again, it might have lasted an hour—not a sign. Dejected, I rose from the table—only to collide with her in the doorway. I sprang back.

She came upon me like a rare and luscious fruit, sleek, roseate and white, bedded in green silk trimmed with point lace; her hair was braided like a wreath about her head and almost touched her brow; her green-gray eyes were like two ripening berries, and there was a celestial fragrance about her.

I stood there, startled and dazed; she stepped aside to make way for me; I did precisely the same thing at the same moment, thus blocking her. She then took a step in the other direction—and so did I—whereupon she burst into laughter, and once again I caught that glassy undertone in her throaty laugh. Confused, I hopped from side to side, still barring her way.

Her laughter echoed after me even when we had somehow disentangled ourselves and I had dashed out of the house.

15

At night the *Dominion* churned down the river, bellowing long and piteously, like an animal in birth pains.

Heavy clouds had hung over the city since nightfall, but no rain had fallen. Now and then the clouds would squeeze out a few orphaned drops that fell among the trees in the rabbi's orchard, but there the matter ended, and a strain of wishing and being unable hung in the air. I tossed upon my bench and my flesh tormented me.

So she laughed at me, laughed so heartily yet heartlessly that my own heart both wept and laughed. And why shouldn't she laugh? Not so long ago I had taken a peep in a mirror at Stissy the Widow's and had caught sight of a nose as blunt as a saddle pommel, dark stubble smeared like mud over gaunt cheeks, and bulging delirious eyes—the eyes of a madman or a drunkard. And a body (this I knew without the aid of any mirror) like that of some hairy beast, patched up from bones and hide!

Perhaps they had even told her the story of the strudel? I suddenly sat up on the bench where I slept, then slumped down again. Nonsense! Whoever paid any attention to me? Who was interested in remembering and repeating what I did or failed to do? Did they as much as notice me? They minded me no more than some stray cat that snatched a bone at their kitchen door.

But, whether the story had been repeated to her or not, had I stolen the strudel or hadn't I? I had, and I had choked on it in secret, and spittle had trickled down my beard. That's the sort of creature I am. And I sinned my sins in a dark anteroom or in the stench of a privy.

On the other hand, what was she, when you came right down to it—an angel? After all, she had a husband, she had a child—and to beget a child one must. The coarse word would have eased matters for me, would perhaps have brought her closer to me. But, oh! I didn't have the heart to use it.

A fortnight went by without my seeing her at all—nor had I been too anxious about it—and once I even skipped a meal at the house where she was staying. I was tired—very tired.

Buni the butcher's daughter put herself in my way quite often, but now I would pass her by as though I didn't even see her. Tsirl, Stissy's daughter, had become even more silent. Had she sensed something?

But on Thursday she herself served me a meal. The cook had gone off somewhere, the mother was evidently indisposed, so the daughter set the table for me and motioned to me to wash my hands. My weariness had not left me, and for that very reason, instead of keeping my eyes fixed on my plate, I let them follow her about and wondered why she now seemed entirely different. She was wearing a loose garment, a robe of some sort, with brightly colored birds and flowers on it. Her hair, done in a single braid, came over her shoulder and fell on her bosom; her face seemed pale, somewhat off-color, puffy. I suddenly noticed a resemblance to her mother, to the good, genial Shaina Leah, something I had failed to see before. It was better that way, more pleasant—and yet, what did it matter?

She became fidgety and lifted her eyes to look at me, but I did not lower mine. This lasted for some time, until the perplexity in her eyes changed to embarrassment.

"Pardon my inquisitiveness," I remarked calmly, "but what is your name?"

A blush started from below her neckline and made its way up her throat, mantling her whole face.

"Why do you ask?"

"Just so. I merely wanted to know."

She contemplated me awhile. Then, lowering her eyebrows, she said, "Hannah. My name is Hannah." And she went out of the kitchen quietly.

I left shortly afterward and followed a side lane to the rear of the house. Then I made my way into the courtyard and saw that my conjecture had not deceived me: the window of her room looked out on the yard, and through the transparent curtain one could easily see what was going on within the room, though it was only dimly lit by a small lamp on a nightstand near the bed. She—Hannah herself—was rummaging in her wardrobe. Then a high-pitched wail, like the piping of a small bird, reached me from within. Before long she sat down on the bed, picked up her baby, talking to it with pursed lips, the way women always do when the baby is very young, unbuttoned her robe—and a full, round, white breast nuzzled the tiny face.

Without any sensuality, only with some such sensation under my heart as that of the suckling baby, I satiated my eyes for several minutes. Then I dashed over the fence and came back to myself.

Could human flesh be so exquisite, so white and serene—and so—
so rich?

16

On the next Tuesday I made an effort to regain that peace of mind
which this day usually brought me. I went without food; all I did was
study, in the synagogue proper. I studied unctuously—I chanted. The
singsong outweighed the words, and the studying was meant to calm
my feelings rather than to enrich my mind.

The following day when I arrived for supper at Buni's house I found
the butcher pummeling his wife. So, those rumors making the rounds of
the town were true. She was running around the table and screaming,
"You heathen! You filthy peasant! May the Lord strike you down! May you
perish from the earth!" But he merely kept after her with a stick.

Disgusted and frightened, I ran out of the house. I decided never to
set foot there again. And, at the same time, I would be getting rid of the
butcher's daughter, who had become used to waylaying me with down-
cast eyes, while I, both indignant and guilty, tried to avoid her.

Within a few hours, however, Buni showed up at our yeshiva. My
heart sank. His roving eyes singled me out and he came over to me.

"Why did you run away?" he shouted and cuffed me a couple of
times; then he grabbed me by the ear and led me out of the synagogue,
demanding that I go with him and eat at his house. All the students had
run out to witness my humiliation. At first I tried to resist, but I was too
afraid of him. When he brought me to his house he placed a dish of
meat before me and ordered me to eat. I did as I was told, choking on
every mouthful, while he stood over me all the time. His wife, her face
bound up, kept pacing the kitchen without a word. The girl was evidently not in the house.

When my plate was empty Buni insisted that I wash my hands before saying the prayer after meals.

"And then you may go to the devil," he snapped. "And don't let me
catch you around here again!"

I withdrew from the rest of the students. In the dead of night I tossed on my bench and moaned as though in pain. As for taking further meals at Isser Tabachnik's house—I could not even think of it. It seemed to me that the whole world must by now be aware of my shame.

During the Sabbath meal Stissy the Widow kept glancing now at me, now at her daughter, but she did not say a word.

That same Sabbath I heard (it was a small town) that Isser Tabachnik's daughter was returning on Sunday to her home in Cherkassy.

The blow must have been stunning: I went about as if in a daze. But I came to my senses in the middle of the morning service on Sunday. I snatched off my prayer shawl and phylacteries and all but ran to the river.

It was nearly too late. People were already running up and down the gangplank. I elbowed my way with difficulty into the enclosure. My eyes found her almost at once in the throng on the upper deck; she was exchanging farewells with her mother and her little sister on the landing. She was a changed being: this time she was in a gray outfit, the jacket tailor-made, something like a student's tunic; her hat was of black straw, wide of brim, with a jaunty feather. Erect, sure of herself, and with an altogether different voice—from head to toe the rich daughter-in-law. The chasm that had divided us before was now yawning between us more widely than ever.

Had my stare attracted her? She turned her head in my direction and for some minutes looked straight into my eyes. Then she turned her head away abruptly, took her baby out of the crib standing alongside of her, put it back again, and called down, "Keep well, keep well! Temke, be a good girl—don't make Mother worry!"

The whistle drowned out her voice. The gangplank was hauled away. The whistle spewed more steam, and the next moment the black water widened between the boat and the landing. Half a mile down the river the steamboat disappeared.

The place where we went swimming was not far from the landing, and I dragged myself there, undressed, and sat down on the sandy bank. Far off across the river something like a huge tuft of cotton-wool formed in the air, then it disintegrated in the sunlight and a new tuft rose up farther away, followed by still others: clouds of smoke from a passing locomotive. But no sound accompanied them.

"The sound will never reach here," I said rather loudly.

The sun shone brightly, the river was ablaze, mirroring its radiance, and I, a naked mortal, sat on the sand with my head sunk on my knees. I sat for a long time, very likely pondering something or other, and, I think, even dozed off for a few moments.

Then I got dressed without having taken a swim.

On my way back I stopped at Stissy the Widow's. "Tsirl," I said, "I've come for my few pieces of laundry. I'm leaving."

Her cheeks and forehead paled.

"Yes," I added, "I am being called home. My father is ill—very ill."

The beautiful eyes in the plain face became still larger. "Your father? But you said you have no father—that you are an orphan—"

"Is that what I said? Well, if I said so, then I must be an orphan. I'm going away, Tsirl, I'm going away. Be well."

I was already in the street when she came out with a parcel in her hand and called after me, "You forgot your laundry!"

"My what?" I said.

She stood there with tight lips, holding out the parcel.

"Good-by, Tsirl," I said in a softer tone. "Good-by."

She said nothing but nodded her head.

An hour later I was back at the landing, standing before the ticket-agent's little window. The ticket-agent, a middle-aged Pole with sullen eyes and an aristocratic blond mustache, asked, "Where to?"

He caught me off guard and stood there impatiently. Let's see: Cherkassy was down the river, wasn't it?

"Up the river," I said.

He eyed me for some time with a sour expression. "As far as Kiev?"

"Yes—yes, as far as Kiev."

I came out on the landing itself. It was early for the next boat and no passengers were yet in sight. The sun was already behind me and the shadow of the landing lay sharp and black on the water. Farther out it was yellow, and over the entire width of the river full-bodied, swollen waves were gliding along—gliding from one end of the world to the other.

1926 (translated by Bernard Guilbert Guerney)

Once upon a time there were a rebbe and a rebbetsin. When the rebbe studied Torah the rebbetsin would say she heard angels chanting, and when the rebbetsin cooked fish for the Sabbath the rebbe was certain that he smelled the odors of Paradise. Both the rebbe and the rebbetsin were equally good, pious, and wise. If there ever was a difference between them, it was that the rebbetsin could almost issue rabbinical judgments, while on the subject of cooking fish the rebbe claimed no knowledge.

God had closed the womb of the rebbetsin. The rebbe would sit in one corner, the rebbetsin in another, and they would plead to God in silence:

Creator of the Universe, heed the prayer of your servant and bless me with a son, so that I may teach him your Torah and good deeds . . .

Creator of the Universe, Lord of the World, hearken to the prayer of your servant and rejoice me with a child, so that I may plant good ways in him and teach him to do your will . . .

And the rebbe would sit down by the side of the rebbetsin and say, "When our son begins to talk, I will myself teach him how to read and the meaning of the words."

And the rebbetsin would add, "When our Kaddish awakens I will say morning prayers with him, and before he goes to sleep evening prayers."

And so the years flew by, and the townspeople began to whisper among themselves, "If a woman has no children after ten years of marriage, the husband must not live with her."

And this was told to the rebbe, and the rebbe answered, "I will not send my wife away, and God will yet give me a son."

The townspeople grumbled and thought of removing the rebbe, but later they decided that if the barrenness of his wife didn't trouble him, it certainly should not trouble them—and so the years went. The rebbe sat opposite the rebbetsin and they talked.

"When our child grows up, I will teach him the Gemarah and all the commentaries."

"When our son will come Fridays from the bath I will honor him with fresh fish, and when he returns from the synagogue on the Sabbath I will meet him with the sacramental wine."

And a while later the townspeople again remembered them and gave them advice. "Adopt a child and bring it up, and a hundred years from now it will say Kaddish for you."

The two of them shook their heads. The rebbe answered, "How can I instruct a strange child in Torah and good deeds if I am not responsible for his sins? And the rebbetsin said, "How will I be able to love a strange child if he has not cost me my blood?"

And both of them added, "No, God will bless us with our own child!"

The townspeople grumbled, called them stubborn, and in time forgot them once more.

And the two old people decided: When our treasure grows up he will issue rabbinical judgments and write holy books . . . When our joy reaches eighteen, we will lead him to the wedding canopy . . .

One after the other, in the flow of eternity, the years passed by. On a morning they were found dead. They were sitting on their beds, facing each other, in the same nightshirts, clasping their hands, like children, around their knees. Across their faces flitted a smile. And in the air of the old house, as though the words still hummed:

When our son will grow up . . .

When our Kaddish will grow older . . .

1910 (translated by Irving Howe and Eliezer Greenberg)

◆ ◆ ◆ The Man and His Servant

1

He seemed really out of place among the people strolling in the fresh air of the park, and so he always attracted stares. Anyone who looked at him was immediately beset by an indefinable fear. Several times each day his wheelchair appeared in the avenues, pushed by a sturdy, fair-haired young servant. He lay slumped in it with his legs wrapped in a warm rug and a kind of cap on his head. He had a rather swollen pasty face with a large nose and gray eyes which seemed almost too calm. He stared straight ahead of him, not looking at anyone.

Nearly everyone avoided him. Only the children would run past him like a whirlwind, shouting and laughing, almost overturning his wheelchair. They simply did not notice him.

He and his servant did not converse. He would indicate what he wanted with one word, and the servant neither looked at him nor answered him, but simply pushed the wheelchair in the desired direction. It seemed as if the blond well-built young man did not notice him either. The link between them was a purely mechanical one.

2

In the evening the park is completely given over to matters of love. If a person of strict morals walks along one of the avenues, his brow darkens. If he goes along a second one, he shakes his head. If he cuts through a third one, he simply shrugs his shoulders. Then he ponders it all, hangs his head, lifts it again and lets out a sigh. The sigh hangs in the air and pulls at his heartstrings.

And it's not just the poor moralists who suffer in the park. Wise men too are well warned not to venture into it, because there are certain avenues in the park which are not really avenues at all. They are actually quite separate worlds, where anything is possible, except reality. If a wise man stumbles upon one of these places, where wisdom is powerless, he will say and do such stupid things that he will be ashamed of them. Yet he will long for them for the rest of his life. A place where water is chattering and greenery is silent—what can be more dangerous? Thus I say: wise man, stay at home.

A young man and two girls start dancing on the smooth asphalt path between the trees. Without singing or speaking he takes one of them round the waist, dances with her, leaves her, takes the other, goes back to the first. They twirl silently, like fantastic incorporeal spirits or shadows. The few passersby stand aside so as not to disturb the silent dance. Suddenly though, there is a low grating sound of wheels on the asphalt, and out of the dark looms a pair of legs wrapped in a rug, an indistinct half-supine body, a swollen face with glassy eyes. The startled dancers scatter in different directions. Only when the wheelchair is hidden by the servant's broad shoulders do the young people gather again, but the dance has been frozen.

On the grass beneath the trees, the darkness is denser and filled with sighs, with secret kisses, with the restrained rustlings of people making passionate love. When the wheelchair with the invalid glides past, it's as if a cold breeze has passed over the grass and, startled, they hide themselves deeper in among the trees. Once a woman's voice called out from somewhere, full of rage and frustration: "Ugh, what an old carcass." She shouted a curse as well.

The invalid did not even look round.

3

Slowly, one day at a time, June wrapped himself round the park, en-
folding it in his hot arms. From early morning on the sun embraced
the garden passionately, and when he left her in the evening, her breath
was filled with a heavy perfume and she tossed and turned on her hot
bed. And when at last she had breathed out all her glowing heat and
was lying cool and peaceful in the darkness of the night, a quiet slumber spread its wings over her, showering her with gentle dreams and
indistinct visions.

The human stream had long since flowed out of the garden through
the many exits, and only the occasional couple still lingered, whispering secrets to each other. A homeless person, sleeping on a bench, nervously stirred in his sleep, probably seeing policemen in his dreams.
An artificial waterfall, hidden somewhere in a dark corner, chattered
ceaselessly. Nobody heard it, and the chatter of that man-made creation, when none of its creators was there to hear it, sounded strange
indeed.

With a low grating sound the wheelchair with the invalid rolled
through the sleeping avenues.

Beside the path, under a wide spreading tree, a lamp impudently
lifted a corner of the night's dark veil. A girl with red hair and a piercing
gaze was coming. When she saw the invalid's glassy eyes, she stopped,
and let out a shriek:

"Oh my God!"

Then her eyes rested on the servant's blond hair and broad shoulders and her face relaxed. She gave him a strange look, an almost im-
perceptible smile, and disappeared down another avenue. Without
speaking, or asking the invalid, the young man turned the wheelchair
to follow her.

The path started rising, leading up to a heavily wooded place, then
unexpectedly climbing up to a bare little hill encircled on three sides
with trees. On the fourth side lies a ravine, in which a fantastic world
spreads out: it seems as if there are trees, hills, valleys, towers, pillars,
palaces all rising up out of a lake, and the surface of the water shim-

mers faintly, half-extinguished, in the starlight. Further in the distance, beyond this vista, a huge city slumbers—so people say.

On one little hill stands an old, broken cannon, a memento of the war which the country once fought for its freedom. The servant stopped the wheelchair opposite the cannon, and went off among the trees, in the direction in which the girl had vanished. The glassy eyes looked at the old cannon. It seemed like the huge body of a long-dead, dried-up snake, or like the skeleton of death itself. Many years ago its innards glowed and spat fire; it fought for freedom. Down below in the valley, where now the water of the artificial lake shimmers, tiny human beings ran about, climbing up to the cannon and tumbling to the earth with shattered skulls and torn bellies from which tangled intestines burst out. Many of them lay with their faces to the earth and their hands stretched out, in mud and blood, like slaughtered dogs. The cannon kept on thundering, and the tiny human beings below ran deliberately toward it. It was a stupendous fight for freedom.

And of all those who manned the cannon so skillfully, only one very young soldier, a still beardless little shrimp who had not even suffered a scratch, suddenly sat down on the ground, chewed his fingers, and screamed and wept bitterly. He only wanted his mother . . .

1910 (translated by Heather Valencia)

The sky on the eastern horizon was dark red like a glowing iron when it is beginning to cool down. The moon was just rising. High in the sky Jupiter was gleaming, and lower down, in the northwest, the Plough spread out. Its distorted square and long broken tail looked as if they were disobeying all the normal rules of design. The Milky Way stretched over the earth like a light gauze ribbon which a fickle hand had carelessly thrown away. Stars twinkled everywhere.

Down below it was still dark, or rather dark gray, and in this gray darkness there was a feeling of chaos: no definite color, no straight line, not a single clearly defined spot was to be seen. The eye seemed to imagine the existence of a field or some kind of open space. Further in the distance hills or shadows rose up—or perhaps it was nothing at all. For one second something did appear clearly when a fiery point suddenly flared up. Something like steps were heard too . . . Soon the little flame disappeared, spurted again somewhere further on in the darkness, and then was swallowed up again. After that the darkness seemed to become even denser at the place where the little flame had appeared for the first time. Something suddenly made a shrieking and ringing sound. Without warning a figure was clearly delineated, but immediately disappeared with a dull thump as if swallowed up by the earth. And then a yellow, semicircle swam up from below the red horizon.

Within a single instant someone pulled the transparent gray cover off the field. It fluttered and twisted itself into long folds and wrinkles. Spirits pursued it across the plain and disappeared in the west. In the middle of the field an old twisted oak tree appeared, as if it had been lowered through the air and stuck into the earth. He stretched his arms out wide and looked with great astonishment at the bright circle which was rising far above the earth and moving serenely across the sky. Behind the oak a black, immensely long, fantastic shadow stretched out.

Long rows of cornstalks stood in the moonlight, dozing and dreaming and from time to time shaking their heads in their sleep. Whenever a ripple ran through them a hushing sound was heard, as if one of them was being told to be quiet and let the others sleep. Meanwhile the moon had risen higher in the sky, and its light grew paler, flooding the whole earth.

A white, built-up rail track stretched between the sleeping fields from the north, coming from somewhere at the end of the earth. It ran past the oak tree and a quarter of a mile further on, beside a signal-box, it turned toward the east and disappeared from view. There the ground, covered with the last trees of the dark and distant forest, rose slightly. Two thin straight lines glittered coldly in the moonlight and ran the whole length of the track. Beside the oak tree, the line on the eastern side was unexpectedly interrupted, but then a few yards further on it resumed. On one side a piece of rail lay as peacefully and impassively as if it were in its proper place. A few minutes were born in the silence and then died again—without sound, or color, or anything happening: the past did not become longer, nor the future shorter. Time flowed on from eternity to eternity.

A low sound quivered in the air and was lost again. It seemed like a mosquito flying past, stinging the silence with its sharp hum. Then a few seconds later the sound came from somewhere else. A slight shiver passed along the metal lines, floated along the whole rail, and continued on past the tree. When it came to the broken piece of track it suddenly stopped and seemed to bury itself in the earth.

The rails trembled more and more frequently. The sound became sharper and clearer, carried along from one rail to the next. Then it broke off. A few of the cornstalks shook their heads in their sleep; a branch of the oak tree bent and straightened itself; a breeze blew across the field. At that moment the whole track shook, as deep in the earth underneath it a muffled noise was heard.

A second, a third noise. With an insistent and measured beat the noises grew. The trembling became faster and stronger as it ran through the whole track, and was cut off at the broken section. Far off in the dark forest a mighty beast ran on, waking the echo among the trees and shaking the air.

Nearer it came! On the other side of the signal-box something flashed. There was a short sharp whistle, powerful and victorious. A glowing eye appeared from behind the signal-box, and, as it curved inward, a second one appeared beside it. Round the bend in the track a string of carriages wound its way gracefully and sinuously, then straightened out like a taut string. The fiery eyes grew bigger and burned with a hellish fire. The whole track shook, shuddered, panted in excitement, as the locomotive ran toward the tree with lighthearted confidence, drawing after itself rings and curls of smoke and steam, like the long mane streaming out from a runaway horse.

The field awoke from its sleep. Cornstalks moved and took on the moonlight tones, now pale as death. The melancholy old oak stretched out its branches toward the track, raised them up, and let them sink down again helplessly. The air murmured and trembled. Convulsions were now passing through the broken rail. From the end of it, hoarse sounds burst out like stifled, despairing groans coming from compressed lips. They burst forth and then sank silently into the earth. It seemed as if the metal was about to break apart with the effort: the accursed, locked lips would *have* to let out a scream! And from the end of the rail sprang out a shriek like that of a living being. And again and again the earth swallowed it and suffocated it.

The mighty steel breast of the locomotive came closer and closer . . .

The disconnected rail lay by the side of the track, gleaming innocently in the moonlight . . .

1910 (translated by Heather Valencia)

◆ ◆ ◆ *Myrtle*

(From a letter)

. . . And if you imagine that you already know the truth—do you really know it?

I can give a thousand replies to your thousand questions, a different reply for each one. Each answer will have within itself, no, each one will *be,* a droplet of the truth, and you will stand bewildered in the midst of this clamoring horde of truths and . . . Oh, what nonsense! There has to be *one* answer if you really want to know anything. I say: there *must* be. I believe in this as I believe in God. Only, what is it? How? Its essence? Its form? All this I do not know.

And if you proceed a little further, you will see that there cannot be one single answer here until there is one single question. And if you go one step further, it will be clear to you that the correctly asked question, the "one and only," is the one which carries its answer in itself. Well, let's leave it there.

I will try, nevertheless, to give some sort of answer. But if, after reading it, you are none the wiser, please don't bear me a grudge my dear friend!

Here, for example, is one version for you.

My world now consists of my writing-desk. A sober dark-green cloth, an aluminum ashtray, a stone inkstand, a notebook of blank paper, a lamp which casts a dull white light, and a little myrtle-tree in a pot. That's it.

My world is pretty small, you'll say? Perhaps it is. Perhaps it isn't. I won't argue with you.

Go through my list of objects again, up to and including the lamp. My relationship to all these things is simple enough: that of property and owner. They serve me well but I don't give them much thought. Even the lamp: I must say it throws a really fine, gentle, cheerful light on my paper, but that's nothing exceptional. Only the little myrtle-tree is different. I don't call her "the myrtle-tree," but "Myrtle."

I became acquainted with her, or rather, we became acquainted with each other, last summer. There's nothing surprising about her appearance. A slender stem with a dry muddy gray rind, a network of little branches with small oval leaves. If you bury your face in the cobweb of branches and leaves—no scent. But now, crush the leaves very hard between your fingers, and they have a pungent smell, like pine needles or something similar. I look at Myrtle and I sense the strong aroma hidden in each of her leaves. It is like the potential in gunpowder, which doesn't reveal itself until it explodes, causing death.

She stands on my table, at the window, which looks toward the west. In the evening the sun sets over the mountain that is just opposite my window. Now the sun is no longer shooting out golden needles and arrows. Its edge is sharply delineated, and every hidden corner of my room is lit up by the fiery red color which suffuses the sun's face. The walls become transparent. Is it possible that this red gold which plays on the walls is not their actual color? Will it really fade in a few moments? And see: every single one of Myrtle's branches and tiny leaves is traced out on the opposite wall!

And my eye turns away from the shadow to my Myrtle at the open window.

Still. Not a single leaf is stirring. The slender stem, the tangle of little branches, the sharp tongue-shaped leaves all look two dimensional, as if pasted onto the shining face of the sun.

Still. The mountain slowly rises up and cuts strip after strip from the fiery disk, cuts and swallows them, one after another. And nothing remains but the fragment of a golden ring. A last spray of golden dust. Then nothing at all.

Still. For a long time a pale mother-of-pearl glow shines through the little branches. Cavernous shadows rise out of the valley and mount up through the air toward the sky. Myrtle and I gaze and gaze at the worlds upon worlds flaring up in the distant sky, further and further into the night. The stillness deepens, becomes palpable. The stillness speaks: Hear, oh Man! Hear, oh Man! Hear, oh Man!

By the end of the summer Myrtle has grown really luxuriant.

Then came autumn. The sun had moved to the left, and at sunset it no longer illuminated the whole room, but only one crooked corner. This made my heart ache. Later on the sky clouded over, the world shrank, and night started arriving early and without any spectacle of changing colors. It was as if it emerged without transition from the cloudy day. Though a few watery sunsets still appeared, they only gave a cold fire, like the arid flush on the cheeks of a consumptive. Then the days became ever grayer, damper, colder . . . brr! My God, the lamp, the lamp!

And a dull milky glow flooded the lower half of my room, while above there were warm pink shadows. Only now did summer start to leave me. As when a frozen limb thaws out, I felt both pain and relief, as well as intense sleepiness and waking dreams. My little room, I don't know when or how, was flooded by a host of strange creatures which created around me a kind of silent commotion; a lively, but soundless din. They were a merry bunch, who helped me to smoke my cigarettes, turned the pages of my notebook, waved and gestured to me and to each other with silent laughter, occasionally whispering something in my ear. They exhausted and stimulated me simultaneously. My notebook of blank paper became thinner and thinner, and beside it a heap of strange pages grew higher. As soon as they were covered with a blossom of little black sticks and rings, they distanced themselves from me, acquiring an independent appearance and behaving toward me as equals. Sometimes I looked at them pensively and with some amazement. A wheel was turning around me, in me, with me. My heart quivered and my breath came in gasps, like in a wind on the high seas.

But all the same a slight unease was gathering. More than once I would suddenly start looking around the room, peering into the corners, or sniffing the air—but there was nothing there. I forgot about this feeling, and the crowd gathered round me again, the white glow rested on everything, and on the blank paper I sensed the black blossoming which would soon appear on the pages. I would suddenly turn quickly and look at the door, searching for the strange, heavy gaze which had just then been pressing on my shoulder—but there was nothing and nobody there. Once, involuntarily, I stretched out my hand toward Myrtle, to pick one of her leaves. My finger touched a branch clumsily, and a host of leaves, like a flock of startled birds, showered down from the branch and scattered over the green table-cover.

I sprang up from my chair.

Ha? What's this? What on earth? . . .

Now I realized what was happening. For some time, (since when, I wonder?), Myrtle had been looking at me with a strangely melancholy expression and her appearance was—how can I put it?—disheveled. Yes, disheveled. Her leaves were as numerous and green as they had been before, but somehow rather more pointed, and the branches appeared through them, like brown, hairy, emaciated arms, worn out by fever. Yes, but why, why?

My eyes roved hastily around the table. The lamp! It had been standing right beside Myrtle for a very long time. I touched another branch, and again a flock of little birds settled on the table-cover with a dry rustling sound. I grabbed a leaf, crushed it in my fingers—dust. I put it to my nose—no smell. Dust and ashes. My legs gave way under me and I dropped onto my chair.

All winter I struggled to keep her alive. I haven't the faintest idea how to look after plants, but I battled, using my instinct and driven by my desperation. The first thing I did was to strip every single leaf off Myrtle, and, oh my friend!, you'll live for a hundred years longer if you have never had to witness a sight like the naked limbs and skeleton of that sick plant. I kept on watering and watering her. I seized every cold ray of the meager winter sun and wrapped it round Myrtle. In short, I did everything I knew and didn't know.

I hated the lamp. The crowd of buffoons had disappeared from my room; my coldness toward them had driven them away. The written pages had become completely alien to me.

This state of affairs lasted a long time. Determinedly, but almost without hope, I watched over Myrtle until at last I had the joy of seeing tiny little shoots, like green poppy seed, scattered all over her stem and branches. I had no strength left to rejoice, but gentle peace filled my heart. Soon the little shoots had sharp points, like hair starting to grow back on the shorn head of a sick person during convalescence. And soon the spring appeared.

Now when I look at Myrtle, my heart is full of hope again. More than that, in fact: it is full of certainty. And yet . . .

A new shoot sprouted at the bottom of the stem and started growing. Initially I looked at it, not understanding what was happening. The new shoot grew amazingly fast, overtook its elders and straightened out into a tall thick stem. Myrtle now has *two* stems, both a little crooked. Oh, I know that the part which is in the earth, right by the roots, is single—and yet . . .

Peacefully and with restrained pride the two stems grow, covered with a whole forest of little branches. The leaves multiply from day to day. I take one and crush it. Its pungent aroma takes my breath away and lights up my eyes. It seems that the smell of bitter almonds has been added to it.

And once again the little tree stands before me, silent and primed, like a loaded gun.

Myrtle, Myrtle—what does the coming summer have in store for us?

1919 (translated by Heather Valencia)

The New World

◆ ◆ ◆ *At Sea*

Whither, o splendid ship, thy white sails crowding,
Leaning across the bosom of the urgent west,
That fearest nor sea rising, nor sky clouding.
Whither away, fair rover, and what thy quest?
—Robert Bridges: *A Passer-By*

NIGHT

At sea—overcast and desolate as though God had not yet created the
world. Between the dirty sky and the blank surface of the water, over the
full breadth of the chaos that is the globe, hovers the spirit of Almighty
God—a severe, hostile, careworn spirit. Restlessly, the thick-dark waves,
capped with gray heads of foam, hurl themselves one upon another.
Harsh is the gloom of the mournful sea, and great its vexation. Little
man, where are you crawling to? Little man, what are you striving to
reach? You've set off over the mighty waters in the shell of a nut. O you
pitiful wretch!

From all possible sides, from the darkness above, from the cold
clamminess below, from the turbid, illimitable ring of the horizon,
mysterious, stark-blind night closes in upon the ship. As the groaning
of the craft is swallowed up in the ceaseless murmur of the waves, the

timid gleam of the portholes is blotted out in the molten intermingling of fog, sky, water and night. Over the vessel's prow and stern, trembling helplessly like children, hover two solitary, lost guide-lights.

Captain, captain! Are we far from land? Can we at least be certain that somewhere amidst this waste of water, dry land can still be found? Is not the earth but a dream?

Far, oh far! Do you see back there behind us, where nothing is visible? Can you turn your thoughts back to the long, long plain where we left behind so many bright and despondent days, so many black and pallid nights? Over there the earth glows in sunshine, and abides as though furnace-forged. And glance over here, on the other side—can you sense the days and nights that are coming to meet us? Behind *their* shoulders a long fragmented strip of land is also sharply etched. Meanwhile, however . . . Aha! Take care! A mountain of water is falling on us.

—Off! . . . Gone! . . .

Songs.

Various songs rise from the ship's deck and are lost in the wind's whistle between the masts, and in the seething waters all around. Scottish songs with the wild skirl of craggy mountains, dark woods, and bagpipes. Graceful Italian melodies, liquescent with sunshine and the passionate glances of women's night-black eyes. "God bless the ship," the seasoned, brine-soaked Englishman prays aloud in a strong low voice. And suddenly a small, thin boyish voice weaves its way forward, struggling to sing its Russian words with the determined strength of a healthy breast: "*Smelo druz'ia! Ne teriaite sily v neravnom boiu*—Be courageous, friends! Don't waste energy fighting an unequal fight!" and on and on. Gradually the voice grows gentler, its tones lower and bolder, and a deep hidden tremor pulses beneath the words: "It is good that a man should both hope and quietly wait" Ah, my beloved song of Lamentations—I recognize you! Eternal, immortal leitmotif, in foreign words, in varied melodies, you unfailingly carve out a path for yourself. Don whatever garments you will, your sorrowful tones betray you at once. Sing, sing, pale gaunt boy with great bright eyes: your chant chimes with the heavy solitude of the somber sea . . .

Ever more deeply the surrounding night closes in upon us. Quietly and fearfully our ship groans; from time to time it sobs like a sleeping child. Yet it sails on. With no trace of a helmsman, driven by secret powers, like a somnambulist the vessel moves onward in its slumber.

Saltier, sharper grows the breath of the swart, turbulent sea. There is no one else on deck. Face to face, the sea and I share a long, long sleepless night.

Come hither, brother! Give me your mighty, ice-cold hand. As great and strong as you are, so small and frail am I. I am as weak and helpless as you are limitlessly powerful. But however fearful your agitation may be, I am a thousand, thousand times more perturbed and restless.

Great is the disquiet of a puny man.

See! You rarely force your way into various of my towns and villages. More than once, on the other hand, I've ventured across your length and breadth, I've searched your depths, and I've found you're too small for me. When you're angered, then—truly!—death glares from your eyes. But for my part, when wildness overcomes me, the lightnings of madness flash from mine!— . . . Ha, ha.

Mu-u-u-u!—the sound was unexpectedly wrenched from the bosom of the sleeping ship.

White fog encircled our vessel, crept onto the deck, over our faces, into our bones. The propeller churned ponderously and with greater precision. A harsh, raw whistle soared from the deck into the fog—a second whistle, a third, a tenth and more. Each went in search of its lost brother, and like them was swallowed up in turn . . . a silent dogged dread. The ear pricks up of its own accord. The eye scans the close distance in vain.

Quiet and indistinct, like an ancient dream, an indeterminate sound emerges from an unknown source: possibly a groan, possibly a protracted yawn from a wide throat. Startled, our ship shudders and responds hoarsely and apprehensively. Somewhat more distinct, a second sound reaches my ear, and on that desolate expanse of water a bizarre duet is set up between two worlds, each hidden from the other. It is difficult to say whence the strange voice emanates: from very far away or from very close by; from the front, or perhaps from somewhere to the side? And before my mind's eye, standing on the deck of that hidden ship I seem to see another, as solitary as I, in a long black coat with a pale face and gleaming eyes, peering intently and eagerly into the bleak, blind fog. And he too appears to see me on the deck of a hidden ship, and our gazes meet . . .

The distant whistle passes to one side and is heard more weakly. Thereafter it is wholly engulfed in the night.

Adieu, my unknown comrade! Greet in my name the eternally wandering Flying Dutchman . . .

Our ship has roused itself from sleep and takes its course more briskly and cheerfully.

The night has grown wet. A thin, pale drizzle of unknown origin drives into the darkness, slowly merging with it, washing it ever grayer. The drab depths blur the vision, making it more and more difficult to distinguish any defined feature. One imagines the air crowded with unidentifiable trembling, fluttering creatures; that soon, very soon, one will glimpse a few soft, rounded forms that evaporate before they come to rest, that die before they are born. That unforgettable crepuscular moment has arrived when the flow of time halts between the night that has been and the day that may be; when the angel of sleep pours out upon the earth the full potency of his enchantment; when during the Days of Awe, sleepy Jews in my shtetl wander like night-spirits along the darkened streets to the synagogue, dreaming as they walk. Several taps of our old beadle's wooden mallet reach my ears, sounds that were born when I was still a child, that for many years sought me across the world, and that have now caught up with me in the middle of the foaming sea—and my heart beats faster in response. The long, long distant past and the brief, transitory present merge. The real world turns into a dream and dreams become reality. The dozing little houses of my dear shtetl twirl and rock around our ship, the old synagogue, its ancient, attenuated guelder rose struggling for life next to it, swims past. My childish heart trembles, waves of water roar, the gall-bitter, maternally tender tones of the prayer "Hear our cry" rises plaintively, and somewhere quite close by the hours of the watch are sounded four times. I awake as from a deep sleep.

The day comes on.

Here and there the clouds, fewer in number, thin to translucency, tear themselves apart, and expose the dull, bleached sky. The fearsome bellow of the waters is tamed: the waves frolic pertly and jauntily, a little uncontrolled, like spoilt children. Far away, there at the edge of the dead night, a vast and radiant being rises up. The day that approaches us will be beautiful.

I kiss your cold dead hand, my dearly beloved mother night! The day that is about to be born will indeed be beautiful, but I shall never forget you in your profound, earnest loneliness.

From somewhere, black as a devil, a sailor with broom in hand suddenly springs up on deck. I imagine that very soon he will either sit astride his broomstick and rise up into the air, or will leap down into the water, transforming himself into a crippled old man, half-human, half-fish. Neither happens, in fact. He rushes past me and vanishes down a hole of some sort as quickly as he had appeared.

The day has come.

SILENCE

Over the sea, the day blazed in all its glory. The mighty blue breast still heaved after the troubled, restive night it had passed, but with every stride the sun boldly took across the sky, the water steadily quieted itself. Behind, a broad, snow-white path of foam, flecked with green and blue, drew out in the wake of our ship and was lost in the clear golden distance; in front, the identically clear golden distance opened up, surveying us from all sides. Our ship was the midmost point of all the world.

Little by little a web of defined connections and relationships was woven among the passengers. People brought together for the first and possibly the last time by shared life on board ship established intimacies, sought status, and spoke slander. A young couple tried to be alone. The history of the world had started all over from the very beginning.

Meanwhile the day grew older. From a wanton youth it had ripened into a serious adult who knew what he wanted, then into an aged person who understood what awaited him and was ready to encounter the inevitable peacefully. The sun had traversed three-quarters of its daily course, and its face had grown ruddy and fatigued. The waters had almost entirely stilled themselves.

Then something happened.

A passenger hunched over the railings, held that posture for a short while, and then dropped slowly into the water, without a word, without the slightest cry. It happened so slowly, so naturally, that in the first few moments those standing around could not grasp what had happened.

For a full hour, sailors in a lifeboat searched for the drowned man. They came back empty-handed, tired and irritated.

Who was he? All had noticed, but none had seen. The passengers crowded together on the deck in a huddled, silent mass like frightened sheep. The ship's steward, a tall, handsome young man with great moist black eyes, stood distractedly in front of them with the passenger list in his hand, calling aloud various names to which people from the crowd responded nervously and rapidly. "John Clifford! Paolo Bernardini! Moyshe Vaynshteyn!" With every new name that drew a response, the general tension mounted and mounted.

—Janko Ravić!

Silence.

—Janko Ravić!

No answer. The steward turned pale. A pair of icy wings fluttered over the deck

—Jan-ko Ra-a-a-vić! The steward called out once more, hoarsely and barely audibly. We caught the name, and the two words "Janko Ravić" echoed over our heads, forcing their way into all the corridors and cabins, lingering for a long time over the whole ship, but always weaker, more smothered, and more hopeless. For a long time we stared down into the calm sea.

In this way Janko Ravić left the world . . . and that was that. From the ship's manifest it was later ascertained that he was forty-seven years old and hailed from Belgrade in Serbia.

What kind of person was he? What did he look like? No one knew. His neighbors in the cabin had taken no notice of him, because he was always silent. No one had even properly seen his face. Apparently he was thin and broad-boned—but then again, perhaps not. Everyone had noticed; none had seen. Now he stood before us like a ghastly secret, like a tormenting riddle: Janko Ravić . . . Janko Ravić . . . What was Janko Ravić?

With its bottommost rim the sun touched the sea and halted for a while. Huge, red, its contours sharply etched, deep in thought, it was evidently dreaming of its youth when, after thousands of millions of risings and settings, it had been born on earth for the first time. What a wonderful period that had been! How good to be a young god—but how great the loneliness of an old one!

And silently the sun vanished beneath the sea.

Mysterious, unfamiliar stars rushed in the alien sky. A tranquil evening flowed over the world. Multitudes of shadows scrambled together from all the corners of the sky, spreading themselves thickly over the water. A dumb silence swam up from its depths, rose, expanded and filled the world. And the sea's silence was as great as itself.

—I had an acquaintance, a painter, said my neighbor on the bench, a graying, stocky man with a faraway look in his blue eyes, who used to paint the sea and went mad.

—Why? I asked him.

—He used to say that when the sea spoke, he could paint it. Fewer or more tints, a softer or a sharper line, all that was human. But when the sea was silent, it told him so much, things he was wholly incapable of representing on canvas. He complained that the silent sea sucked the marrow from his bones, while the speaking sea disturbed him more and more with every passing day. To his ears, its discourse had come to sound like brash, commonplace babble.

I glanced more attentively at my neighbor. He spoke calmly, monotonously, like one half asleep. It seemed to me that he was looking out to sea but at nothing in particular. Having held his peace for a while, he began again.

—This same artist had a beloved. That is to say, *he* loved a young woman who did *not* love him. She was given to chatter, song, laughter, and could not endure his silence. But when the artist went mad, the young woman grew to love him. From then on, she too stopped speaking. She took him into her home, and on stormy days, when the sea spoke, they were never seen outdoors. Only during calm, soundless days and nights, she and her ailing beloved would sail far out into the sea in a little boat, and spend hours there. I've no idea what they did, but each time she returned she was paler. I don't know the end of that story either. I haven't yet worked it out.

My neighbor rose from the bench and crossed to the other side of the deck.

—And what's the moral of all that? I shouted after him.

He gestured vaguely as though to say, "Oh, leave me alone!"

A strange fellow!

The ship rocked. I dozed off, and someone murmured in my ear:

—I knew a painter who used to paint the sea, and he went mad. His name was Janko Ravić.

THE ICEBERG

Bright warm days strayed randomly over the sea.

On dry land, the days of the Omer were now being counted, and where no human feet had trodden, sharp blades of grass crept from the soft, aromatic earth, rising and leaping upward to the far distant sun, still faint and transparent, like the first soft hairs on the fresh face of a boy. On dry land, the days of the Omer were now being counted, and on the half-bare branches of the trees, like frozen drops of dew, sprouted green, full buds, tightly packed and rolled up, bearing within those dark shadows which the trees would later spread round themselves. Here on the smooth surface of the water, no hillock, no sapling, no tiny blade of grass—no single object except our ship on which the eye might come to rest. Yet there were colors and sounds indeed, thousands of colors and thousands of sounds, being created every minute, every second, and colors and sounds such as the dry land had neither seen nor heard before. The blue canvas of the sea was spread out below, the silk of the heavens was stretched out above, and the day, with a golden paintbrush in hand, swept about in the air between them, painting and tinting, coloring and combining, without cessation. At night, from the blue-blind distance, something murmured, spoke, sounded.

What? None of us had the faintest idea, but strings quivered in each of our hearts, and in our heads it seemed as though songs were being sung, or stories told, or thin dreams were being woven and spun.

And the air was warm and soft, like oil.

Suddenly, one warm, golden morning, a thin, sharp, chill current from a place no one could identify swirled past on one side.

From the very first days of our voyage I had noticed two fellow passengers on board, a young couple.

She had a head of straw-blonde hair with a face not pretty, but warm, compassionate, intelligent and open, an average-sized, well-set figure with sturdy rounded shapes, and a somewhat mischievous smile on her lips. Everything about her bespoke a worldliness that was a little wanton, but was also healthy, full-blooded and human at the same time.

He was handsome, his features delicate and pale, his nose elongated, and his eyes sharp and far-seeing. His thin nervous fingers were continually on the move, tugging at his small dark mustache. He wore his overcoat unbuttoned and his shirt collar unfastened.

When they strolled across the deck, she clung to his arm; when they sat in a corner gazing out to sea, she nestled close to him, joyful sparks dancing in her eyes, the corners of her lips trembling with suppressed, vivacious, exuberant laughter. For his part, he took obvious pleasure in her open, playful little face and often whispered waggishly into her ear, whereupon she would desperately bite her lower lip, and finally burst into the kind of laughter that made all of us feel lighthearted.

In the evenings, it was their custom to sit for a long time in the stern of the ship on a thick rope coiled up in the shape of a bagel. Almost always, when the silken folds of night's cloak had settled over the sea, and undefined sounds merged and twirled about high above the ship, sometimes cracked and scattered, sometimes knotted and woven into a hushed but disciplined, passionate chorus, he would break into song, and his melodies trickled like water-drops, churned like torrents, chimed like bells. Those were strange songs! Wild and raw they leaped from the ship and cut far into the night. Sometimes they seemed to be drawn from anger and arrogant laughter; sometimes they caressed and tickled, like a mother making her infant laugh. The passengers were dumbstruck. One, a fat merchant who had an extraordinary passion for apples and ate them continuously when he was not asleep, would be frozen in his seat, a morsel of apple in his mouth, his eyes bulging in fright, seemingly at a loss about what to do with the bitten fruit in his hand. These songs made me feel uneasy: at one and the same time they were utterly alien yet heartwarmingly close.

Then the flaxen-haired young woman would fall silent, huddle into herself, grow smaller, and slowly withdraw a little from him, as her face registered loneliness and bewilderment. Once she cried out in anguish: "Oh, if only I could have at least one song of my own!"

All aflame, the sun burned in the sky, the air moved in gentle languor, like the breath of a sleeping child, yet at sea it grew colder and colder. One sensed that in the vicinity, somewhere very close, was *someone* whose approaching proximity excited hidden fear in everyone. In trepidation we all looked at the sea, at the sky, at one another, and again at the sea, waiting and trembling . . .

The graying passenger with the faraway look in his blue eyes recounted:

"For long consecutive months God showed his mighty hand in the distant north. With immense exertion the sea grappled with His cold iron fist as it bore down on its mighty breast. It threw itself about, turning and twisting and straining its unquiet bones and muscles with immense effort, and was frozen in its mighty striving, with ungainly, contorted and dissevered limbs, with deadly fear and the terrifying agony of death stamped upon its visage. Under the dead glare of the frozen sky, steep shattered mountains soared and bottomless valleys gaped on all sides of the world, while between them, furious winds whistled their devilish songs, smiting everything around with clouds of stabbing needles of snow. By night a fiery hand rose from the north, ascended to the zenith, overlaid half the sky with its fantastical sheen, and its giant digits moved silently and slowly, hovering like priestly fingers raised in benediction over the lifeless world. From time to time the winds and storms concealed themselves between the icebergs and fell dumb for a while, and then the silence was profound, fearfully profound, the air sharp and immobile, like stone, and only God, solitary in His proud loneliness, gazed out steadily at this desolate world.

Swiftly and frighteningly God had shown His hand over the distant north.

The solitary old polar bear, a powerful exemplar of his species, that had previously experienced something of God's wrath on his world, spent virtually the whole of that winter in his cave of snow and ice. With every passing day the strips of fat beneath his hide grew thinner and thinner. A heavy drowsiness numbed his limbs and filled his head with lead. Dimly he heard the wind and snow shrieking and moaning between the towering icebergs. Occasionally the blast reached a pitch of such piercing shrillness that the sleeping bear could no longer contain himself and subconsciously emitted a snorting roar, only to lose himself almost immediately in his near-drunken stupor. Finally he felt so weak that he could no longer even doze; his eyes opened of their own accord, and for a long time they stared dully through the opening of his cave at the enormous mounds of snow that had erupted all around, like the graves of giants. He cautiously raised his head, stirred one of his forepaws, began slowly to thrust forward, and crept out of his cave, threadbare and disheveled, a moving bag of bones.

Something was going on, but what he did not understand. It was bright—too bright. Winds gusted, somewhere something was cracking, and the ground underfoot shuddered. The bear understood little of all this and began blundering over the ice, scrabbling about here and there in the snow, seeking he knew not what. He found nothing, and when it grew dark, he dozed off again. When he awoke, it was broad daylight once more, and again he searched for something but, as previously, found nothing. This time he was angered, and for a long time roared at random into the air. By the second night, the cracking and juddering had intensified, everything around seemed to be vibrating and buckling, and the bear's sleep was greatly troubled. Toward daybreak, the uproar abated somewhat. The bear left the cave and set off in search of food, but having gone forward a short distance, he reached only water. Sniffing at it, he turned aside, and loped away for a considerable time only to reach water yet again. Many times he changed direction, but wherever he turned, he found only water. His cave was located at the foot of a towering mountain of snow up which the bear now clambered, rising up on his hind legs, confused and disturbed. From the summit he saw that his kingdom was tiny and encircled by expanses of blue water. Bare white icebergs, scintillating and stabbing against the sun, floated far in the distance. The bear had absolutely no comprehension of what this meant. He raised a paw and emitted a long, terrified, plaintive roar, hollow and smothered as though from an empty barrel.

For days and weeks the iceberg floated still further away, wandering from sea to sea, from waterway to waterway, and at every stage it steadily and inescapably neared its own death. More than once it lost its balance and overturned, exposing deep, gaping wounds in its gigantic body. The snow had long melted from its bulk. Now it consisted of pure, clear, translucent ice, in some places rinsed and rounded, in others peaked and razor-sharp. It moved forward, its cold breath preceding it and announcing its coming. It moved forward, and mutely related what a fearful winter had passed in the distant north, how heavily the sea had been battered, and how lonely God was in those distant places.

All were on deck. All clustered together, turning their strained gazes toward the sea on which they could as yet discern nothing. From a distance I saw my young couple and moved closer to them. He stood in his unbuttoned overcoat with his open shirt collar, very pale, paler than normal. She—next to him. Over her shoulders lay a warm shawl and on her narrow brow hovered a cloud, like a premonition of something evil settling on her head. He looked out at the sea. She looked at him.

To the right of the horizon, a glowing golden streak suddenly thrust itself out of the water; a gleaming sword pierced the sky, overturned, and was abruptly extinguished. Several seconds passed. The crowd on the ship did not draw breath. Then once more there was coruscation in the distance. This time a sharp spear was flung upward and shortly thereafter a second, and then a third. A moment later the entire iceberg, lambently aflame, was etched sharply on the sea. The sun attacked it furiously, shooting it through and through with long, thin, incandescent arrows. Plucking the arrows from its wounds, the iceberg flung them, now frozen though still gleaming, back into the sun's face. Silently and bitterly this battle for life and death raged. Rotating slowly and displaying all its floating ordnance, the mountain moved onward to its death in the cold, proud, radiant friendlessness in which it had been born in the distant north.

It floated past on one side and gradually began to disappear. And then my glance fell once again on the young couple. She stood alone with outstretched arms and trembling lips, looking up at him with tearful eyes. He stood not far from her, avidly turning his own wide-open, sparkling gaze from the distantly disappearing ice-mountain to the close, homely face of his beloved.

LODESTAR

It seemed to me that years had passed since we had taken leave of the shore. Our ship continued to sail ever onward, seemingly with a purpose as nonexistent as the trail it left behind. At noon each day a placard was put up that showed how far we had traveled and how far we had still to go, but little by little we lost interest in that announcement. All around was water and more water, water, water everywhere, day in and day out, and it was easier to think that our ship was rotating around itself, going no further and making no more progress than a clock. Dull folk, irked by this tedium, drank beer and vehemently cursed the endless voyage. Even the weather set in: there was no storm, no fog, only unvarying bright days, blue nights, and fresh breezes.

Only now did we start to feel that we were beginning to know the sea. At the very moment we registered this anomaly, eternity winked at us, and a suspicion awoke among us that the sea had been like this, exactly like this, thousands and millions of years before, day after day, year after year, century after century. Sadness filled our hearts, and none among us was certain of its cause: the eternity of the sea or the brevity of our lives.

I do not know how the children of other nations dream of the sea. Possibly they dream of frightening spirits, sea serpents or mermaids— those full-bodied females from whom may God protect every faithful believer. Between ourselves, they are all wholly innocent creatures. In the worst case, one might expect them sometimes to carry off to their crystal palaces on the seabed some handsome blond fisherman with a weakness for the siren-song of women, while his young wife, sitting at the spinning wheel and looking out for her heart's beloved, weeps her eyes out for the pity of it. For my own part, I keep remembering that axe which fell into the sea thousands of years before the time of Rabbah bar Bar Hana, and which even in his day had not yet touched the bottom. Very likely it has not done so even in our own time, and when I imagine that axe still plummeting ever downward and never coming to ground, I shudder.

Happy is the man of learning! Firstly, he knows everything, and secondly he knows what the sea is. The sea is water. Water and nothing else. Had we a beaker holding so many and so many cubic centiliters of water, we could replicate an ocean. I, however, am no learned man, so I still dream that when the Master of the Universe is left all alone, face to face with His great creation, when no single human eye, let alone the eye of a man of learning, roves over the vast expanses of water, then He, if it were possible, loses heart at what He himself has created. And in this way, Creator and created each stare at the other, and both are silent, and the sound of their silence stretches from one end of the universe to the other, enduring until one stronger than either of them arrives: the man of learning with his vessel of so many and so many centiliters' capacity.

And so once more, as with so many other times, night fell, and the sea shimmered under the gleam of the stars.

In a corner on the ship's upper deck I noticed my neighbor, the passenger with the broad shoulders, graying hair and blue eyes. He was lying on a sail spread out over the deck, gazing up into the sky. Lying down next to him, I noticed a smile on his face. In response to my question, he held his peace for a while, and then answered nonchalantly:

—If you wish, I'll tell you.

". . . The sharp, glaring light finally drained from the earth. In places, somewhere on the peak of a mountain or in the shaggy head of a tree, a weak, reddish sheen lingered, but little by little it darkened, extinguished itself and was seemingly sucked into the air. The sempiternity drew closer and silently gathered the earth into her lap. That moment was born when people say: the night has come.

In reality, nothing has come; something has simply gone. The eye-searing sun with its fanfare of rays and tumult of colors deafens and blinds the earth, concealing this endlessness from her. In the glare of daylight, every earthly trifle shambles boldly forward, leaps full into your face with the insolence of a boor, and makes you think that some kind of bane is dancing before your eyes, making your heart beat faster, dragging you by the lapels, while an importunate voice rasps oaths and threats in your ear: 'I . . . do you hear? . . . As you see me alive! . . . I . . . let yourself worship! . . .' With the greatest exertion the mind pursues something ostensibly very important, very close by, something that is the core of the matter yet which slips away every time, driven off by the flash and flurry all around. Like an unexpected storm the day pours down on the earth, forcing its way through, maddening and confusing it—then fades away. Then from all corners of the world shadows fly to-gether, dark noiseless shadows that blanket the earth ever more thickly. The trolls and goblins of the day evaporate and the earth slowly revives and recovers her normal state, taking her place in the universe, in the blue endlessness. And people say: the night has come.

Once more—for which of how many times?—the stars strode into the heavens and betook themselves to their tasks: to behold, simply to behold. Some gazed straight down on the earth as though it were truly the midpoint of the world; others looked one at another; and the third lay far, far away, yonder, where neither your eye nor mine will ever reach, where the solitude is at its most intense, and where all is more disparate than you can imagine. Only one star had the capacity to send its glances everywhere at one and the same time: to the earth, to its brother stars, and also far yonder where neither your eye nor mine will ever reach. And this was 'Lodestar.'

Its name derived from its pure, pale-green countenance. Not one of the biggest, nor one of the smallest. None of this star's brothers pos-sessed so profound a glance, one that seemed to say: 'I've seen a fine number of things since I've been gazing down from here!' It had looked down when the earth had not yet come into being, had gazed on when the earth was brought into existence, and had seen the manner of the earth's creation. It had watched when on earth there was as yet nothing to see nor yet anyone to do the seeing. Its green gaze had blended into the fire of the newly born planet, had later shattered into millions of sparks on the immense ice plains of the earth's cooling crust, had for one millennium after another followed all the transformations the earth had undergone before life appeared on it, as also when that life manifested itself and began to evolve. And when the first human being on his first night on the earth lifted up his eyes to the heavens, he met the profound glance of a star as ancient as time. He was left shocked and astounded. Through that glance the star related what it had seen on the earth, before the earth, and beyond the earth.

That first glance seared the soul of man, kindling a fire within him, a sharp longing for that place yonder where the solitude is at its most intense and where all is very, very different. A wild, raw, yet harmonious cry tore from man's breast. Lodestar's glance had reconciled the sacred with the profane: mankind's cry was transformed into a hymn destined to fall silent and to vanish from the earth only with man himself.

Thus did Lodestar's beaming glance accompany man while he built his life on earth. Courageous sea-voyagers, steering their ships over the deep waters, sought and found their direction with the help of the stars in general and of Lodestar in particular. Those in love sent their sighs and the fragrance of their youth to it; poets offered it every tremor of their souls in tones, colors and lines. The star absorbed all of this into itself, returning it to succeeding generations, so that for every new generation, the content of its glance grew richer and deeper. Numerous star-gazers from many generations spent their nights staring at Lodestar through their lenses, studying its past, present and future. They discovered wondrous things: it was the biggest of all the stars and the one furthest from the earth. This they proved arithmetically with the help of a long series of complicated calculations. They computed its weight, its size, its orbit in the universe, the dust of which it was composed and its distance from Earth. This last computation was the most wonderful of all: the star was as far off as the time it took for its beam to reach the Earth: 9,347,657,000 years, 52 days, 18 hours, 49 minutes and 22 1/2 seconds. This is what the learned proved, and ordinary mortals were agape at their wisdom and at God's wonders.

And thus, on the evening I am now telling you about, in a country, in a city, in a garden, on a bench, a young man was sitting with a beautiful young woman gazing at Lodestar. And everyone knew—and why shouldn't we know as well?—what it means when a young man and a young woman gaze at Lodestar. They had only just met that very evening, and had spoken about clothes and books, about God and the world, and after they had spoken about all this, they had fallen silent. Now they felt heavyhearted and their eyes strayed to Lodestar, and for a long time, in silence, they drank in its profound, green-golden glance.

Suddenly the young man rubbed his eyes, transferred his gaze to the young woman, and then back to the sky. The young woman rubbed her eyes and glanced at the young man and then back at the sky. Thereupon they both rose from the bench amazed and a little frightened.

Before their eyes, Lodestar had suddenly disappeared. It had extinguished itself, like a candle.

When the young man and woman parted at the door of her dwelling, she yawned, thinking that when he spoke spittle sprayed from his mouth, and in his heart the young man blasphemed against God because in the very front of her mouth she was missing an upper tooth.

The next morning the disappearance of Lodestar was reported in newspapers throughout the world, whereupon the learned took the matter in hand.

The first hypothesis enunciated by a famous person asserted that Lodestar had died a natural death. It had cooled over and been extinguished, 'just as the sun of our solar system will one day be extinguished.' Afterward the world was privileged to witness with what venom and keen intellect a colleague from another country, also famous, exposed the former's ignorance: even a child could understand that a natural death did not occur so abruptly. If there were even the shadow of probability in this conjecture, one would long before have been obliged to notice that Lodestar was growing dimmer and dimmer. In conclusion, this colleague put forward his own hypothesis: there had been a massive catastrophe in the firmament, the collision of two solar systems, and as a consequence, the destruction of one, or of both.

A third scientist then came forward to wonder how it was possible not to understand what was as clear as daylight: that such a catastrophe would have set off a chain reaction in the heavens: falling stars, wandering comets, exploded and scattered pieces of the destroyed worlds. No. The matter must and could be scientifically explained in quite another way.

The issue grew ever more problematical and complex. It became apparent that the basic principles of certain scientific theories were questionable, and their various opponents and supporters joined battle with girded loins. The dispute steadily grew wholly tangential to Lodestar. In truth, to the man in the street who knew little about science, the matter was somewhat distasteful, for as it is written, 'His dead lay unburied before him' and mankind's bereavement should have been respected. Arguing over the corpse of one that had taken and given so much caused genuine emotional pain. But there are certainly other stars, no less old, no less honorable, and, I mean—what can one do?

People began to forget.

Let us assume that somewhere in a medium-sized provincial town there might be a student who had gone off the rails from the start: that's to say, he didn't study, he played tricks on the teacher, drank beer like a German and persecuted the female students with what were, by their own admission, unwelcome attentions. One night this young man was staggering along the road, gesticulating and talking to himself, articulating in fine, high-flown language the protests of a wounded heart against the cruel barmaid in the little tavern he had only just left. Suddenly, God knows how, he called to mind Lodestar, its unexpected end, its long, rich career, its size, its great distance from the earth: '9,347,657,000 years, 52 days, 18 hours, 49 minutes and 22 $\frac{1}{2}$ seconds!' he murmured to himself with rapture and tender affection, although I imagine that in his drunken mind the figures came out somewhat muddled. 'More than nine million years used to pass before its rays reached the earth . . . nine million . . . a ray . . . nine mil— . . .' The student suddenly stopped dead in the middle of the road. In one moment he had sobered up, and despite the fact that his body was shivering from the cold, he wiped sweat from his brow. Running over to a street lamp, he snatched out a notebook and pencil and began to write, his hands trembling feverishly.

The next day in the town newspaper there appeared in bold type a short comment, printed in place of a leading article:

'Science is currently deeply preoccupied with explaining the cause of Lodestar's disappearance from our skies. We wish to call the public's attention to another aspect of this earth-shattering event. The same scientific inquiry has calculated and proved that en route to the earth, the rays of Lodestar spent 9,347,657,000 years, 52 days, 18 hours, 49 minutes and 22 $^1/_2$ seconds. This means that its last ray left the star more than nine million years ago. In other words, Lodestar has been dead for more than nine million years, long before human beings appeared on the earth, quite possibly long before the earth itself even existed. That means, further . . . but the further implications of this fact are already quite obvious to everyone . . . '

This observation flew round the whole world.

In that year many accidents occurred at sea.

One captain, steering his ship by the light of the starry sky, suddenly clutched his head and stared up at the peaceful, shimmering stars with distrust and hidden fear. He began to give a variety of contradictory orders to the crew who were standing at the helm. To this day, what became of that vessel is unknown. Another captain made the same grimaces, and in disgust smashed and then hurled away his ship's compass. Such or similar things befell many captains of various ships on all the seas. In the end, some ships ran onto the rocks, others were involved in collisions, and some simply disappeared forever.

In that year there were no weddings—none, not a single one. As long as young men and women sat about chatting in the evenings, they were occupied. No sooner had they fallen silent, however, and as their custom was, had raised their eyes to the stars, than they were abruptly confronted with a vision of horror. It seemed to them that the dead eye sockets of long-drowned corpses were staring at them, that yellow teeth were gibbering and grinning and cackling with skeletal laughter.

Of the thousand million and more people living on the earth, 347 of them reacted to this event as to their own personal injury. And what exactly did they do? They went off and took their own lives. Ninety-nine of them shot themselves, 68 took poison, 54 hanged themselves and the rest chose other modes of violent deaths. All left behind letters, written more or less in a literary style, in which appeared the words 'Schopenhauer' and 'Lodestar,' not always logically juxtaposed, and almost all of these missives closed with a warm, friendly piece of advice to the whole world to follow them along the same road. As a result, no one in that year committed suicide for such conventional reasons as unhappy love affairs, gambling or bankruptcy, so that to everyone's astonishment, the number of suicides that year was conspicuously smaller than usual.

The stars gave light as before, but the people—the people blundered over the earth lost, confused, like sheep in a conflagration . . ."

My neighbor had been silent for a long time. The ship beneath us rocked gently as we lay gazing at the stars. Vague thoughts bumbled about in my head.

Only on the bright morning of the next day did I ask my neighbor about the end of the story. He laughed.

Ah, you've taken it seriously! he replied teasingly. Naturally, science triumphed. "Quite possibly," the learned explained, "we are living under the glow of dead, long-extinguished worlds. It is possible that the first person on earth was already being guided by the light of a corpse. But living or dead there are quite enough stars to serve us for all practical purposes. A ship can be steered merely with the aid of a compass, let alone by the stars, and as regards love—what need is there of stars for love? Hee-hee!!" Since people were eager to convince themselves, they did.

In truth, sometimes even today the captain of a ship, his entire being unexpectedly sensing the sea—the sea!—all around and beneath him and the distant shining worlds above his head, loses himself for a while. It also happens that a lover catches sight of a blackened tooth in his beloved's mouth. There have also been cases of suicide for which it has been impossible to discover any logical reason. But the captain reminds himself that he must bring his merchandise to port on schedule, the lover makes haste to achieve his goal, and the suicide is forgotten.

In short, the old student is still a student. He drinks as much as or more than before. The young women who encounter him squeal, though not sooner than necessary. The barmaid has mellowed. And sometimes, when our student returns home from the tavern at night and is overcome with maudlin emotion, he stops opposite a lamppost, from which the swollen red eye of a smoky kerosene lamp glares back at him, theatrically spreads his arms, and in a heartrending voice exclaims:

—O Lodestar, Lodestar!

THE SCENT OF LAND

A pale good-natured visage floated into the sky and a pale glow flooded over the sea.

Good evening, my quiet, dreamy Fairy! You are still the only one capable of liberating a light sigh from my oppressed heart. Much water has flowed since that time. Remember? Since then I have become much "cleverer," less "sentimental." Life, which has estranged me from laughter, has taught me to mock. But here in the middle of the wide ocean, between ourselves, when no one can see or hear us—you follow? I want shyly to confide a secret to you: all this is nothing more than my father's long coat which I, a child, have donned in order to look like a father. Yet the coat trips me up and embitters my life. And the spectacles you see—what for? It's said that spectacles are better than eyes, so I obey. But in reality I'm the same child you once knew. I would willingly weep when I'm slapped, I would willingly wince when my heart trembles, and when life grows too ugly to endure, then I sigh, looking at you, and I feel easier. I greet you from the depths of my heart.

Have you now come from that dry land I've long abandoned? What have you seen there? You once used to tell wonderful stories, so tell.

She smiles quietly and sadly.

I have seen—

In a little room, in a cot next to a bed on which the young mother is sleeping, a little child lies crying. The mother does not hear.

The tiny lips are wide open, averted and contorted. The tear-filled eyes stare in deep, dumb terror at the greenish stripe I have drawn over the wall opposite. In life's troubled moments, the child is accustomed to the sight of a pretty, loving head with two cheerful warm eyes bent over the cot. Now it does not see them, and the weak little voice howls its distress for a long, long time, as though it will never stop.

Are you enough of a child to feel its loneliness?

I have seen—

A young couple strolls slowly along a quiet, secluded avenue that I have bewitched. Hand in hand they walk: he gnawing his lower lip, she unable to control a trembling corner of her upper lip. They do not look at each other and are silent. They have only just quarreled and already their hearts are drawn to each other, but neither wants to be the first to make up, though the silence brings no benefit to either. I leave them quietly, knowing that two hands will find each other in the dark with no more difficulty than in the light.

Are you young enough to remember how sweet such sorrow is?

And hear—

I come from the land you are leaving, from the shtetl where you dwelt, from among the people to whom you were born. There I glanced into the window of a poor room and I saw—

In the middle of the night a weak old man with a long white beard has left his bed, and half naked he stands stooped over a second bed on which his beautiful daughter is sleeping restlessly. The girl's cheeks glow fiercely, her hair is tousled, periodically her breast heaves and gasps feverishly. Every so often a nervous tremor convulses her entire body. She sees troubling, hateful dreams, but the old man has no heart to waken her to the even more hateful reality. In the darkness of the night he stands looking down at his pure flower on which a coarse, brutish hand has left a filthy blemish, and his knees buckle under him, his old head shakes in helpless senility, and his lips move silently, distorting themselves in such childish bitterness that the heavy curtain of burdensome years suddenly falls from one's eyes and one sees distinctly that selfsame child that cries so forlornly in the silence of the night, but a thousand times more desolate and powerless.

Are you old enough to understand this old man's grief?

Oh, let it be! These are all tales and fables, I think! Such things as never were or could be! Do you understand?

In mortification the Fairy hides herself beneath a pale cloud.

The moon rose above the ship, overtook us, and glided off toward that country to which we were sailing.

Greet in my name those who are waiting for me, as also those who are *not* waiting, who do not yet know me, and whom I do not know of, yet with whom my ways will nevertheless intersect and weave together, who knows how closely.

A quiet murmur rises from all sides.

It seems to me that gathered together here are all the nights that have lived and died on the lap of the sea, that they are standing in circles, in groups, listening to one another, conducting a conversation, restrained, muted, but in haste and agitation. What do they want? What do they want?

Suddenly, quite suddenly, as though cut off, everything fell silent. What had happened? Difficult to say. Possibly—from somewhere far away, on the shore, the unexpected crow of a cock shot up, as from a rifle, and its velocity carried it out here to the sea. It was a strange morning cry that made one imagine some kind of curtain had swiftly risen with a silken rustle: here, look.

A strong, warm breeze sprang up to meet us, split itself against the prow of our ship and began gusting evenly and ceaselessly against its sides. Steadily the sea heaved into motion. Small waves rose up, breaking against one another with a thin, glassy tinkle and leaving behind them a trembling echo. A soft, liquid song rose from the sea, ascended higher and higher, flooded our ship and swallowed up the roar of the propeller. Bright, distant worlds looked down from the bleached sky, and their green-golden luster mingled with the song of the sea.

"When the morning stars sang together."

And involuntarily I added my own voice to the heavenly chorus, the tremulous voice of a human being at sea.

A human being on the sea! . . .

In the morning the sun burned brightly. White seabirds appeared and encircled the ship. A hubbub filled the deck. The restless business spirit of land hovered in the air and the crowd prepared to disembark. The enchantment of the sea disintegrated like gossamer.

A yellowish, sandy strip of land stretched out to starboard, ran forward, turned back, straightened itself, and finally embraced us on three sides. The new world pressed itself upon us. The impatience and restlessness grew. What's it like over there? Is everything the same? Everything the same? Everything the same? . . .

A gigantic female figure, its hand upraised, appeared to larboard. The Statue of Liberty's gaze was tensely directed toward the city, so near but yet so far. Situated a little further up in the bay, Ellis Island with its Castle Garden bared its teeth angrily in our direction: Don't move! Stay where you are!

Sea, oh sea, on *your* surface human beings ought to have been born. Sea, my sea—I shall still return to you!

1910 (translated by Joseph Sherman)

♦ ♦ ♦ *The Chair*

"Bedbugs also have a right to life," declared one of Mendele Moykher Sforim's characters. But Jake Bereza disagreed.

1

At twilight the airplane flew over Union Square, its red banner proclaiming to the world: "Children Cry for Castoria!" In equally fiery letters the Amalgamated Bank trumpeted to the world her mission and tidings: "4-$\frac{1}{2}$%!" The crosstown 14th Street trolley rumbled from west to east and cut loose a hoarse rasp. From a window over Child's Restaurant someone whooped into the street below, "You won't put that over on me! I hate smart-alecks!" Under the bridge, the express subway thundered and shook the bowels of the earth like a sharp earthquake.

A gramophone emptied into the street the lamentation of a baritone accompanied by a guitar:

I ask her—which way uptown?
She answers—she lives next door . . .
Ta-ra-ta-ta-tam—tarita—tat-am—
Tarita—tarita—taratam!

This was Union Square.

2

On the eastern side of the Square, near the "leftist" cafeteria, a small crowd was gathering, and a cop bore down on it, feigning benevolence and courtesy, but brandishing his short, thick, nightstick. The city had been rocked by demonstrations, and the police had not hesitated to wield their clubs, often brutally. No one was certain what action Governor Fuller of Massachusetts might take at the last minute. All day the newspapers had been hewing and crying: "RIOTS IN BUENOS AIRES," "POLICE FIRE ON DEMONSTRATORS IN PARIS," "MOSCOW AFLAME WITH RED BANNERS," "BOMBS EXPLODE AT THE AMERICAN CONSULATE IN BARCELONA." Night on the 22nd of August, 1927, was falling. It was the night of Sacco and Vanzetti.

3

The cop had elbowed his way into the crowd, rocking from side to side, his broad shoulders battering open a path for him. Seeing two other cops approaching, he ordered no one in particular: "Break it up. Move on. You're blocking traffic. Come o-on!" A pedestrian turned sharply, browless, bloodshot simmering eyes on him and snarled, "Don't p-pushh!"

"The Law" instantly lost his composure and hurled himself at the bloodshot eye, but Jake ducked under the flailing elbows and reappeared at the door of the cafeteria. The cop gave chase, but Jake flung open the door and scooted inside. The cop appraised the situation and turned away.

4

Eyebrows are not necessary for life. But when the cheeks under the browless eyes begin to twitch, it is vexing. And if in his vitals a hellish resentment smolders, and he is unable to pinpoint exactly against whom his wrath is directed—it is very, very galling.

And Jake is constantly vexing his vexations. Whatever he is counseled, he is tempted to answer, "No matter," and regardless of what he is offered, his immediate reaction is rejection. In the factory he is at odds with everyone, but here in the cafeteria, for some reason, he is shielded by a great deal of patience. He is considered somewhat crazy. This is their perception of him, Jake Bereza, the fur salesman: yes, he quarrels with the "lefties," but he also hangs out with them. He had, for example, voted against the strike of the furriers, but then participated, being beaten by the police during the riot near the Forward building. Even now he is an ardent backer of the union, despite being locked out for his support.

Jake surveyed the cafeteria. Who should he hook up with? Jake was still worked up about the cop: a smooth-faced, idiotically young "non-Kosher" and shady faced Irish pagan! Although at the moment he would have been able to vent his rage at anyone.

The cafeteria was packed, mostly with laborers, but also with a sprinkling of intellectuals, writers, artists, and newspaper men, who as always, were sounding the "pulse of the public." Primarily Jews, but also Russians, Ukrainians, Italians, Negroes, and even one—the only authentic American—a genuine Yankee, Jeremiah Wilson, a longshoreman and a sailor on a shoreline-hugging ship that plied the waters north of New York to Cape Cod and beyond. At the table where Wilson took his meals, Jake found his element, the brotherhood he loved to badger.

5

At the table:

Jeremiah Wilson, the bony sort, with long arms and long feet. By nature, quiet. A pensive man, a bit astonished at the outlandish, astonishing life that swarms and teems around him. The jolly type, although to him the "foreigners" are—oh, just a hair!—"strange"—odd, that is, and their attitude to him is a shade—or a drop!—flattering, subtle and restrained, and cautious. Both sides would have been reluctant to acknowledge these feelings, which they wanted to overcome but were unable to.

Pete Molovan, a Bessarabian peasant, who fled shortly after the Romanian occupation because of some sort of conflict with the new authority. Here in New York he works in a warehouse on a dock along the East River. Pete hates the East River. To him it is less a river than a dark, foul slop for ships and barges, which marks the grimy border between Brooklyn and Manhattan. The river just lies there in suspended animation, not seeming to go anywhere. It rarely speaks, and never, it seems, raises its voice. Now and then, someone throws himself head first from a bridge. The East River swallows him with a crisp gulp—and it's over, since this is a river without passion and without joy in life. This river is devoted to business. Can you compare it in any way to the Dnieper, or even the Bug? From time to time Pete throws a sidelong peek at the river, with a contempt as expressive as a spit in the face.

The Ukrainian maiden Nastia, Pete's bride, who is the Jewish family Fish's domestic in the Bronx. Nastia now speaks English, is called Nettie, wears high-button shoes and sports a boyish "bob." Her cheeks are no longer doughy, but milk-white and firm. Her eyes are still wide and enticing, although on occasion they sparkle devilishly, and then she turns beautiful. Here in the cafeteria she sits, silent but attentive to her own interests. It seems she harbors unusual notions, this Nettie. She herself does not know how she has come to be here—does she belong, or not?

The coal miner Luke, a Negro, whose father for years had wandered the southern states spreading "God's Word" among his brethren, baptized countless numbers in the waters of the Mississippi, and lived in unbelievable need. Nevertheless, despite his fiery faith, he had no influence on his son Luke, whom he had named after the Apostle. Luke instead was drawn to the movement of Marcus Garvey, who had expressed the wish to lead the Negroes out of America and into Africa, "as God had led the Israelites out of Egypt." After the movement had self-destructed with scandals and corruption around the transatlantic voyages, Luke took to wandering from city to city and from job to job. In the coal mines of Pennsylvania, he became a Communist. But in him there remained a certain lingering qualm about the brotherhood of the whites and the Negroes. As a legacy from his father, from time to time he would slip into a vocabulary somewhat flowery and biblical, and then he would lapse into "brother" rather than "comrade," while quoting citations which he had made up at that very moment.

6

Comrade Yossl, the representative of The Industrial Union of Foodstuff Employees, approached the table, a piece of paper in hand, his face glowing. "Here," he said, "read this," and passed the page to Wilson. It was a proclamation of the Communist Party to the workers of America to energize their support in the struggle to secure the freedom of Sacco and Vanzetti. Only an avalanche of protest had a chance of forcing the Governor of Massachusetts to spare their lives. The proclamation ended with Sacco's words about Vanzetti, addressed to Judge Thayer: "Sacco's name will live in the hearts of men and in their gratitude . . . when the wind will have long blown away the dust of your bones, when your names, your laws, your institutions and your false Gods will remain only distant memories of a shameful past when one man was a wolf to another."

Wilson read the proclamation aloud, and his voice vibrated, sharp and dry, occasionally breaking. It was obvious that the prophetic pathos of the final words stirred his blood like torrid and dynamic music.

Jake Bereza had turned despondent. Bitterly, he said, "Not our business. Better to make sure workers aren't lured into 'their' unions. Two Italian anarchists, what do they have to do with us?" Jake had spoken in Yiddish.

"What did he say?" Jeremiah Wilson demanded. Comrade Yossl translated. "He says that we don't have to defend the two Italians. In his opinion, that's the obligation of the bourgeois radicals."

"Not true, brother Jake," horned in the Negro Luke. "You're lost in the confusion of the ungodly. It's written, 'Workers of the whole world, unite!' I'm asking you, is that written or not?"

His naive paraphrase of the slogan, which laid bare his innermost feelings, embarrassed the bystanders: they couldn't ignore his challenge, or answer it.

Stubbornly Jake muttered, "Are we supposed to run down every misstep of 'their' world? Look for fleas in every mangy dog?"

"M-m no," Wilson said reflectively, shaking his head. "When they say, 'Not your business,' they're telling us, 'You can go to hell.' But it is our business. And if a few of the straight shooters among the bourgeoisie want to help, why shut the door in their face?"

7

But Jake was no longer listening. Restlessly, his eyes ranged over the large sweep of the room, his ears picking up a voice at the neighboring table. The tone alone incited him: languid, self-satisfied, and content with itself and the world.

"And I'm telling you, 'they' had no right to raise such a ruckus. They should have stayed out of it." Thus spoke Jacob Lapidus, a columnist for the *Day* newspaper, his scribblings as a rule dripping with the "wisdom of the ages." For example, "As concerns the dead—either praise or nothing." In conversation he displays his wit with, "What more can one do?" or "I have the honor of—" Opposite him sat Yalkut, a middle-aged man with a red birthmark on his cheek, the remains of a lock over his ears, and around his bald head a curious loop of hair, resembling the forage headpiece of the Zaporozhe Cossacks. His expression was weary and tense, which usually accompanies Weltschmerz and a sour stomach. At the same table, Izzy Fishler of the United Charitable Organizations, lanky, thin, gnarled like a slice of stale bread, and Jonah Margolis, head shaved to the gray skin, with macabre, protruding and invariably red ears, and with a drunk's addled eyes because he was constantly humming the first line of a lyric bubbling in his mind without being able to pin down what followed.

Sarcastically, Izzy Fishler said to Lapidus, "And who are 'they'? Do you mean the Communists? Oh sure . . . rely on you? The anarchists should become your cause?"

"What do you mean, mine? American liberalism. By now the influential American liberals would have won the battle, if not for their wild, uncontrolled agitation, which has offended American public opinion. As soon as the 'Reds' find their way into a mix, the average American chokes. We have to fight it out on the basis of justice, along with the uncorrupted American freedom-loving institutions, and not stir up the mob. Mark my word—the two poor devils will be finished off. And what makes you think that will break the anarchists' heart? They're only looking for a reason to attack the existing order, and casualties won't slow them down. It's simple—they're political rabble of the worst sort."

Suddenly, a face with one frayed eyebrow popped into view. "Okay . . . granted," the face said. "But they're our politicians. What do you want us to do? Not pay attention to yours?"

And the face melted away.

Lapidus was stunned. Yalkut studied Jake carefully, mute and eager, the creases rippling his forehead, showing that he was deep in thought. Finally, he said, "Listen to me. Recently I happened to hear several storekeepers on Burnside Avenue complaining that they 'can't earn a nickel.' And when I asked them what were the conditions of their clerks, did they make a living, they answered naively, 'We're not talking about clerks. Their problems are for them to solve.' Get it? Trying not to look like smart-alecks, the storekeepers sat themselves down in the same boat as their employees. And this fellow here talks about our politicians . . . That is the same—"

After a moment, Yalkut added thoughtfully, "I've come to understand several simple things clearly, which actually are really not that simple, but which fall in place into a large picture, even though on the face of it they're far removed and contradictory. Still, I can't seem to warm up to self-instruction. So where does guilt lie, with the Torah or with the student?"

Lapidus shrugged. Impatiently, Jonah Margolis turned away; the formulation annoyed him.

8

At the door of the cafeteria, Mrs. Fish of the Bronx loomed. She smiled a greeting across the room at her maid Nettie. Pete Moldovan smoldered, resenting any closeness between Nettie and her bourgeois boss. Mrs. Fish did not approach their table, but summoned Jonah Margolis with a crook of her finger. He rose, obviously unwillingly.

She said, "Would you like to come with me to a meeting of a few women of the committee?"

Margolis frowned, "No, I'm not in the mood."

Glaring at his large, protruding ears, Tillie Fish, in her rage, was tempted to wring them, or worse.

The ways of the female soul are veiled; that is to say, not exactly veiled, but inscrutable, like the Bronx streets, which will lead you to who knows where if you follow them in a straight line. The slight Tillie Fish, homely but clever, had met the poet at some gathering, and that same night he accompanied her home, embraced her and tried to plant a kiss. She refused. He persisted. She held her ground. What could she do? As fate would have it, she had chosen today to give in to another temptation, and before leaving the house had nibbled away a few layers of an onion. No matter what she'd tried, she could not get rid of the odor. There was no way she would let him get a whiff of that stench! Offended at her frigidity, Margolis bid her an irksome good-bye. Tillie took it in stride; he'd get over it. Come to think of it, it was better that way—let it not be too easy for him.

But Margolis did not get over it. She ran across him often, but he was cold and kept his distance. Tillie was disturbed and even lost some sleep. Something was topsy-turvy. She was in high spirits when someone lost sleep over her. She never expected too much from a man—beyond his losing sleep over her. But this—what a miscarriage!

Tillie took stock. Tillie always took stock. She came to a conclusion, and organized a committee of women to push Margolis's books. With this, Margolis became slightly more friendly, but that was all. Tillie was burning to have Margolis at her feet, but as he refused to submit, she eventually found herself in the predicament of longing to throw herself at his feet. And even his protruding ears—no, nothing more than his protruding ears—now caused her heart to skip a beat.

"So that means, you'd rather not?" Tillie had said.

"No. You know what kind of day this is? Nothing interests me. You know what? Let's take a walk on Broadway and take in what's going on."

Tillie's eyes blazed. "Oh, I'd love that!"

9

Jake Bereza, a restless soul, invariably agitated, had never been as inflamed as tonight. What, even if this were a black year, are they all babbling about this evening? And why, even if this were the blackest of years, is it irritating him so much? Why should he saddle himself with the two Italian clods, who had stumbled into the web of the Capitalist spider? Was he to take them for a pair of prodigies? Listen to this bit of wisdom: "When men were wolves to men!" Wolves? "Men are bedbugs to men and they suck blood—drop after drop—because each has to suck out his share. From time to time he's a wolf—a bloodthirsty, savage wolf, who simply enjoys other people's woes. That is a p-p-p-pro-problem! Oh, these ponderous words! But a bedbug, it drains, and drains and drains—it's clear—to stay alive. So how can it change? Oh, my head!"

He went out into the street.

At about eleven in the evening, the press of the crowds in the streets was so great that the police became skittish, and to a man stopped functioning. But the crowd was not rowdy or behaving badly, a bit tense, but certainly not explosive. In Union Square they waited, silent as posts, expectant. Expecting what? They expected something—they thought—from Governor Fuller of Massachusetts—himself a "liberal"—at the helm—the fate of Sacco and Vanzetti resting in the hands of one man. If he wished he could acquit, and just as easily, he might not. But how is it possible that he wouldn't? It seems that the country—the world—wants him to. The spirits of these two hovered over the continents, and certainly that meant something! Sacco-Vanzetti. Two names in one, but two different paths. Vanzetti is exalted by the slogan, "A good cobbler but a bad fishmonger." He speaks for both, Vanzetti. And Sacco—he is silent for both. The rock. To Jake it occurred that there were methods, and strains of silence. You can be silent and under the lash of a whip . . . or the restraint of a yoke.

10

From somewhere, a clock tower struck twelve.

They all heard it. Union Square was silent. A few streetcars rattled and clanged but finally were forced to come to a stop; there was no way to cut through the jammed square. Noon, and still no word from Governor Fuller. That means . . . that indicates . . . suggests . . .

A shudder, hidden and undisclosed to human eyes, raced across the telephone wires of the world: "The dam has burst." It was silently noted in the editorial offices of the newspapers, but the public in the streets and squares could only guess. Yalkut felt the hair stiffen on the nape of his neck. Beside him at the door of the cafeteria, the tall figure of Jeremiah Wilson loomed, remarkably long-limbed. The Negro Luke broke out into a cold, clammy sweat, in spite of the sweltering evening. Jake Bereza had vanished.

In the village of Charlestown, near Boston, workers erected a structure by hand—to what purpose? Why had they laid brick upon brick, patiently and carefully. And in that building, in view of the entire world, there was a process, now, of exterminating two live, simple souls . . . who draw breath . . . who sense . . . who dream . . .

Five after twelve—

Ten after twelve—

A quarter after twelve—

Eighteen after twelve. A megaphone blared overhead, from the window of the "left center," restrained and toneless:

"Sacco . . . Vanzetti . . . dead . . ."

A moment of silence. The throng hushed, as if a thousand throats had been strangled.

Then the megaphone, in the same dry, weary tone, added an afterthought:

"Sacco . . . remained . . . calm . . . eleven minutes."

Abruptly, the concrete details loosened the crowd. Later, no one was in a position to render a clear account of what took place in Union Square. A chaos of hands, fists, heads, feet and limbs. A throaty rumble as from a waterfall. From the northwest direction of Times Square, echoes of gunfire. In a corner of Union Square, Luke rocked on a subway grate, arms raised high above his head, muttering malediction and anathema, condemnations of his father's, on sinners; "The curse of God, the God of Abraham, Isaac and Jacob, shall fall upon your heads, and shall His wrath pursue you, you Devils in sheep's clothing, forever and ever, A-men."

Not far away Jake Bereza growled in cold fury, "They roasted his insides for eleven minutes. Eleven minutes! Okay . . . we'll remember that. We won't let them off the hook that easily. We won't forget until

. . . until there is no trace of them left on earth!" Jake was no longer aware of what was spilling out of his mouth. Nor could the cop understand what Jake was saying, but with drunken, bloodshot eyes he loomed threateningly over Jake. Instinctively, in the bat of an eyelid, Jake shied away and tucked his head into his armpit. It did him no good; the cop's nightstick ripped into his shoulder. At that moment, the bony, raw-boned fist of Jeremiah slammed into the cop's jowl, and Pete Molovan's peasant knuckles crashed into his other cheek. Nettie/Nastia jerked Pete to her side with the strength of a powerful and desperate peasant, hissing in her native tongue, "*Du-u-ren ti! Kikamora Li-i-zesh!*" At the same time, the echoes of the shod hooves of the mounted police echoed through the Square from the direction of Broadway, along with the warning siren of a fire engine from 14th Street.

11

Late that night, Yalkut rode home to Brooklyn on the I.R.T., wrinkled, shriveled and alarmed by the limitless tyranny of man. Beside him rode Jacob Lapidus, and over the hurtling, metallic clatter of the subway, he drilled into Yalkut's ear, "Didn't I tell you, didn't I predict that this rabble and their agitation would ruin the two poor Italians! You can see for yourself. You—" Yalkut shot out of his seat. "Please, Lapidus! Leave me alone! . . . Leave . . . me . . . alone! . . . "

Late at night, Jonah Margolis was scribbling at a desk in a hotel. Tillie Fish sat at the edge of the bed, frightened but cheerful, her large eyes drinking in Jonah. Margolis put down his pen, and read aloud:

Oh, eleven minutes are an eternity ** and death's a long road ** my ship rides a sea of pain ** these past eleven hellish days. ** Oh pilot in the wheelhouse ** when will mother night appear ** and wrap us in her cloak. ** In mute-and-deaf-and-blind repose, ** in the tomb's frozen froth**

Margolis considered a moment, his forehead furrowed, "English . . . Kiplinglish . . . vile!"

Fuming, he flung the sheet of paper aside and launched himself at Tillie like a wolf.

Late at night, Jake Bereza, in his room on Elridge Street, stripped and threw himself face down on his bed and ground his nose into the sheets. He had a habit of sleeping with a pillow under his stomach, which dropped his face lower than his body. The position soothed a kind of nagging ache that constantly roamed his viscera and had the ability to tame the anger that constantly fired his throat and palate.

With a drawn-out groan and sigh of relief he'd dropped into an abyss and in an instant rose again to the surface, a hand having locked on his shoulder. He vaulted off the bed and asked, "Is it time?" He was greeted with silence, and in the silence lay his answer. The warden, Jake thought, resting his eyes on a string of metal buttons. In the open grate of the cell the turnkey stood, keys in hand, mute and with lowered eyes, his silence carrying the same message as the warden's.

Jake followed the turnkey through a long, narrow corridor to a mantel holding a flickering memorial candle—yes-yes, a wick in a cruse of oil. They have to conserve electricity, he thought. They have other uses for it . . . Then they stepped gingerly into a large, square room, without a window, and Jake immediately noticed a black, iron chair— "so . . ."—where the executioner was cheerfully fussing with small chains and buckles, and three or four witnesses were whispering to each other.

"Sacco, Vanzetti," the warden greeted Jake, "there's a reverend here, a Jewish rabbi . . . he will deal with you according to the laws of Moses and Israel."

The rabbi was in a wheelchair. The warden pushed him from behind and the rabbi rolled toward Jake.

"Sacco-Vanzetti!" the rabbi shouted, "beh-beh-beh-beh!"

Stunned and mute, Jake scrutinized him. What was he to make of this?

The warden wagged his hand across the rabbi's eyes and nose, and shoved him against the wall. The rabbi clung to his wheelchair, stiff and unmoving. How extraordinary, Jake thought.

"Sacco-Vanzetti!" the warden said to Jake, his tone haughty, aristocratic, "Sacco-Vanzetti, would you be good enough to sit in this chair, at your pleasure . . ."

"Oh, with all due respect," Jake answered, mimicking his intonation, and taking his seat in the hard, cold chair. Jake wondered how had he come to master an aristocrat's accent? From his father the Hebrew tutor and his grating gabble when he tried to carry on a conversation with the neighboring Gentile woman on the other side of the ocean? Usually on Thursday evenings, when their own bread was gone? His meditations strayed: the same neighbor, from whom his mother would borrow the Gentile girl—what had been her name? . . . It seems, the equation had been; one week his father would be out of bread, his neighbor not, but the next week . . .

"Oh!" Jake broke into his own thoughts. "I beg your pardon, Reb Warden, but this shoulder of mine . . . don't lean on it, I beg you: it is bruised . . . it's . . ."

The warden, who had lashed Jake's feet to the iron chair, now pinned his forearms to the armrests, leaning heavily at the same time on Jake's injured shoulder.

"That shoulder is sensitive," Jake said politely. He thought: they're so considerate in this place! The warden pretended he had not heard, and maintained the pressure on Jake's shoulder.

"I beg your pardon . . ." Jake started to repeat, and suddenly lost his voice.

The warden was looking him straight in the eyes with such tormenting elation, and sinister malevolence, that Jake understood: this is not a game, they're looking to do away with him, he is about to lose his life, he is facing murder! Jake realized, this was an inconceivable injustice, impossible madness; another, a person much like Jake, had come to the conclusion that he, Jake, should die, that he had lived long enough, that from this day forward nothing would be left of him but a cold corpse. But how could Jake be so sure, and how could he prove it? What if the tables had been turned: and the warden had been sitting in the chair, and Jake was fussing with him? The hair rose on the nape of Jake's neck and his blood ran cold. The warden lowered a sort of iron bonnet on Jake's head and was closing in with his finger on some sort of button on the wall, when someone with pen and notebook in hand burst in. "I'm a representative of the press. The public has the right to know everything. Sacco-Vanzetti!" he sang out, leveling his pen at Jake. "In their name, in this your most trying moment, I give you my word, in allegiance to the trust in me by the general welfare, I will report the truth as you see it, the whole truth, and only the truth. Tell me. What blade do you use in your razor? Gillette? Gem? Or something else? Answer!"

"Gee . . . Gillette," Jake answered through trembling lips. "No. Gem . . . no, I . . . I don't remember!"

"He doesn't remember," the reporter said, making a record in his notebook. "He doesn't remember," the warden said. "He doesn't remember," chimed in a chorus from the knot of people in the comer of the room. The warden repeated, "He doesn't remember." The reporter spun mechanically on one foot, like a door on its pivot, and vanished from the corner of Jake's eye. Resolutely, the warden leaned into the button on the wall, grasped Jake's battered shoulder again in his left hand, and looked him in the eye—arrogantly, avariciously and brightly. Jake could not withstand the leer and closed his lids.

Warm, narrow rills like sweat began to ebb and flow over his skin. Nothing to worry about. It was, only . . . hmm . . . somehow pleasurable. No, that wasn't true: here and there large drops clung to the skin and inflamed. That was not comforting. It pricked the shoulders, under the armpits, tormented his right hip, burned his ears like long exposure to a severe frost. His entire body was on fire, and an aroma reeked from him. Not exactly sweat, but a strange corrosion . . . pheww-w-w. On his hip a bead was eating its way into his soft flesh, burrowing and tormenting. That would seem a triviality, but it would not let up for a second, and was becoming unbearable. If he were able at least to reach it with a soothing finger, or change his position for an eye blink! But aside from being lashed to the chair, the blood in his veins was now flowing slower than hot pitch, and no matter how he strained against his bonds, he was unable to stir an inch. He must do something. He could beg the warden to scratch his back, but he feared to face his savage glare . . . even for a warden this man was a brute! It would seem that a warden could also have . . . oh! hell . . .

Unable to restrain himself any longer, he opened his eyes. Gone! The warden had vanished, the room had dissolved, nothing was discernible, and it was black as tar! His skin was broiling, his shoulders battered, raw and racked, there was a continual ringing in his ears. Jake groaned and vaulted from the bed.

But he was alive! His groping fingers found a matchbox on the table. He rose and with jittery fingers struck a match and lit the burner of the gas lamp on the wall. The flame threw a sheen across the filthy bedspread, bringing to life a stampede of tiny brown stains, scattering in panic in all directions, to the edges of the bed, under the cushions, into the murky shadows, anywhere it might be possible to find "cover" or camouflage, like soldiers being shelled. In Jake the terror of his dream exploded in an eye blink, turned into churning wrath. He threw himself on the bed and unleashed an assault on the bedbugs, thwacking and grinding with ferocity, gnashing through tight lips: "Trying to escape, are you? You want to live? Thrive on my blood . . . my blood?" A rabid, half-naked wild man in reeking underwear, his eyes flooded red and his hair disheveled, he fumbled on the bed in the feeble light and stifling air. Red splotches cropped up on the bedspread in swarms, and an ugly, putrid aroma rose and spread to all sides. The bedbugs scurried and sauntered, in numberless squadrons. It was impossible to annihilate them all. Jake felt vile enough to vomit. He leaped up from the bed, tore at his hair, threatened the bedbugs and the world with a tightly clenched fist, and snarled into the stillness of the night, "Damn you! Damn you! May the plague take you all!"

1934 (translated by Reuben Bercovitch)

1

At dusk, a man with a sullen face ordered some pancakes at the hot food counter of The Automat.

A girl with bare, brown arms, in a white apron with a linen cap over her hair, flung the order over to the cook, turned toward the far side of the counter, and suddenly gave the customer a warm, open, let's-be-friends smile.

The face stayed sullen, the rounded shoulders tried to hump themselves, to express still more sullenness, but the belly made that impossible. The girl's mouth drew back and tightened, the smile was gone—automatically, as is only fitting in such a restaurant. She took a spoon and stirred one of the steaming pots, stirred a second pot, raised her black-haired head with its long, not especially pretty face, and then gave another smile. This time it wasn't so simple—it was inviting, childlike, unsure. Childlike also were the weary, longing gaze, the thin arms, stretching pityingly down from the shoulders, and the thin collarbone around the meager neck. The face itself was much older; she could have been sixteen, or twenty-six, or older still. The sullen customer looked at her for a while, disconcerted. Gradually the sullenness left his eyes, the way frost leaves a window, and the bulldoggish chin lost its stiffness. On such a face, that was a smile—an inviting smile. Thank God!

The girl was more cheerful now, and reacted nimbly and energetically to the orders given by other customers. The man with the sullen face got his pancakes, with honey and butter, and sat down at a small table near the hot counter. He worked methodically—first putting the pats of butter between the hot pancakes so that they would melt, then pouring himself some coffee from the automat faucet set into the wall, and finally taking off his coat and hat and putting them on a hanger. He sat a good while at his table, unmoving, with his rounded shoulders sunken as if from exhaustion. At the top of his head there was a bald spot shining with an ivory light, which the slightly silvered hair on either side was striving in vain to hold back. He ate slowly, lost in thought, now and then taking a look in the direction of the girl. Once he sullenly shrugged his shoulders: "a lot of nonsense!"

He had already put on his coat, but then his hand, extended toward his hat, fell back to his side. He went to the hot counter, pointed without looking at some dessert, and calmly asked the girl a question: When would she be finished with work? Suddenly a wave of expression, of cunning flowed across her face, like a gust of wind over a pool, and with a quick look at the clock on the wall she said, "In an hour." He gave a mournful nod, left his dessert untouched on the table, and went into the street.

2

The lights had already been lit. The air was sharper than during the day, but the evening was still mild. There was much movement on the streets; it was the absolute peak of rush hour. He roamed the streets around the Public Library, with an absorbed look and smoothed forehead, in hidden stillness. The surge all around was very near, but at the same time was cut off from him, as if by a thin curtain he carried with him as he went. Once his calm demeanor was disturbed when he came face to face with a young lady with blond hair and gray eyes. Both persons turned pale. He touched his hat, she asked him how he was, he said, "Fine, thank you, and how are you?" She invited him to accompany her, and he declined with regret—he had, he said, an appointment to meet someone in a few minutes. Behind the courteous, restrained words, both their glances were pointed and hard, like rapiers in the hands of duelists. The lady left, her back straight, her head haughty, and he—somewhat hunched and overcast. Then his face was smooth again and a faint smile lifted up a corner of his mouth. He stayed that way until he saw on a clock that he was five minutes late. With unhurried steps he turned back toward the restaurant.

She was standing outside, looking into the window of a shop near the restaurant. She wore a gray-brown jacket and a brown hat which didn't suit her. Her face was serious, wearing its older expression, the one belonging to a twenty-six-year-old. A momentary smile in his direction changed all the lines of her countenance. Then suddenly it was gone. What mobility! Southern blood, perhaps?

They took 42nd Street, walking west, toward Broadway. Her walk was dignified, proper—on a first glance one might have thought her a young Jewish woman, poor but respectable. But a second and then third glance would have shown clearly that she was the creature of a wholly foreign world—Spanish, perhaps, with a mix of American Indian.

"Have you been working at that restaurant long?"

"My second week. But just half days. You can't make a living from it."

Aha! A hint! "You can't make a living." Two incomes . . . He made a sour face.

"And what should I call you? What's your name?"

Her face changed again, with a strange suddenness, as if from some inward explosion. These sharp shifts were unnerving, as if she were grabbing a button or pulling a sleeve. In truth her movements were quite restrained; only the line of her mouth snapped like the edge of a whip, and waves of laughter leaped out at the corners of her eyes.

"Jenny. Jenny's my name."

"Jenny! No . . . What do you mean, 'Jenny'?"

She took offense at this.

"Why not? I'm an American! Born here in New York! Sure!"

"Right, right, I'm not saying . . . but you look to me like you're from the South—Spanish, maybe?"

Her swarthy forehead turned swarthier.

"Okay, yes, my folks are from California. But I'm a New Yorker! Born here. Born right here."

With her left hand she gestured to the side, toward the southwest.

That was probably true. Her speech was full of errors and slangy, but no different from that of the average working girl—American, New Yorkish.

3

He suggested having some ice cream, and sitting at one of the parlor's tables, she became more relaxed. She didn't, she said, know any Spanish. Her folks, sure, they spoke Spanish with one another, but she herself knew only a few words. Oh, the prayers—but those were in Latin. Sure.

He too was now more cheerful, and pressed her:

"But listen, what kind of a name is Jenny? I mean, really. Every Jane, Jeanne, and Joan is Jenny. Wouldn't you rather be called Juanita, maybe? Or Isabella? Or why not, say, Dolores?"

She looked at him uncertainly.

"I'm an American girl."

"Sure," he said reassuringly, "a real American girl. But say it yourself: Do-lo-res. Now that's a name with a ring to it. You know what? I'm going to call you 'Dolores'!"

She was suddenly pleased and stretched her hand across the table and put it over his.

"*Olrayt!* Dolores, if that's what you want. Ha ha ha! Dolores! . . . but what should I call you?'

In tone, they had gone over to *du* or the informal "you" in Yiddish, although modern English does not have particular words corresponding to the formal "*ir*" or informal "*du.*"

"Me?" His tone was suddenly a little cooler, but he soon returned her smile. "No, you won't be able to pronounce my name. Just try: Lakrits-pletsl."

"L . . . Lak . . . proudprrr . . . ," she sputtered amidst repeated laughs. "No, never, what did you say again? Ha ha!"

"See what I mean? No, Dolores, my name doesn't matter. Or—just call me Manny. That's easy to pronounce, and it's better than Morris, or Michael, or even Sidney. So let's—hmm . . . a movie. Want to go see a movie?"

She was delighted. "Oh yes! *I'd love to.* Let's go."

They went out into the street and set off for Broadway.

On the way, he noticed her looking longingly at a flower shop. He went in, and brought out a rose for her—a single rose, not yet fully opened, but full and compact.

"Thanks, darling!"

In the theater, after she took off her coat, she removed the rose from her buttonhole and pinned it in her hair, on the right side of her head. Somewhere he'd seen a painting, a Goya, perhaps, with a Spanish lady with a rose in her black hair. No similarity here to that lady's face, and yet . . . in the faint light of the darkened theater . . . even her expression was different! Hmmm . . . a strange race.

4

In front of the curtain, in a spot of purple light, a tall, fat man in black tails, with a smooth, round, feminine face, sang in the unexpectedly thin little voice of a "little angel." The lips of his narrow mouth opened like a samekh—more up and down than across. He continued, sweetly and languidly:

Give my regards to mother,
tell her I can find no other,
who'd love me as much as she di . . . d!

Someone sobbed in a nearby seat. Jenny-Dolores' mobile face worked continually, and her cavalier for the evening looked at her furtively, with a faint smile at the corner of his mouth. Afterward there was, of course, "Somebody's Waiting for Me," and at the end a song about how the tobacco leaves are like gold and the cotton blossoms like snow, how the "darkies"—that is, the Negroes—do nothing but eat red, juicy watermelons, and dance by the light of the blue moon, and how all this happens down de Mis-sis-sip-pi!

All this was very nice. It did seem odd to him that the three songs were apparently all sung to the same tune, and that it was apparently the same tune he had heard a year ago, and two years ago, and six years ago, in all the vaudeville houses; only the words were different. Or perhaps he was wrong, and the words were the same too?

After the two-hundred-pound little angel had exited, gathering in his few sheaves of applause, a Negro entered, whom all real Negroes would have envied—so black was his face, so red his lips, so white his teeth, so large and round his eyes. He sang a Negro song. What the hell . . . wasn't that the same tune yet again? He danced a jig, and was gone. From opposite sides of the footlights a girl swam out dressed as a red lily, and a tall, slender, gray-haired dandy dressed as if for a ball, twirling a walking stick in his fingers. The two sang duets and danced next to each other, and both the dancing and the duets very clearly insinuated what they had to insinuate. Dolores giggled, then finally couldn't hold her feelings in, and with a muffled scream pressed herself against her cavalier's arm. Not to respond would have been boorish.

God, Manny's God, came to the rescue, and the vaudeville ended. The theater got even darker, the curtain rose, and on the screen appeared a newsreel, called *The World Before Your Eyes*. Yale and Cornell are playing football, and Cornell wins. Hurray! A celluloid factory in Columbus, Ohio, has been destroyed in an explosion. The damage amounts to two million dollars. A kitten in a cellar survived, and sits snuggled in a policeman's elbow. A wounded firefighter has been admitted to a hospital, and the bodies of the missing workers have not as yet been found. Miss Marian Terrance, of Tacoma, Washington, has gone over Niagara Falls in a barrel. She's wearing knickers and smiling with white teeth. There are scenes of rice fields covered with water in Japan. Men and women stand in water above their ankles, and dig with their hands in the mud. The annual English Derby has just ended. A horse named Lightning takes up two-thirds of the screen, his pricked-up ears quivering on his narrow head. In Los Angeles, California, a young man has been sitting for seventeen days fastened to a chair on the top of a high pole, on the roof of the Commercial Bank building, betting that he'll be able to last twenty-four days. Old John D. Rockefeller plays tennis and hands out dimes. Paris lays its annual wreath on the tomb of the unknown soldier. "Lindy" flies six hundred miles in his airplane to reach the site of his wedding. Jack Dempsey trains for his match with the Peruvian champion Zapatero. An automobile race. A motorcycle race. A baby exhibition. President Coolidge blinks with his fish eyes right into the theater. With the broad brim of his cowboy hat, it's difficult to deduce from his forehead what whirlwind thoughts might be blowing around in his mind.

Oops! The survey is finished. *The World Before Your Eyes.*

Now comes The Comedy.

Someone is running. Falling. Getting up and getting hit on the jaw. Running. Falling. Getting up and hitting other people on the jaw. Running again. Losing trousers and bits of clothing. A flowerpot falls from a window onto someone's head. Running and bumping with his nose into—ouch—a policeman! Running back and falling into a barrel of water. Running still, and then treating himself to a brick in the head. A last, fateful run: into his own wife! Then he rolls his eyes in a fearful, impossible way, till the whites occupy the entire space, from eyelid to eyelid, and he falls backward into a lake. Some gigantic bubbles come to the surface. Ha ha ha ha ha!

"You like it, kid?" smiles Manny, looking at his companion.

"*Oh, it's so funny,*" and Dolores' mobile face sparkles with a thousand ripples of laughter. The people around her laugh for a long time, and can't stop. A gift from God, the sense of humor.

From behind the spectators' backs, the program's main attraction flows and settles on the screen: *The Red Scarf.* Let's see . . . a young reporter for an American paper uncovers a crime and wins the heart of a banking heiress. Or maybe . . . no we're somewhere in Europe, in the twelfth century. Two proud knights, one rich and one poor. The former is proud in direct proportion to his wealth, the latter, in proportion to his poverty. So what will happen? Which of the two prides will . . . but let the high-born lady worry about that. What's true is true. She is beautiful, the lady, in her long gown and high coiffure, with pearls in her hair. And noble, too, oh how noble! Interesting: does so heavenly a creature ever eat? Or, let's say, does she . . . But no, no, no! Manny looks over at Dolores and the smile freezes on his lips. Jenny is looking at the lady with wide-open eyes, her whole face almost prayerful, and she whispers in the silence: "Jesus, Maria—she's so lovely!"

"Dolores," Manny murmurs in her ear. "Forgive me, Dolores. If I weren't so smart, I wouldn't be such an idiot."

"Huh?" says Dolores, not tearing her eyes from the scene. "Shh, darling—look up there—why aren't you looking?"

"I'm looking, I'm looking. Why wouldn't I be?"And he does look, but at her, it's at Jenny that he looks. Beneath her black hair there's the shimmer of an ear, a dainty ear, and right beside it, like a dying ember, the rose in her hair is glowing, as if growing out of the hair itself. He takes her hand between his two hands, and she responds with a faint, absorbed clasp. Gradually his head sinks down. The two sit close to each other, though in different worlds.

5

"Oysters," Manny decided as they left the theater. "Let's have some oysters!"

Dolores follows, silently, the shadow of a pensive smile on her lips. Outside it was colder, and small, scattered snowflakes drifted in the air. In the big *lunchroom* with its "popular prices," it was warm, bright and noisy with all the after-theater customers. Manny ordered oysters "in their shells," Dolores an oyster chowder. She ate with the exaggerated etiquette of the "real" New Yorker: narrowed her mouth, took small sips, held the slice of bread delicately, and with just two fingers, picked at it like a bird. For dessert she had red, sweetened gelatin in whipped cream. Manny observed her from under his eyebrows. Once he said,

"You live with your parents?"

A cloud passed across her forehead, and was gone. She was silent for a moment. Then she said softly,

"You know, if you work in a restaurant, you see all sorts of people."

As simple as that! Ignoring a question that was perhaps too intimate, and introducing a new subject on her own.

"What makes you say that?"

"Oh, nothing particular, just remembering . . . One day in the automat, someone comes in, a little guy, skinny, homely. With glasses, in a round hat a good five years old, a threadbare coat. In a word, a real sight, a bum. Must be one of these Russians, maybe? All he eats is pancakes and syrup. Oh, right, that's probably what I remembered, you had pancakes too, but this guy, that's all he eats. Pancakes and more pancakes, and that's it. A real show. I don't even wait for his order any more. He just smiles, and I put in the order for pancakes. Right, a smile, he has a nice one you know. That is—how to put it? A smile like other smiles? But no . . . a really fine smile. So what did I want to tell you? Hmm, yes. He sits down at a table, not too close, not too far, eats his pancakes and looks at me. And why does a guy look at a girl? No mystery there! He looks and that's as far as it goes. To tell the truth, at first I tried to encourage him a bit. A couple of times I smiled back. I wanted to know what sort of guy he was. But he smiles back and doesn't say a word. I tried again. Same story. So what are you looking at? Go on, look! He was getting on my nerves a bit. There was something between us . . . just like that, silently. He comes in often, has his pancakes, looks, says nothing. But if he doesn't come in for a while I miss him! *Did you ever* see anything like that? Ha ha ha!"

She was more cheerful now, more playful, and as they left the restaurant grabbed him beneath his arm and pressed against him.

"So now, young lady," said Manny, "time to go home."

She let his arm fall, straightened like a tightened string, and looked at him wordlessly. Amazed. Hurt.

"Why the look? It's late. Time for you to go to sleep. And for me too."

She remained silent, and he, uneasily, stepped away from her, then back. She took hold of his sleeve.

"Take me with you. Take me somewhere."

"Mm . . . no," he said gloomily. "I . . . it's not my style."

"Meaning what?"

"Not my style! You can't understand. And where am I supposed to take you to? Say I have a wife and kids at home, eh? I'm supposed to bring you home to my wife??"

"But . . . in a *hotel!*"

"A hotel? Hell! A hotel? I hate hotels."

He was upset, and paced impatiently around her.

"What kind of a man . . . ?" she wondered.

"What kind of man? A man like other men. Not a lot worse than other men . . ."

Suddenly he had an idea.

"Listen," he said. "I understand . . ." He put his hand into a pocket, but her southern eyes were suddenly full of fire, her mouth twisted, her face the opposite of beautiful. He understood, and stood still, discouraged. She bridled, shook her head, and said,

"Good night. And thanks for a nice evening."

Before he recovered himself, she was ten steps away.

"Hell!" He grimaced, as if from a sour taste in his mouth, and ran after her.

"Wait a minute. I . . . come on, don't get me wrong. I'm a golem. Why are you running away like that?"

She took smaller steps, but kept walking.

"Hey, listen—I'm a little crazy, you know, couldn't calm myself down all at once." He took her by the arm. "Come on, come on, we'll stroll a bit. Then—we'll see."

The snow was now falling less heavily, like light, warm down, descending without hurry, drifting in the air and then the flakes settling each one in its own place, as if just for a moment, ready to rise again and fly away elsewhere. Fifth Avenue was beginning to turn white, between mute, high walls. Now and then an automobile slid by, with a muffled, silken rustle. You couldn't say that New York was sleeping, but rather—what, exactly?—that it had settled itself in an armchair, an unlit cigar in its fingers, too lazy to think.

At 59th Street, Manny called a taxi. The brief sullenness that had come between them, moments ago, had removed any trace of strangeness, but there was no inclination to talk. In the car, he embraced her with one hand, she snuggled up to him, and so they sat until the taxi stopped by a big apartment building in the Bronx. She took a surprised look at the entryway. Not a hotel. But she said nothing. They made their way across a large, lower *hall* and reached the stairs.

"Take my hand," he said, "and take your time. You'll have to climb, and then climb some more."

The corridors and stairways were well lit, empty, quiet. She leaned her head against his shoulder as they climbed up, though the bright emptiness, from floor to floor, like a couple returning home late at night from a party at the house of good friends.

6

The day is so hot that the grassy earth under Manny's body is as warm and yielding as a wool blanket. The day is so bright that through his closed eyelids he can clearly see the green valley far beneath, the pale blue sky, as if bleached with light, around and above the whole world, and the rich foliage of the chestnut tree high above his head. He is lying on his side, his left hand under his cheek, and resting with every fiber of his being.

It is very quiet. But somewhere nearby, off to his side, a bee is humming in a small, thin tenor, "Scar-let-red! . . . scar-let-red!" Meaning what?

Pensively, he taps his right hand across the ground next to him and encounters something that utters a faint, frightened peep. He snatches his hand back. On the ground is a tiny little bird, turning about with its beak and yellow round eyes. Pink skin can be seen through the sparse feathers. Still a baby. He must have fallen out of the nest. Again he puts his hand on the tiny baby—cautiously, tenderly. The bird wriggles weakly, almost imperceptibly, but clearly without fear, is quiet, and then wriggles again. Now the wriggling is more frequent, regular and quiet, trusting. So just don't be afraid! Don't-be-afraid, be-afraid. Afraid-afraid-afraid.

Inside his head, toward the back, there is a thought lying, which he has to draw out and look at closely. What is it? Oh, yes: how is it that he can see with closed eyes? If it's so bright, what will happen if his eyes are open? Curious. And he starts to open his eyes straight into absolute darkness. Unbelievable! Quickly he closes them again: darkness, blackness. He opens them again: blackness, darkness. Beneath his hand, the bird is still wriggling—quietly, regularly, the way a human heart beats. Beneath his hand beats a human heart.

He wakes up.

Night. Lying for a while with one's eyes open, one sees that it is not so black, not at all so dark. The light from the stars stream through the double windows to him in the bedroom, and the night itself is saturated with a white, soft, diffused light—the snow on the street, clearly. The nearby walls appear, with a few dark patches on them, pictures. The table. A chair. On the ground a dark heap: clothing, women's clothing, thrown there in eager, joyous forgetfulness. He twitches, smiles, and strongly draws a breath of air into his lungs.

She is sleeping quietly, curled up, snug beneath the covers, warm. Her heart beats noiselessly, but as it should; the expended powder is being remade. Interesting, how often homely women have beautiful bodies! And vice-versa—

He slipped out of bed and, in a sleeping gown and slippers, went out into the second room, closing the doors behind him. There, in the darkness, he felt for the electric switch, then pressed it. This was the larger of his two rooms, very sparsely furnished, with only a single picture on the bare walls: a landscape of Isaac Lichtenstein's. Two doors in a corner led respectively to a bathroom and to the miniature kitchen, the *kitchenette*.

He washed out his mouth, drank down a glass of water, smoked a cigarette. Then he looked in the mirror and grimaced. What a mess! His sleepy, swollen, ugly face, eyes creeping out of his head, with a sprouting of grayish stubble on his chin—hell! A hairy chest, a little round belly, a body that seemed fleshy, though . . . In vexation, he waved his hand and moved over to the window.

"—A white and frosty night. A few minutes ago a warm, sunny day, just as real—for me. And what do I know except 'for me?'—'Scarlet-red.' A delicious word, 'scarlet'; fills the mouth like Malaga wine, or a bit from the heart of a fresh, juicy melon. Scarlet-red. There must be more words—Wait—cornstalks—gold—yes: 'The ear of corn is green and gold . . . the poppy scarlet-red.' Yes. 'The ear of corn' . . . 'Life asks no questions . . . ; death asks the questions, of the dead.' Aha! 'The Song of the Women Reapers.' Where is that from? Who was it who . . . And why did it come into my dream? And what's the meaning of, 'death asks the questions?' Hmm . . . unclear.

"That child of man on the bed. Turns out that: love that is bought— is still love. Go figure. Tender—hot—capricious—playful—deep and real. How can that be? The child of man needs a sunbeam, some playfulness, some fun. And so simple, so physical: something good to eat, a kiss, a tickle. And the truth is, I've never seen a naked soul stroll along Broadway that way, minus its pants. For that matter, I haven't seen a body going around all by itself. The Ninth Symphony, or Tristan, or whatever else there may be—without an ear of skin and meat they're nothing, and stuffed kishkes console the . . . soul. How can that be? Ah, you old synagogue idler, picking up a girl in the street, and then philosophizing about her!—"

A few blocks away, the elevated and tramway cars were already thundering along. Heavy wagons creaked in the snow. The day was near.

He strode around, in his soft slippers, along the diagonal of the room, from corner to corner.

—"The little one there, yes, the child of man, still desires. Oh, come on, we've heard that refrain before. What was it I wanted to demonstrate? Love that is bought is still love. Show the child of man a shekel and it starts singing psalms. But the joke is, that the psalm is genuine. It's a shekel, sure, but no sooner has it begun but . . . ha ha ha! What does that mean? Was I misunderstanding? My whole life long was I misunderstanding? My whole life? That would be too easy. Too easy is useless. Too complicated—is also useless. So where do I stand? Where is the beginning and where . . . *Oh, hell!* . . ."—He spat, having swallowed a bit of the lighted cigarette, and from vexation at the whole tangled knot.

The blue-white day came into the house through all its windows. Manny silently opened the door to the bedroom and went to the bed. Dolores lay on her back, one hand beneath her neck, one of her cheeks glowing red. She was breathing quietly, and he looked at her in surprise, confused. And suddenly, without warning, she opened her eyes. For a while her eyes showed only that they understood nothing. Then they flared up. Then they became darker. A smile slithered between her lips, and her eyes became even darker.

7

Manny brought in the milk from the hall, and the smell of a "goyish" breakfast wafted through the apartment: eggs, bacon, fresh coffee.

"Dolores, breakfast!"

"Coming . . ." she answered from the bedroom. She sat on the bed, pensive, as she got dressed, in violet underwear, naked from the waist up. A young body, almost boyish, the head, unexpectedly, belonging to a grown woman, the black hair loose, the eyes staring, the mouth open, self-hypnotized. Then, finally, with difficulty, she tore her gaze away from some point in the room, and sprang out of bed. She picked up the heap of clothing and ran through the front room into the bath.

They sat in silence, both occupied with their own thoughts. Meanwhile the sun peeped in from a steep roof opposite, and flung on the floor a radiant, golden sword, straight, sharp, with a long point. It happened so suddenly that both turned around, and with pricked-up ears listened for a metallic clang. It did not come, and they exchanged glances with faint, vague, wandering smiles. Soon afterward Dolores finished eating, put on her hat and coat, and in a businesslike way powdered her face in the mirror. Manny got up, and from a desk drawer took a couple of bills and handed them to her. She stepped away from him, shook her head: "No."

He grimaced, impatiently.

"Come on, take it."

She threw her hands back, like a child.

"But . . . why not?"

She was silent. Then, with difficulty, straining to get the words out: "I . . . this time I went—for myself."

"For yourself?"

He thought this over. Then he stepped over close to her and said softly,

"Listen . . . take it, it'll come in handy. A gift, understand? Or . . . okay, let's put it this way: buy yourself something nice, to remember . . . No. Buy yourself a nice silk blouse, something that goes with your nice tender skin—tenderly—like that."

They stood for a while, one next to the other, in silence.

Then not looking, she stuffed the money into her bag and said, "Goodbye."

He took her hand, and brushed her fingers with his lips. His manner was both playful and ceremonious, the proud knight, it seemed, in his dressing gown, a shiny bald spot on top of his head, and the highborn lady, in New York, in the twentieth century. But Jenny of 10th Avenue received the gesture without a smile, earnestly, almost haughtily. She gave a shake of her head, went toward the door, opened it. There she turned back toward him for the last time. From behind her glance, from some place very far away, a wave of such intimacy, such closeness, came upon him that he squirmed. Quietly she took one step back, then closed the door behind her. He threw himself forward—and then, quickly, stood still. My God! What's all this? What was all this?

1931 (translated by Lawrence Rosenwald)

♦ ♦ ♦ *Notes*

p. 6   At that time the whole country was feverish with excitement: He is referring to the revolutionary turmoil in tsarist Russia during the fall of 1905.

p. 13   The servile bodies tremble, as if under the lash, but the dark, thin faces and the dark feverish eyes are lit with the red fire that wreathes the mountaintop: Compare Exodus 19:16: "And it came to pass on the third day, when it was morning, that there were thunders and lightnings and a thick cloud upon the mount, and the voice of a horn exceeding loud; and all the people that were in the camp trembled." See also Exodus 20:2–4: "I am the LORD thy God, who brought thee out of the land of Egypt, out of the house of bondage. Thou shalt have no other gods before Me. Thou shalt not make unto thee a graven image, nor any manner of likeness, of any thing that is in heaven above, or that is in the earth beneath, or that is in the water under the earth; thou shalt not bow down unto them, nor serve them; for I the LORD thy God am a jealous God . . ."

p. 14   Who was it that said that a thousand years was more than a day?: A reference to Psalm 90:3: "For a thousand years in thy sight are but as yesterday when it is past"; and 2 Peter 3:8: "that one day is with the Lord as a thousand years, and a thousand years as one day."

p. 14   self-defense corps: The self defense units comprised Jews and Christian sympathizers who were organized, mostly along party lines, to resist the pogromists.

p. 17   They shall be frontlets between your eyes: Compare Deuteronomy 6:8: "And you shall bind them for a sign upon your hand, and they shall be frontlets between your eyes . . ."; this passage has traditionally been understood by Jews to refer to the requirement to wear phylacteries, placed both on the arm and, more importantly for our purposes, on the forehead.

POUR OUT THY WRATH

p. 24   Four Questions: The "four questions" are the questions related to the Passover service that are traditionally asked in a joyful spirit by the youngest child at the seder.

p. 24   "*Shfoykh khamoskho al-hagoyim, asher loy yedo'ukho*—Pour out Thy wrath upon the nations that know Thee not!: At the end of the Passover meal, the door is opened to welcome the prophet Elijah. When the door is opened, those attending the seder recite verses from Psalm 79: 6–7, 69:25, and Lam. 3:66. The folk belief is that Elijah, who is visiting Jewish homes, then sips of the wine that has been prepared for him in a special cup.

IN THE DEAD TOWN

p. 34   But compare the month of Elul: Elul (corresponding to September) is the final month before the High Holidays when the Jewish calendar and holiday cycle begin anew. During Elul, in anticipation of the upcoming holidays, the Jewish horn, or shofar, is daily blown in synagogue. It is a month of intense introspection and penitential prayer.

THE KISS

p. 47   *Vot Durok:* "A fool!" These quotes are all in Russian, but the idiomatic Russian of a native Ukrainian speaker.

p. 47	*Eh, ty, vstovoy:* "Eh, you, stand up!"
p. 47	*To shtsho:* "So what?"
p. 47	*Rebyata:* "Guys"
p. 48	*Shto ly:* "maybe"
p. 49	*Haspodi pamiloy nas:* "Lord, forgive us!"

WHITE CHALLAH

p. 56	The Jewish government: "The Jewish Government" was a common, anti-Semitic term for a Jewish intent to enact laws that justified stealing from the Gentiles and cheating the government; to convene secret conclaves in the dead of night; and to otherwise conduct activities both self-serving and subversive.
p. 57	They burned the towns of: This is an inversion of the Exodus from Egypt. Most of the place names are fictional.
p. 59	The cries of the victims: The term *korbones* denotes both "victims" and "ritual sacrifices."

THE JEWISH REGIME

p. 60	The Jewish Regime: A richly ambiguous title. This novella opens with the description of a Jewish community that sees itself as covenanted to God, a *melukhe*, or Jewish-kingdom-in-exile. But with the rise of modern anti-Semitism, Jews were accused of being a state-within-a-state, a separate "regime," part of a worldwide conspiracy designed to cheat the Christians, break their laws, and take over the world.
p. 60	a little pale after the fast: This refers to the fast of Yom Kippur.
p. 61	Book of Life: Between the Jewish New Year and the Day of Atonement, a period of intense introspection, it is believed that the names of those who are truly penitent will be inscribed by God in the Book of Life, thus ensuring their life for the coming year.
p. 63	It is merely a harmless diversion: Gershon uses rather "learned" Aramaic words here, presumably to impress the rabbi.
p. 64	He's a real count, eh: A reference to the Russian novelist Count Leo Tolstoy (1828–1910).

p. 67   He recited "Shema koleynu," hear our voices: "Shema koleynu" is recited on all public fast days. "Afafuni metsukot" (Hardships have surrounded me), composed by Kalonymus ben Judah of Mainz, is a penitential prayer specific to the Ashkenazi rite. In a rare memory lapse, Shapiro has the rabbi recite a passage from the Book of Jonah that begins with the word "Afafuni." This has been corrected in the translation.

p. 69   Is that so! And who created the world: The rabbi's rebuttal is a paraphrase from the famous Voice from the Whirlwind section in the Book of Job.

p. 69   All for the Sanctification of the Name: A bitterly ironic reference to the Jewish laws of martyrdom, which require a Jew to choose death rather than commit idolatry, adultery, or murder.

p. 74   *Ve'es hadom loy soykhlu:* All three passages that Gershon cites are citations from Deuteronomy 12. See verses 16, 23, and 27. Gershon may also have been thinking of a similar passage in Genesis 9:4, part of God's Noahite commandments.

p. 76   Blood—matzos—Passover: The accusation that the Jews use Christian blood to make their Passover matza was used throughout the Middle Ages and early modern times to justify anti-Jewish riots. This in turn calls to mind the Cossack revolts specific to the Ukraine. Bogdan Chmielnicki in the mid-seventeenth century, and Gonta at the end of the eighteenth, were Cossack commanders who led uprisings against the Polish nobility in the course of which vast numbers of Jews were massacred. "Haidamacks" are the eighteenth-century Cossacks.

p. 77   And before the writing had begun to fade, the war had started: This refers to World War One.

p. 78   The police commissioner, official forms, Cossacks: The Cossacks were Ukrainian soldiers traditionally used by the Tsarist authorities to carry out their orders and to keep control over the general population. In Jewish collective memory, the Cossacks are associated with the massacres carried out under Chmielnicki during the Cossack Revolt of the seventeenth century.

p. 87   The defeated army was retreating: The Jewish population of the

Pale of Settlement and Galicia lived on the Eastern Front between the warring sides. As the Russian army advanced and retreated along the Eastern Front, its multinational forces massacred, pillaged, and raped the Jewish civilian population. As recounted in this story, Jewish soldiers were helpless to stop the carnage carried out by their comrades-in-arms.

p. 94   He sat there for a long time: The calendar of destruction that this story documents has circled back to Elul, the month before the Jewish New Year.

SMOKE

p. 102   *Mahorka:* a term for cheap tobacco.

p. 105   Slavita: (or Slavuta), a town in the Ukraine, was an important center of Hebrew publishing during the nineteenth century.

EATING DAYS

p. 117   Eating Days: the term for the free meals that local Jews would provide for resident Yeshiva students, as a way of supporting the study of Torah. Playing on this term, Shapiro titled the story "Gegesene teg," which literally means "Eaten Days," i.e., days consumed by other passions.

p. 121   Litvak: The term is here being used to imply someone who is overly rational and intellectual, at the expense of simple piety.

AT SEA

p. 159   Whither, o splendid ship: The Yiddish poem, of unacknowledged authorship, which Shapiro provides as the epigraph to this story, is here replaced with a stanza from "A Passer-By," a poem by the British poet Robert Bridges (1844–1930). The original poem is: A ship is sailing on the open sea, / Sailing and rocking hither and yon. / Where from, o ship? Where to, o ship? . . . / On the broad sea, a ship goes forth . . .

p. 160   It is good that a man should both hope and quietly wait: This refers to Lamentations 3:26.

p. 162   Hear our cry: This prayer is part of the *Shimenesre*, the Eighteen Benedictions, a central section of the liturgy that observant Jews recite thrice daily on all weekdays.

p. 166   On dry land, the days of Omer: This refers to the seven-week mourning period between Passover and Shavuot in which the forty-nine days counted are symbolically understood to represent the forty-nine steps taken by the People of Israel from the depths of spiritual impurity in Egypt to the giving of the Torah on Mt. Sinai.

p. 172   Rabbah bar Bar Hana: A third-century Talmudic sage famous for his remarkable legends, known as the "*aggadot* of Rabbah bar Bar Hana," which are mainly found in the tractate *Bava Batra* (73a–74a). These tales purport to relate what Rabbah saw and heard during his many journeys by sea and land. They are characterized by hyperbole and amazed contemporary scholars. Although Rabbah ascribes some of his stories to sailors and Arabs, he begins most of them with the words, "I myself saw." The story of the axe is typical:

> "Rabbah bar Bar Hana further related: Once we traveled on board a ship and we saw a bird standing up to its ankles in the water while its head reached the sky. We thought the water was not deep and wished to go down to cool ourselves, but a voice from heaven called out: 'Do not go down here, for a carpenter's axe was dropped into this water seven years ago and it has not yet reached the bottom. And this is not only because the water is deep but also because it is rapid.' R. Ashi said: 'That bird was Ziz-Sadai, the wild cock whose ankles rest on the ground and whose head reaches the sky, for it is written: And Ziz-Sadai is with me.' At the Messianic banquet at the End of Days, the flesh of the legendary bird Ziz will be served to the righteous together with that of the Wild Ox and Leviathan. (Babylonian Talmud, *Bava Batra*, 73b; adapted from the Soncino translation)

p. 171   Lodestar: "A star that shows the way; a guiding star; that on which one's attention or hopes are fixed" *(Oxford English Dictionary)*. Shapiro's Yiddish coinage is "Helshtern," literally, "Bright Star."

p. 176   His dead lay unburied before him: In the Yiddish text, Shapiro cites
         the Hebrew formulation, *meyso mutl lefonov,* "one whose dead lies
         before him," and thus invokes the ritual law derived from it. *Mish-
         nah Berakhot* 3:1 teaches that "one whose dead [close relative] lies
         before him" (i.e., is not yet buried) is exempt from the recital of the
         Shema, from laying tefillin, from praying three times a day, and in-
         deed from all the precepts laid down in the Torah.

p. 178   Schopenhauer: This likely refers to the cult of suicide that arose
         among Arthur Schopenhauer's (1788–1860) followers.

p. 181   When the morning stars sang together: A reference to Job 38:7.

THE CHAIR

p. 183   Bedbugs also have a right to life: See the tenth chapter of *Fishke the
         Lame,* in S. Y. Abramovitsh, *Tales of Mendele the Book Peddler,* ed. Dan
         Miron and Ken Frieden (New York: Schocken Books, 1996), 111–12.

p. 184   It was the night of Sacco and Vanzetti: On August 23, 1927, two Ital-
         ian anarchists, Nicola Sacco and Bartolomeo Vanzetti, were exe-
         cuted in Massachusetts for crimes allegedly committed in 1920.
         On that day, the communist newspaper *Freiheit* carried banner
         headlines: "Brandeis Refuses to Stop the Execution of Sacco and
         Vanzetti. Workers, Bring Your Work to a Standstill at Three O'-
         Clock Today and Come at Four to Union Square. Fight to the End
         for Sacco and Vanzetti! No Worker Dares Stay in the Shop Today
         and All Must Come to Demonstrate!" See Ruth R. Wisse, "Drown-
         ing in the Red Sea: The Lasting Legacy of Jewish Communism,"
         unpublished paper.

NEW YORKISH

p. 198   The Automat: The details of the sentence make clear that Shapiro is
         referring here to a particular restaurant, called "The Automat." The
         odd thing is that the restaurant in question is not in fact an au-
         tomat, but a classic cafeteria.

p. 199   Fine, thank you, and how are you? Shapiro uses the formal second-
         person pronoun, *ir.*

p. 201   *Olrayt:* This is in transliterated English in Shapiro's text. All such words are indicated in the translation by italics.

p. 201   In tone, they had gone over to *du:* This sophisticated remark, inserted into the text by Shapiro himself, reminds us of a remarkable feature of Shapiro's story. His choices about when to use the formal pronoun, and when to use the intimate one, are skilled and expressive. But clearly the characters are imagined as speaking English, not Yiddish, and the shifts between the Yiddish pronouns express Anglophone tonalities.

        In relation to the phenomena being described, then, an English translation of Shapiro's story is the original, whereas the Yiddish text is a translation.

p. 201   Lakritspletsl: In Yiddish this means "licorice stick." Possibly a veiled, ironic reference to I. L. Peretz's celebrated ballad "Monish" (1888), in which the balladeer complains that rendering the erotic realm in Yiddish is as off-putting as eating "licorice stick." The encounter between Manny and Jenny-Dolores can be read as a New World rewrite of Peretz's "Stories" (1903). See *The I. L. Peretz Reader,* ed. Ruth R. Wisse (New Haven: Yale University Press, 2002), 200–12.

p. 202   little angel: It is not clear what Shapiro might mean by calling the singer a "little angel." In the context of the singer's "round, feminine face," though, it seems plausible to think that "a little angel" might refer to a gay man.

p. 202   *samekh:* a letter of the Yiddish alphabet that is more or less in the shape of a circle.

p. 202   Give my regards to mother: This song is in English transliterated into Yiddish.

p. 203   a Negro: The Yiddish word is *neger.* The word is similar in connotation to the English "Negro"; the usual pejorative term is not *Neger* but *shvartser.* Hence Shapiro's pointed satire, directed not against African Americans but against blackface minstrelsy.

p. 205   Oysters: They are not kosher. Nor will be the bacon Manny cooks up the next morning.

p. 207   *golem:* Originally, an artificial man, most famously the one created in Prague in the sixteenth century by the Maharal; colloquially, a clumsy or awkward person.

p. 209   the expended powder is being remade: The Yiddish is *es produtsirt zikh oyfsnay der oysgeshosener pulver.* A mysterious phrase. It might, as Harry Bochner suggests, refer to Manny's renewal of sexual desire; on the other hand, the structure of the sentence suggests that the phrase refers to Jenny, and her own awakening.

p. 209   Isaac Lichtenstein: Born in 1888, he was a prominent Jewish American artist of the 1940s.

p. 210   "goyish": means Gentile, not only because the bacon is forbidden by the laws of kashrut, but also because the whole style of the breakfast is American rather than Jewish.

♦ ♦ ♦ *Glossary*

Bima: The synagogue pulpit.

Borscht: A soup made primarily of beets and served hot or cold, often with sour cream.

Challah: Egg-rich yeast-leavened bread that is usually braided or twisted before baking and is traditionally eaten by Jews on the Sabbath and on holidays.

Chanukah: (see Hanukkah).

Cossacks: Members of a group of frontiersmen of southern Russia organized as cavalry in the czarist army. In 1648, the Ukrainian nationalist Cossack Chmelnieki led brutal pogroms against the Jews that radically decreased their numbers in Poland.

Day of Atonement: See Yom Kippur.

Day of Hosannas: The seventh day of the Sukkes festival. Seven circuits are made around the altar, at each of which a special Hosannas hymn is recited.

Days of Awe: Rosh Hashana and Yom Kippur.

Days of Repentance: The ten days between Rosh Hashana, the Jewish New Year, and Yom Kippur, the Day of Atonement—a time for introspection and penitence.

Elul: The Jewish month corresponding roughly to September. The shofar is blown daily in anticipation of the high holidays.

Gemarah: The second part of the Talmud, which consists of discussions and commentaries on the basic part, the Mishnah. Sometimes the term is used to refer to the Talmud as a whole.

Golem: An automaton in human form, created by magical means.

Goy: A non-Jew, a Gentile.

Goyim: Plural of goy.

Haggadah: The text of the home service read during the seder ceremony on the first two nights (in Israel the first night) of Passover.

Hanukkah: An eight-day Jewish holiday beginning on the twenty-fifth of Kislev (third month of the civil year) and commemorating the rededication of the Temple of Jerusalem after its defilement by Antiochus of Syria.

Hasidism: A populist mystical movement that arose in the middle of the eighteenth century in Eastern Europe. It centered around a charismatic leader called a zaddik or rebbe, and placed great emphasis on religious enthusiasm and the personal knowledge of God.

Havdalah: A ceremony that marks the end of the Sabbath or of a festival. Blessings are made over wine, spices, and a braided candle, symbolizing the separation of the sacred from the ordinary.

Kaddish (Aramaic for "holy"): A mourner's recitation.

Kasha: A porridge made usually from buckwheat groats.

Kheyder (literally "room"): A Jewish elementary school for boys, often convened in the teacher's room.

Kiddush: A prayer over wine.

Kishke: A Slavic sausage akin to Polish sausage.

Litvak: A Jew from Lithuania. The term denotes someone of a rationalist, skeptical and anti-Hasidic temperament.

Matza: Unleavened bread eaten during Passover.

Matzos: Plural of Matza.

Melamed: A teacher in the kheyder.

Passover: The eight-day festival that marks the beginning of spring and commemorates the deliverance of the Israelites from Egyptian slavery.

Phylacteries: Small leather cases containing passages from Scripture that observant Jewish males affix to the forehead and left arm during weekday morning prayers. They are signs of the covenant between God and Israel.

Pogrom: An organized massacre of helpless people, specifically the massacre of Jews in Eastern Europe.

Prayer Shawl (Tallis):   A garment in the four corners of which fringes have been knotted, worn during morning prayers by observant Jewish males over thirteen.

Purim: The holiday that celebrates the rescue of Jews from the Persian Haman.

Rebbe: The term for a Hasidic leader.

Rebetsin: The wife of a rabbi or teacher.

Rosh Hashana: The Jewish New Year, traditionally regarded as the day of the creation of the world.

Sabbath: The weekly holy day of rest, which begins at sundown on Friday and ends at sundown on Saturday evening.

Sambation River: In Jewish folklore, the river on whose banks the twelve lost tribes of Israel settled.

Seder: A Passover service at home that recounts the liberation of the Jews from Egyptian bondage.

Shabbes: See Sabbath.

Shimenesre: (Hebrew: Shmona-esreh): Eighteen benedictions recited in silent devotion at each of the daily services, also known as the Amidah.

Shiva: A traditional seven-day period of mourning the dead that is observed in Jewish homes.

Shlimazl: Unlucky person, ne'er do well.

Shofar: The horn of the ram (or any other ritually clean animal except the cow), sounded on Rosh Hashana and Yom Kippur.

Shoykhet: Jewish ritual slaughterer.

Shtetl: Any Eastern European market town inhabited largely by Jews.

Shtetlekh: Plural of Shtetl.

Siddur: A Jewish prayer book containing liturgies for daily, Sabbath, and holiday observances.

Sukkah: A booth or hut erected for Sukkot (see sukkes) in which, for seven days, Jews "dwell" or at least eat.

Sukkes: The autumn festival that commemorates the tabernacles that the Israelites inhabited in the wilderness after the Exodus. A blessing is made over the Four Species: lulav (palm), hadas (myrtle), aravah (willow), and etrog (citron).

Tallis: See prayer shawl.

Talmud: A collection of post-biblical writings based on academic discussions of Jewish law by generations of scholars and jurists over several centuries and in several countries.

Tamuz: The month of the Jewish year corresponding roughly to July.

Ten Days of Repentance: The days between Rosh Hashana, the Jewish New Year, and Yom Kippur, the Day of Atonement—a time for introspection and penitence.

Tfilin: See phylacteries.

Tisha B'Av: The ninth day of the Hebrew month of Av, commemorating the destruction of the Temple in Jerusalem in 586 BCE and in 70 CE.

Tkiye: One of the sounds blown on the shofar during Rosh Hoshana and Yom Kippur.

Torah: The Pentateuch, the Five Books of Moses; it is also a term for Jewish learning in general.

Treyf: Non-kosher; not conforming to dietary laws.

Tsholnt: Traditional Sabbath stew.

Yarmulke: A skullcap worn by observant Jewish males at all times.

Yeshiva: An institute of talmudic learning.

Yom Kippur: The Day of Atonement, holiest day of the Jewish calendar. There are five services: Maariv (Kol Nidre, on the eve), Shakharit, Musaf, Minkha, and Neila.

Yortsayt: The anniversary of a death.